MOTHER
OF ALL TALES

DAILY LIFE BANTER. WRAPPED IN HUMOUR, AS VIEWED BY A DAUGHTER

SUPREET DHIMAN

First Published in September 2019

ISBN: 978-93-5347-970-1

BLUEROSE PUBLISHERS
www.bluerosepublishers.com
info@bluerosepublishers.com
+91 8882 898 898

Cover Design:
Mohd Arif

Typographic Design:
Namrata Saini

Distributed by: BlueRose, Amazon, Flipkart, Shopclues

Layers

This book is a celebration of life lived and rejoiced by my mother,
my maker.

This book is dedicated to everyone who feels I have written
about their mother. So while reading if you find any flaws,
please direct complaints accordingly.

Acknowledgements

If you find this book should never have been written, then please get hold of Pranav Kumar as he never had a doubt about the roaring success this book would be, even though 27 publishers thought otherwise! I am as much grateful to my dear author friend Anil Menon, who gently tried to tell me to keep #mymothersdiary as a personal memoir, as I am charmed by the enthusiasm of my much valued friend Mr. K.J.S. Chatrath, who found my notes a refreshing way to cherish our mothers. I also acknowledge Dr. J.M. Jerath who edited the draft, duly bribed with 'stick-jaw' made by my mother. Apparently this is what his own mother used to make all those decades ago. Vivek Kumar burnt the midnight oil to remove the imperfections from the book he fell in love with as he read every page. Thank you C.J. Singh for creating a cover for the book that left us all speechless.

I am immensely grateful to all the friends on Facebook who for years kept reading my notes on my mother, and yet kept mum whenever they met her in person. Your patience enabled me to give the biggest surprise to Mum, in the shape of this book.

Most importantly, I thank every mother who contributed to laying the foundation of my being and brought up children who became the pillars of my life. You have collectively nurtured this troublemaker; now, live with it!

Prologue

My mother stands as tall as her 5-feet frame permits, weighed down by 70 years worth of experiences her life has thrown at her. At times, she caught them neatly, occasionally had some pleasant surprises which charmed her no end, sometimes she managed to dodge some shrapnel, and then, let's admit, at times she got hit right in the face. However, not even once did life manage to dislodge Mum from her pedestal of grace and dignity with which she continues to rule life, with a charming smile and a twinkle in her eye.

Born all those years ago in 1946 in Ludhiana to a loving mother and a revered father, Mum was the fourth of six siblings. As was the norm in those days, she grew up in a large, joint household where food was cooked for at least 20 every day. While her upbringing was conservative and traditional, Mum had great fun getting her schooling in place and breaking the rules every now and then – a streak she retained even after getting married into a large, respected entrepreneurial family with a rigid rulebook to follow, where food was cooked for at least 30 people every day.

There is something quite entertaining about my mother's birth, which remains hotly debated. Even decades later, my mother, a produce of 1946, and a first cousin born in 1947, have not settled their war of words surrounding their birth. My mother claims, 'Main aayi te azaadi mili'[1] while the cousin categorically declares, 'Jaan de! Tu te gadar paaya si, azaadi te

---

[1] ਮੈਂ ਆਈ ਤੇ ਆਜ਼ਾਦੀ ਮਿਲੀ (I took birth and brought independence with me.)

main le ke aaya si.'[2] Sitting on the fence, we simply enjoy the arsenal they fire at each other, while staying out of the firing range!

As a young woman of 20 with dreams in her eyes, Mum joined my father to establish their own little nest amidst the joint family of 21. The basic principle that no one should ever leave home without food ruled the vegetarian roost in Mum's marital home too. Guests were welcome to stay as long as they wished. You can just imagine the piles of clothes to be washed when no one had heard of the washing machines and tonnes of vegetables to be peeled, chopped and cooked on a daily basis, when LPG was looked upon as a combustible device to be avoided at all costs! Despite the enormity of physical hard work that was pooled in by each family member, all one hears about is the fun they all had every day, in dodging the elders and spoiling the youngsters, while saving their own skin along the way. Ours was a household straight out of a well-made Punjabi film, with every character played out in real life, every day. This is the kind of life my mother has seen, where your identity is merged with your family name, where living for family members is the norm, where life begins and ends with the family.

This epitome of sacrifice, who has taken utmost care of her family and her own self to the best of her abilities, once tripped and grazed her knee as she fell down during her evening walk. Mum quickly picked herself up and walked home where we cleaned the minor laceration with an antiseptic lotion and smeared her knee with anti-everything concoctions. The following day she had the mandatory tetanus jab done and the wound healed in no time. Unfortunately, the cosmetic healing

---

[2] ਜਾਨ ਦੇ! ਤੂੰ ਤੇ ਗ਼ਦਰ ਪਾਇਆ ਸੀ, ਆਜ਼ਾਦੀ ਤੇ ਮੈਂ ਲੈ ਕੇ ਆਇਆ ਸੀ (Leave it! You are responsible for brining the mayhem of partition. It was I who brought the independence.)

hid a monster that wrecked Mum physically and emotionally. She was diagnosed with Staph infection, the nasty drug-resistant bacterial infection that kept breaking Mum's soft nourished skin into massive painful boils all over her body. For three months, she underwent multiple courses of intensive antibiotics, including intravenous ones twice a day, but the boils as big as her palm kept reappearing. Eventually she landed in the ICU where, to make matters worse, her body started reacting to the medicines, making her condition even more precarious. Finally, this pillar of strength threw in the towel one night at the hospital. She was tired of fighting and that broke my heart.

Here was a woman who had put her little nest together, after the massive joint family separated 10 years into her marriage. A wife who had nursed my father single-handedly when he lost use of his left arm for 9 months because of a viral infection and then again for a year when he met with a near-fatal accident. I was seeing this formidable lady fall apart, who had nursed me to health for 6 weeks when I was quite lost to dengue. This pillar of strength was losing ground, who had held the fort at home for months, while we had no diagnosis for my brother's debilitating headaches. A resilient graceful woman who had seen family fortunes wiped out twice, yet taken the riches and rags in her stride. This was a woman who had never said 'I do' to the vows of 'in sickness and in health, for richer and poorer' but laid down her life without asking anything in return. And here she was now, speaking in a delirium about the sum total of her life.

It was past midnight as the nurse finally switched off the light in the hospital room after Mum settled a little. Exhausted, I also lay down on the couch next to her bed. Suddenly I heard a very feeble quivering voice through the darkness. Mum was reminiscing about the things she wanted to say to her father whom she lost when I was a year old. She had reached her parental home in Ludhiana by the evening but our maternal grandfather whom I affectionately call nana, gave up the fight before she could get to the hospital to hug her father one last time. Mum was thinking of her own mother with whom she could not spend as much time as she would have liked, especially towards the fag end of nani's life. I thought I would get up and hold her in my arms to tell her that she has been a splendid daughter, living her life by the values her parents raised her with, but Mum's continuous mono-dialogue stopped me.

Mum started mumbling about her wedding and the years thereafter, about us, her children. I suddenly became very still. Something in me prevented me from even breathing in case that broke Mum's drug- and fatigue-induced spell of release. I knew Mum would survive, but I wanted Mum to just let it all out. I have no idea when was the last time any of us stopped by to listen to Mum. I can't recollect when was the last time we asked her how she was doing or coping with her life. We just kept living our lives, taking Mum for granted. Nothing could ever happen to Mum. She would always be there.

With tears streaming down my eyes, I heard how proud Mum felt when my brother was born because not only was he a very gorgeous child, he was also an extremely dutiful son. For 6 years, my handsome brother was the envy of the household, till I made the grand appearance as a breech baby who was declared dead at birth. Mum remembered how I refused to let go and screamed my lungs out 15 minutes later. Indeed! Persistence has been my trademark since birth!

Mum spoke about the times when our home was being built in 1978 and she felt as if her own Rome was under construction, her own home finally in this whole wide world. She mumbled how happy she felt as her kids progressed in life, how joyful it was to have a houseful of children and grandchildren.

Suddenly in her delirium she started wailing and apologised to me, 'I am sorry I could not do much for you, my child.' I was awake but did not have the courage to say anything to her at all. My Mother, the reason for my being, the one who brought me in to this world, was apologising to me as she felt that she had not stood by me enough, she had not supported me enough, while she was the reason I am still around, in this country, in this world! I let Mum be. I had no words to convey to her that I needed nothing more than just her presence in my life. We both eventually fell asleep, with heavy hearts and exhausted heads resting on soaked pillows. Mum was later released from the hospital and went on to make a full recovery. Neither of us ever mentioned that night to each other or to anyone else for that matter. It lies buried in our souls.

However, that night became a turning point in my relationship with my mother. We may fight over anything and everything under the sun, but we all agree unanimously that if there is one person who can be credited for keeping our family of seven together over the last four decades through all the highs and lows of life, it is none other than my mother. Having come so close to losing her, perhaps I, subconsciously became more aware of her being. In an effort to understand her beyond the spoken, I started paying closer attention to her expressions, her choice of words in order to decipher what she actually wishes to convey. Slowly I was able to gauge her mood by just looking at her. Over a period of time, I truly started enjoying the little things Mum does and how she behaves when faced with certain scenarios or dilemmas.

Of recent, I started jotting these amusing yet poignant everyday incidents down. This book is just a simple salute to her, an effort to rejoice in the mundane life of my mother. It is an attempt to celebrate the life, lifestyle, and life perspectives of a 70-year-old Punjabi woman, who has always been a daughter, a sister, a wife, a mother, a grandmother, and a housewife. I am hoping that just as writing these logs and compiling this book has brought me closer to my mother, it brings you closer to your loved ones too.

Every life is a very precious gift with a hidden expiry date. Obituaries and eulogies are meaningless if we could not make our dear ones feel loved while we have a chance. Let's make an effort to cherish our loved ones while they are still around us!

ik pagal budiya

Maañ se ik bachche ne pūchhā

Chāñd meñ ye dhabbā kaisā hai

Maañ ye bolī

Chandā beTe

Jis ko tum dhabbā kahte ho vo to ik pāgal buḌhiyā hai

Bachche ne māsūm āñkhoñ se

Kuchh lamhoñ tak maañ ko baḌī hairat se dekhā

Aur ye pūchhā

Maañ jab maiñ chandā beTā huuñ

To mujh meñ bhī ik pāgal buḌhiyā hogī

Maañ ne us ko bheñch liyā

Us ke lab chūme

Gardan chūmī

Māthā chūmā

Aur ye bolī

Haañ tujh meñ bhī ik pāgal buḌhiyā hai

- Rahi Masoon Raza

Pride and a Little Prejudice

Mother is who wakes up earlier than usual to make stuffed paranthas[3] for the long trip ahead, packs a travel-friendly packet of knick-knacks to help you beat hunger pangs on the move. Mother is who stuffs a few hundreds, fifties, twenties and tens into your jacket's pocket, as she does not want you stranded for 'smaller' notes in a strange city. Yes, she had obviously frisked through your wallet to check if you had enough cash and the composition of the cash behind your back! Mother is who hugs you tight, wishes you well and waves you off with her blessings on a bitterly cold morning as you sit in the cab to catch Shatabdi for Delhi. Mother is who will not send you a 'good morning forward', but a little personalised note to say, 'Rock it Baby!'

Mother is who will not keep calling every hour to check where you are, what you are doing, or even if you have eaten. She knows her grooming is at work! Mother is who will remain awake till 10 pm, and then call you just once to see if you can speak, catch up a little, and will then blow kisses through the

---

[3] ਪਰਾਂਠਾ (Stuffed and pan-fried Indian bread).

phone to say goodnight. Mother is who will call you during your return journey to ask if you would like a parantha or rice for dinner.

Mother is who sends a text message to you saying, 'Waiting, give me a missed call when you reach home.' She understands you are returning home after days, must be tired, possibly hungry and definitely cold. She does not want you to have to wait in the cold verandah for someone to get the bearings around to open the door for you. She stays awake well past her sleep time, till almost midnight, to open the door for you.

Mother is who waits for you with a fist full of smaller notes right there in her hand, in case I have used up all the cash currency to pay the cabbie. Mother is who sits by the cold window herself to hear the iron-gate open and run to your cab to help you with the luggage. You notice she has lined up your night clothes neatly, geyser is on, hot water bottle is already in the blanket and there is a glass of hot cinnamon-ginger-honey water to warm your cockles, so to speak.

Mother is in whose arms you finally fall for that big beary hug to fill your heart with the warmth of the world. She is the one who can stitch all your pieces together and cleanse your greasy soul in less than a blink. Just when you pick up your bags to go to your room, Mother is also the one who hands over something round, like a little round steel tiffin box in your hand and says, 'Kithe challi? Pehlaan gate nu taala la ke aa!'[4]

Regardless, how can we not love the hands, which tend us like tiny daisies, even when we have grown up into those large, un-shapely banyan trees? It had been a productive but

____

[4] ਕਿਥੇ ਚੱਲੀ? ਪਹਿਲਾਂ gate ਨੂੰ ਤਾਲਾ ਲਾ ਕੇ ਆ (Where you think you are going? Go lock the main gate first!)

quite a crazy week, which kept me on the road for long hours. This, of course, meant that I became susceptible to either skip or binge on food and missed my date with my drinking water bottle often. All of this worries my mother no end as it took her over a year to nurse me back to this level of fitness since chikungunya struck.

However, despite being a typical emotional Punjabi Mother, she held on to her horses every day, till the clock stuck 6 pm and that is when she would call to gently establish my coordinates. Thereafter she would patiently wait for me to ring the doorbell after 8 pm and greet me with a tight hug.

Alas! every good thing comes to an end they say, as it did for me too one fine evening. Mum called around 6 pm to find out if I had had my lunch somewhere and unfortunately I blurted out, 'Nahin'.[5] That's it. All hell broke loose! 'Eh kadar hai Maa di? Ker ditti meri saari mehnat suaah? Kinne maheene lagaa ke tainu kharra keeta si. Akal hai ke nahi kuch? Eh shareer khatam ker lena tu! Kise ne nahin tainu puchhna je pher manje utte pae gayi!! Neyaani reh gayi hunn? Kehna mannan wale din te jammi hee nahin na!!'[6] Before Mother Superior could add any more dialogues in her maternally colourful lingo, I quickly truncated the call by telling her that I was going to get home late and had reached the venue for my next meeting!

---

[5] ਨਹੀਂ *(No).*

[6] ਇਹ ਕਦਰ ਹੈ ਮਾਂ ਦੀ? ਕਰ ਦਿੱਤੀ ਮੇਰੀ ਸਾਰੀ ਮੇਹਨਤ ਸੁਆਹ? ਕਿੰਨੇ ਮਹੀਨੇ ਲਗਾ ਕੇ ਤੈਨੂੰ ਖੜਾ ਕੀਤਾ ਸੀ. ਅਕਲ ਹੈ ਕੇ ਨਹੀਂ ਕੁਛ? ਇਹ ਸਰੀਰ ਖਤਮ ਕਰ ਲੈਣਾ ਤੂੰ! ਕਿਸੇ ਨੇ ਨਹੀਂ ਤੈਨੂੰ ਪੁੱਛਣਾ ਜੇ ਫੇਰ ਮੰਜੇ ਉੱਤੇ ਪੈ ਗਈ!! ਨਿਆਣੀ ਰਹਿ ਗਈ ਹੁਣ? ਕਹਿਣਾ ਮੰਨਣ ਵਾਲੇ ਦਿਨ ਤੇ ਜੰਮੀ ਹੀ ਨਹੀਂ ਨਾ! *(Is this how much you value your mother? You have poured water over all my efforts. It took me months to get your pain-ravaged body back into health. Can't you use your brains for once? You will ruin your health and then no one will be there to look after you if you fall sick again. You are not a kid anymore. Oh Lord! Why am I wasting my time? Why do you always have to go contrary to the instructions I give you?)*

Still reeling under the barrage of the motherly abuse I had endured in the evening, I finally reached home around 11 pm. Mum opened the door to me but the customary hug was missing. I can't deny that I deserved this cold treatment. I quietly went to change into my jim-jams and as I headed towards my bed, I found freshly warmed dinner by the bedside and hot water bottle in my blanket.

This is how my mother stands by me every step of the way. She stands tall when my work is appreciated. Blessing me profusely is her way of saying, 'I am proud of you.' If someone questions my work, she turns her back towards them and says to me, 'Let your work be a slap on their face.' When she sees me struggling, she makes sure everything from my food to clothes and even shoes are in order, so that I don't have to sweat over the little stuff. She often says, 'Je Ma parrhi-likhi hundi te tere daftar de kamm vi kardi. Hunn jo main ker sakdi haan, uss naal hee tera saath devaangi.'[7] Little does she know, she is my pillar of strength. I owe my being to her courage and her passion for life is my sole inspiration.

And then you catch your Mother Darling looking at the daily newspapers. Hindustan Times (HT) was celebrating its 18th anniversary with a pullout on fitness, featuring CATS (Chandigarh Adventures, Treks and Sports). CATS is the adventure group I had formed in 2007 with the support of Mr. Vivek Atray, the then Director Tourism of Chandigarh with the sole purpose of getting people to leave the concrete jungle behind once a month and realign themselves with Mother Nature.

---

[7] ਜੇ ਮਾਂ ਪੜ੍ਹੀ-ਲਿਖੀ ਹੁੰਦੀ ਤੇ ਤੇਰੇ ਦਫ਼ਤਰ ਦੇ ਕੰਮ ਵੀ ਕਰਦੀ. ਹੁਣ ਜੋ ਮੈਂ ਕਰ ਸਕਦੀ ਹਾਂ, ਉਸ ਨਾਲ ਹੀ ਤੇਰਾ ਸਾਥ ਦੇਵਾਂਗੀ (Had your mother been highly educated, then she would have done your office work too. However, I will support you with what I know best.)

CATS brought together socially conscious and environmentally friendly individuals to raise environmental concerns through adventure sports activities such as hiking, biking, trekking, white water rafting, paragliding, and camping. With 'Explore, not exploit' as our motto, we have undertaken more than a hundred activities everything from Leh down to Bundelkhand and the backwaters. Members of CATS slowly brought their better halves and then their children along to the activities. Coming back to the news coverage, HT wrote about CATS along with a picture of yours truly, the Big Fat CAT.

As I sensed a little smile playing at the edges of Mum's mouth, I also felt a little pride on her relaxed forehead. When Mum figured out that the proud mother had been caught 'red-handed', Mother Superior quickly put the paper down, turned around and quipped, 'Meri hee paali hoyi ethhe pahunchi hain.'[8] As I rolled my eyes and was about to turn around, she caught hold of my hand and blew a flying kiss towards me. That's how my Mother Darling says, 'Love You Kiddo!'

Her pride in CATS does take some unexpected turns. The other morning Mother Darling entered the room and declared with great drama, 'Munni tu te ker tyaari Triund jaan di.'[9] Though always up for travel and trekking, this is not something I wanted to hear on a cold, wet and grey miserable morning, especially when one does not feel like even getting out of bed and had resolved to work from home! Feeling intrigued and befuddled by her sudden declaration, I looked up from my laptop and asked her meekly, 'ki hoya?'[10]

---

[8] ਮੇਰੀ ਹੀ ਪਾਲੀ ਹੋਇ ਏਥੇ ਪਹੁੰਚੀ ਹੈਂ (The credit for you reaching this stage goes only to me. I am the one who brought you up to reach this far in life.)
[9] ਮੁੰਨੀ ਤੂੰ ਤੇ ਕਰ ਤਿਆਰੀ Triund ਜਾਂ ਦੀ (Kid you better start making preparations for Triund.)
[10] ਕੀ ਹੋਇਆ? (What happened?)

Raising her plump arms up in the air, giving whatever little twirl her portly body could offer, Mum let the cat out of the bag, 'Oh rang-barangi vaddi saari chhatri jehri tu Triund trek ton le ke aayi si na, ohde hath-paer jahe tutte laggde ne. Chal uth navi leya ke de Ma nu.'[11]

To give you an idea, Triund Peak is at a height of 2800 metres, nestled away in Kangra district of Himachal Pradesh. To reach Triund one needs to travel by road for 7 hours from home (Chandigarh) and then trek for another 3-4 hours each way on a good day to kiss the peak! Mum wanted me to do all this for an umbrella. 'There's a thing called Amazon mother?' I let out of my mouth and I was suitably rewarded with a clip around the ear for making this suggestion.

I happen to be a product born in a patriarch atmosphere where women from Mum's generation were encouraged to study only as long as it enhances their matrimonial prospects. Hence, my mother could never achieve her dream of graduating. Yet, my mother's constant claims about her not being well read fell apart when I saw her reading through my thesis on incest abuse. While the rest of the world was full of apprehensions about my decision to work on incest abuse in the country, my mother never had any doubts. You would be surprised to read what she had to say to me after reading my thesis.

I refer back to what happened in the spring of the year 2016, when I had already been researching incest abuse as part of my Post Graduate Diploma in Human Rights & Duties at Panjab University since six months. I picked this topic after

---

[11] ਉਹ ਰੰਗ-ਬਰੰਗੀ ਵੱਡੀ ਸਾਰੀ ਛਤਰੀ ਜਿਹੜੀ ਤੂੰ Triund trek ਤੋਂ ਲੈ ਕੇ ਆਈ ਸੀ ਨਾ, ਉਹਦੇ ਹੱਥ-ਪੈਰ ਜਹੇ ਟੁੱਟੇ ਲੱਗਦੇ ਨੇ. ਚੱਲ ਉੱਠ ਨਵੀਂ ਲੈ ਕੇ ਦੇ ਮਾਂ ਨੂੰ *(That colourful umbrella you bought during your last Triund trek, it seems to have fractured all its limbs. You better get going to Triund as Mum needs a replacement.)*

much debate. I guess at some level I picked up incest abuse because no one wants to talk about it.

As mentioned already, I was deterred by almost everyone you can possibly imagine: nearly all my professors, my learned academician friend Vipin Dewan and my cop friend whom we affectionately call Boss.

It took long hours of heated arguments and fact finding to come to an agreement about what incest actually means and how can it even be defined. Vipin had felt that given the subject is such a taboo, even two people won't respond to my research questionnaire and he did not want me to waste time. Boss was afraid for my personal safety as he felt that given this is so deep-rooted, sooner or later I would be at the receiving end of those who are benefitting from this practice. My professors I guess wanted me to pick up a topic that was easier to manage. However, taking things easy was not my style!

I would never forget a phone call I received one evening from the gentlest of souls, Dr. N.N. Wig who is revered as 'The Father of Psychiatry' in the country. I had met him in the afternoon to share the research work and we had a long discussion over a cup of coffee. He asked me to leave the thesis behind for him to read, which I assumed he would do at his leisure. Much to my amazement, within hours he called to congratulate me for working on such a challenging subject.

In the same breath, he offered his expertise as a psychiatrist to anyone suffering from mental trauma arising out of incest abuse. Most importantly, he accepted my request to support the work by guiding me through the maze of this dark social taboo. Suddenly I had found an anchor for my work, which no one wanted to touch with a barge pole. I remember he would often introduce me as 'a very brave girl', yet, he would warn me in the gentlest of tones to expect the brickbats along with the bouquets.

Indeed the journey was pretty tough, as no one wanted to use the word 'incest', not even in my own family. My own brother, who has an inquisitive mind and has an opinion about quite a few things under the sun, has never participated in any discussion about incest I continued to have over the last few months with friends, philosophers and guides. I tried to engage his children as it is important for children to know about incest abuse but they seemed a little too embarrassed. I expected nothing at all from my mother as she studied only till class 10 before she was married off to my father and incest is a word, which not many have heard, not even those who have experienced it themselves! Coming back to the research, I marched ahead supported by a small team and the research was launched without much fanfare. To our surprise, on the very first day 100 people filled the questionnaire by clicking on the link http://bit.ly/END-incest-research

For the sake of my coursework and to complete my Post Graduate Diploma, I analysed the data and presented the topic 'Incidence, Impact, Awareness & Reporting of Incest' in a thesis for the examiners during the viva voce. I remember I had left it at a prominent edge of the centre table in the room, as I did not want to forget to pick it up, just as I had forgotten to take my pencil box before sitting the exam a few months earlier!

My mother has an old habit of reading through the newspaper along with her morning cup of tea. She has been following this ritual since decades. However, that day, Mother Darling picked up the thesis instead. I felt amused and wondered what questions she might ask or what she might say to me about 'this work' or 'my topic'. Mum kept on sipping her tea while flicking through the thesis. I kept one eye on my laptop and the other on Mum, who was not turning the pages en-masse. Mum was actually reading the pages. Curiosity was killing the cat but I dared not breathe and break the mirage or the chain of thought.

After half an hour of scrutiny while still putting the thesis on the table Mum said, 'Next time if you are including a section on newspapers reporting the cases on incest, let me know and I will give you the newspaper cuttings.' Not a word more, not a word less; just one rock solid suggestion in support of my research, encouraging me to continue my work beyond the viva voce. The credit for the mounting evidence through 'incest crime log' we run on our Facebook page goes purely to Mother Darling. (https://www.facebook.com/endincest/).

The page led to a full-fledged project raising awareness about incest abuse across 11 Indian states and union territories within a year. Mum also financially supported the project by becoming the first official donor to form the End Incest Trust shortly afterwards. With mothers like these around, how can the daughters fail?

Despite the Mother Hen's constant oppression of her meek little Chicken, I do know that deep in her heart she is quite proud of what her Chicken has been delivering on various fronts. CATS is like that much-loved National Cadet Corps (NCC) team that has pitched tent at home and she looks forward to meet the main volunteers. Within months of starting CATS, we started donating blood in three well-organised camps every year. With 1700+ registered blood donors,

CATS has become one of the largest voluntary blood donor's groups, run a helpline 24/7 for blood needed in emergencies, support cancer patients in PGIMER (Post Graduate Institute of Medical Education & Research), Chandigarh, and send donors to 10 regional hospitals too. Needless to say, we have become one of the trusted names for blood needed to meet medical emergencies in the region.

Even a decade later, even though Mum takes great pride in the fact that not only I organise the blood donation camps, but also that I myself donate blood regularly. However, her maternal instinct takes over the moment I step home and she loads me with fresh juices, milk shakes and coconut water to make up for the fluid loss.

If this was not enough for the adventure enthusiasts, soon we formed Can and Will Foundation, a registered charity to undertake the project eduCATe Scholars whereby we began to mentor, guide and support the education of students who had cleared class +2 with 85%+ marks, had fire in the belly to achieve something but lack of finances prohibited them from achieving their professional career dreams. With a budget of Rs. 10 lakh per year, a sum raised entirely by the members without any CSR or government funding, we have been able to raise an army of 168 eduCATe Scholars till date, some of whom include doctors, engineers, chartered accountants, and computer scientists. Since CATS believe in working quietly without seeking publicity, when a local Digital Media House, Bigrox Media, approached me to shoot a small video about the origins of CATS and how we have progressed, I was obviously nervous. The short and crisp video was soon made available online. After sitting over it for a few days, I finally gathered the courage to show it to Mum.

After settling Mum down with her favourite cup of mint-ginger tea, I even fetched her glasses so that she does not miss any detail from the video. Little did I know that in my enthusiasm, I was digging my own grave! Mum quietly watched through the video and said, 'It is a GREAT VIDEO. Do congratulate the team who made this video. Everyone spoke so well. I like how they have made the effort to speak with different people and taken their opinions. WELL DONE.' Hearing this made my day and as I was about to switch off the laptop, Mum demanded, 'Dobaara Dikha'[12] and hearing this I knew my fate was sealed. Just a selection for you:

1. Chalo, je khapp paa ke aande ho, te koi bhalaa kamm vi ker hee lainde ho![13]

2. Vipin vekh kinna sohna boleya. Pata laggda hai koi parrya-likheya insaan hai. Sikh lai kuchh![14]

3. Ravideep sachhi Nawanshehr to aaya si khoon dein? Uss da khayaal rakhya see na poora?[15]

4. Eh college de bachhe te malook jahe laggde paye ne. Marjaani ehna da vi khoon peeta si.[16]

5. Jolly kol camp te jaan ta time hai, chachi nu milan da time nahi hai. Koi na![17]

---

[12] ਦੋਬਾਰਾ ਦਿਖਾ (Show me again.)

[13] ਚਲੋ ਜੇ ਖੱਪ ਪਾ ਕੇ ਆਂਦੇ ਹੋ ਤੇ ਕੋਈ ਭਲਾ ਕੰਮ ਵੀ ਕਰਦੇ ਹੋ (Good that you do something for the society also while having fun.)

[14] ਵਿਪਿਨ ਦੇਖ ਕਿੰਨਾ ਸੋਹਣਾ ਬੋਲਿਆ ... ਪਤਾ ਲੱਗਦਾ ਹੈ ਕੋਈ ਪੜ੍ਹਿਆ ਲਿਖਿਆ ਇਨਸਾਨ ਹੈ ... ਸਿੱਖ ਲੈ ਕੁੱਛ! (See how well Vipin spoke? One can clearly discern that he is a well-read person. Learn something from him.)

[15] ਰਵਿਦੀਪ ਸੱਚੀ ਨਵੇਂਸ਼ਹਿਰ ਤੋਂ ਆਇਆ ਸੀ? ਉੱਸ ਦਾ ਖਿਆਲ ਰੱਖਿਆ ਸੀ ਨਾ ਪੂਰਾ? (Did Ravideep really come all the way from Nawan Shehar city? I hope you took good care of him.)

[16] ਇਹ ਕਾਲਜ ਦੇ ਬੱਚੇ ਤੇ ਮਲੂਕ ਜਹੇ ਲੱਗਦੇ ਪਾਏ ਨੇ ... ਮਰਜਾਣੀ ਇਹਨਾਂ ਦਾ ਵੀ ਖੂਨ ਪੀਤਾ ਸੀ? (These college kids look really frail. Don't tell me you took their blood also!)

[17] ਜੌਲੀ ਕੋਲ camp ਤੇ ਜਾਣ ਦਾ ਟਾਈਮ ਹੈ? ਚਾਚੀ ਨੂੰ ਮਿਲਣ ਦਾ ਟਾਈਮ ਨਹੀਂ ਉੱਸ ਕੋਲ. ਕੋਈ ਨਾ! (Jolly has time to go to the camp but he has no time to come and meet me. Don't worry, I will take him to task.)

6. Akshi di Mumma nu mere vallon mubarakbaad deni hai. Kuri bahut syaani hai.[18]

And then came what I was dreading the most:

7. Bright colours paa leindi tu? thorri hor sohni laggdi pher.[19]

8. Lokee kehnge ma khan nu nahin dindi, taan hee kuri di awaaz nahi nikkaldee payi.[20]

There, there now. If you think what would a septuagenarian housewife know about business generation ideas, read on.

One day while massaging a smelly oily concoction into my joints:

Mum: Dekh maalish naal kinna farak pai reha hai.[21]

The Chicken: Pher meri ma da hath hai.[22]

Mum: Company da naam koi changga jeha soch lae.[23]

The Chicken loved Mum's entrepreneurial thought process. Mum defies all logic of age and enthusiasm. I felt absolutely proud to be her daughter. Without looking at me, **Mum continued:** Main hunn sochdi haan ke 500 da rate taan hona hee chahida hai.[24] The Chicken smiled indulgently.

Mum added further: Tael da paisa alag.[25] The Chicken had a huge grin on the face by now.

---

[18] ਅਕਸ਼ੀ ਦੀ ਮੰਮਾ ਨੂੰ ਮੇਰੇ ਵੱਲੋਂ ਮੁਬਾਰਕਬਾਦ ਦੇਣੀ ਹੈ. ਕੁੜੀ ਬਹੁਤ ਸਿਆਣੀ ਹੈ. (Do compliment Akshi's Mum on my behalf. She has raised a very responsible girl.)

[19] ਬ੍ਰਾਈਟ ਕਲਰ ਪਾ ਲੈਂਦੀ ਤੂੰ? ਥੋੜੀ ਹੋਰ ਸੋਹਣੀ ਲੱਗਦੀ ਫੇਰ (Could you not have worn bright colours? You would have looked even more pretty!)

[20] ਲੋਕੀ ਕਹਿਣਗੇ ਮਾਂ ਖਾਣ ਨੂੰ ਨਹੀਂ ਦਿੰਦੀ ਤਾਂ ਹੀ ਕੁੜੀ ਦੀ ਆਵਾਜ਼ ਨਹੀਂ ਨਿਕਲਦੀ ਪਈ (People might feel that I don't feed you enough, that is why your voice is so feeble!)

[21] ਦੇਖ ਮਾਲਿਸ਼ ਨਾਲ ਕਿੰਨਾ ਫਰਕ ਪੈ ਰਿਹਾ ਹੈ (See, how beneficial massage is proving for you?)

[22] ਫੇਰ ਮੇਰੀ ਮਾਂ ਦਾ ਹੱਥ ਹੈ (Well, these are my mother's hands after all.)

[23] ਕੰਪਨੀ ਦਾ ਨਾਮ ਕੋਈ ਚੰਗਾ ਜੇਹਾ ਸੋਚ ਲੈ (Think of a good name for the company.)

[24] ਮਾਂ ਹੁਣ ਸੋਚਦੀ ਹੈ ਕੇ 500/- ਦਾ ਰੇਟ ਤਾਂ ਹੋਣਾ ਹੀ ਚਾਹੀਦਾ ਹੈ (I am thinking that rate must be at least Rs.500/-.)

[25] ਤੇਲ ਦੇ ਪੈਸੇ ਅਲੱਗ *(Cost of oil should be charged extra.)*

Mum: Tax rate tu pata kareingi ke main Monica nu puchhan?[26] The Chicken almost fell off the bed. Matter was getting serious now.

Mum: Tip alag ton honi chahidi hai.[27] Just as she said this, Mum tugged at my beleaguered shoulder a little harder making me wince aloud.

The Chicken could not help adding: Galat tareeke naal maalish karan khaatir 100/- kattye gaye.[28]

Hearing this Mum twisted my elbow 'a little' and the Chicken shouted, '100/- hor gaye!!'[29] Mum looked straight into my eyes by now and gave an oily clip around my ear. I could not escape as my arm was in her other hand.

The Chicken screamed: Client assault kaaran lawyer fee 250/- rupaye!! Tussi te ker leya business! 50/- bachhe sirf tuhaade kol.[30] Mum was done by this time and I peacefully slept the night away. That oily concoction and Mum's hands is a magical combo for the joint pains. I slept like a baby.

Every morning after our tea and newspaper formality, Mum usually does the massage round, but this particular morning she made no effort to grab her chair and oil jar. Then she had her bath and got dressed. She chose a new suit to wear and asked me to match a lipstick, which I dutifully did. All done I eagerly looked at her and asked if she was ready to do the magical massage on my creaky joints. Mum threw a nonchalant glance

---

[26] ਟੈਕਸ ਰੇਤ ਤੂੰ ਪਤਾ ਕਰੇਂਗੀ ਕੇ ਮੈਂ ਮੋਨਿਕਾ ਤੋਂ ਪੁਛਾਂ? *(Will you find out the tax rate or should I ask Monica direct?)*
[27] ਟਿਪ ਅਲੱਗ ਹੋਣੀ ਚਾਹੀਦੀ ਹੈ *(Tips have to be extra.)*
[28] ਗ਼ਲਤ ਤਰੀਕੇ ਨਾਲ ਮਾਲਿਸ਼ ਖਾਤਿਰ 100/- ਕੱਟਿਆ ਗਿਆ *(Rs. 100/- deducted for massaging in the wrong manner.)*
[29] 100/- ਹੋਰ ਗਏ! *(Rs. 100/- more deducted!)*
[30] ਕਲਾਇੰਟ ਨੂੰ ਮਾਰਨ ਖਾਤਿਰ ਵਕੀਲ ਦੀ ਫੀਸ 250/- !! ਤੁਸੀ ਤੇ ਕਰ ਲਿਆ ਕਾਰੋਬਾਰ! ਸਿਰਫ 50/- ਬਚੇ ਆਪ ਕੋਲ (Rs. 250/- deducted for assaulting the client. Prime example that you are out of your depth when it comes to running a business! Do you realize that you made only Rs.50/- after all this.)

in my direction and left the room, '50/- waale ton karwa lae!'[31] Boooohaahaaaa!!!!!!!!

Since my episode of chikungunya was turning chronic, I was trying almost every possible medicine and concoction under the sun to overcome the excruciating pain — right from trying ayurvedic medicine from Karnataka to boiled herbs to homeopathy. Apart from that smelly oily concoction Mum massages religiously into my joints, the second thing that I found the most refreshing was this watery concoction. You need to prepare it only once in the morning and just keep adding hot water to it the entire day. In addition to the prescribed herbs, I was fond of putting 'things' in my water bottle, such as a pinch of thyme, holy basil leaves, a squeeze of lemon, a sliver of lemon grass, a thread of ginger, primarily anything which is readily available in the kitchen.

Since being abandoned the previous day on account of challenging my Mother Superior's business plan, the poor Chicken with one arm painfully wrapped around the waist slowly got up to make her water bottle. As Mother Darling saw me adding rose petals from a bouquet into the bottle, she quietly walked up to me with some holy basil leaves in her hands and addressed me as menacingly as her cute face could conjure, 'Eh paani hunn tu kalli nahi pi sakdi!'[32] Done deal I say! Someone bring along the oil jar please.

Given Mother Darling's melodrama over my health and my commitment with my dear friend Binnie to get fit for her next trek, I went to the local park and this sight made my heart swell. There I found this tailor Ahmed who had set up a temporary shop

---

[31] 50/- ਵਾਲੇ ਤੋਂ ਕਰਵਾ ਲੈ! (Go get the massage done from the one who charges Rs. 50/-.)
[32] ਇਹ ਪਾਣੀ ਹੁਣ ਤੂੰ ਕੱਲੀ ਨਹੀਂ ਪੀ ਸਕਦੀ (You can't drink this water alone now.)

at the edge of the community park. He could not afford to pay the rent to a shopkeeper nor wished to part with his hard-earned money as commission to another tailor, so he devised this alternative. He bought a second-hand umbrella for roof and tarpauline for flooring. He has done 'setting' with the electricity guys having an empty corner in the room where he stores his sewing machine and paraphernalia for free at night. He shuts shop when it rains. It has been a month and he does roaring business taking advantage of the 'location' and rent-free 'shop'. As Mother Superior said, 'tussi saare MBA fail.'[33]

It might have taken me and my team months to turn denial into acceptance as far as prevalence of incest abuse in our society is concerned, but it has started happening, I was invited as one of the panellists for a 'conversation' co-hosted by the Canadian Consulate and the British High Commission. It was an engaging discussion on safe spaces for women online. It was attended by the Consulate General of Canada and the British High Commissioner, along with more than 50 concerned and conscientious citizens of the city. Human rights activist Sanam chaired the panel that included a lawyer, a youth activist, a politician, a transgender and yours truly. The idea was to look at the online space from all possible angles and perspectives.

After I returned home, Mum asked me about my day and I told her about this panel discussion. Without showing any photos, I told her what transpired. At first Mum smiled and gave me a kiss. Then suddenly dark clouds of doubt appeared on her face. Even before I could probe, she asked, 'Othe koi sunnan wala vi see ke aape magaj-maari ker ke aa gayi?'[34]

---

[33] ਤੁੱਸੀ ਸਾਰੇ MBA ਫੇਲ (All you MBAs fail.)
[34] ਓਥੇ ਕੋਈ ਸੁੱਨਣ ਵਾਲਾ ਵੀ ਸੀ ਕੇ ਆਪੇ ਮਗਜ-ਮਾਰੀ ਕਰ ਕੇ ਆ ਗਈ? (Was there any audience to listen to you or you just blew your own trumpet and returned home?)

Mum finally got convinced about the veracity of the event only after seeing the photos and media coverage in over half a dozen newspapers the following morning!

I can't deny that I do like lazy Sundays. No rush to have a bath and get out of the house. No need to wear anything but your comfy jim-jams. So as I was roaming around, almost aimlessly, soaking in the nothingness of a Sunday, all 5' and nothing of my Mum jumped right in front of me. Startled, I stepped back but I did not succeed as there is only so much one can press one's body into the kitchen cabinets. I tried to dodge her by stepping sideways and she moved with me in tandem. I finally threw the towel and asked her, 'Savere-savere Mumma?'[35] Mother Darling curled up her podgy hands into tight fists and wedged them into her non-existent waist, 'Laggi savere-savere di. Mumma nu good morning keeti ajj??!!'[36]

I suddenly realised that I had not tossed a flying kiss in her direction and tried to move out of her way again. Alas! She would have nothing of it. Instead, she moved a step closer to me. Feeling literally threatened as my ears were within her grasp now, I yelped, 'Lao good morning … hunn jaan deyo mainu!'[37] Mother Superior was not impressed, 'Iss terah taan nahin jaan dyungi tainu ajj.'[38] My mind started reeling as though it was a lazy balmy cold Sunday, I was still working from bed to complete a paper I was supposed to email 2 days ago! What was it that Mum wanted? Does she want to visit a friend? Go eat chaat? Walk in the Japanese Garden? Or just

---

[35] ਸਵੇਰੇ ਸਵੇਰੇ Mumma? (First thing in the morning Mum?)
[36] ਲੱਗੀ ਸਵੇਰੇ-ਸਵੇਰੇ ਦੀ … Mumma ਨੂੰ good morning ਕੀਤੀ ਅੱਜ??!!' (What do you mean first thing in the morning? Have you wished Mum a good morning today?)
[37] ਲਓ good morning .. ਹੁਣ ਜਾਂ ਦੇਯੋ ਮੈਨੂੰ (Alright … here … Good morning … Now let me go please.)
[38] ਇਸ ਤ੍ਰਹ ਤਾਂ ਨਹੀਂ ਜਾਣ ਦੇਉਂਗੀ ਤੈਨੂੰ ਅੱਜ (With this kind of attitude I won't let you go at all.)

go out for a furlough in the car? And since I was in jim-jams with no mood to change, none of these options particularly appealed to me.

Hesitatingly, the Chicken asked, 'Pher?'[39]

Mother Superior thundered, 'Punishment milegi hunn tainu!'[40]

That's it. She confirmed my worst fears. I would have to burn the midnight oil to finish the already long-pending document. Mother Superior would have me, embarrassingly so, certified as LASTMINUTE.com. Before I could open my mouth to plead guilty and seek forgiveness, she announced the sentence, 'Ikk tight jehi hug de hunn apni Maa nu … Eh sazaa hai teri.'[41]

Relieved, I loved and hugged all 5' and nothing of my Mother Darling in the kitchen, till the warmth of her hug brought back colour in my cheeks. In the same breath I must admit though that it is a bit of a challenge to hug the almost 5' circumference that comes with the territory; my mother, my maker, my caregiver, my everything.

---

[39] ਫੇਰ? (Then?)
[40] Punishment ਮਿਲੇਗੀ ਅੱਜ ਤੈਨੂੰ! (You shall be punished today!)
[41] ਇੱਕ tight ਜਿਹੀ hug ਦੇ ਆਪਣੀ Mumma ਨੂੰ … ਇਹ ਸਜ਼ਾ ਹੈ ਤੇਰੀ (Give one tight hug to your Mum … This is your punishment.)

Mothers are like buttons, they hold everything together.

- Unknown

The Precious Bond

I went to bed on the last day of the year, closing the chapter on yet another year with much unwritten and even more left unsaid. Time stops for no one they say, it marches on; and so it did to bring 2016 to a close too, closure be damned!

The first morning of the New Year sauntered in bright and crisp through the bedside window. However, since it was a double holiday of a Sunday combined with 1st January of the year 2017, I had no reason to stir out of the bed at the crack of dawn. Unlike my father of course, who keeps checking time through the night to finally wake up around 3.30 am Honestly, if anyone gave him breakfast at 6 am, he would leave for office before you could say 'Jack Robinson!' May God bless the alarm clock of our home!

To be truthful, my authoritarian father is nowhere near as challenging as a dear friend Riyaal's grandfather is, whose advancing years had made him a wee-bit more insecure of his well-being. This handsome nonagenarian while going to the washroom every couple of hours through the night would keep waking up his professional grandson each time to repeat the same instruction, 'Don't forget that you have to make tea for me at 6 am!'

May God bless my mother too, who also belongs to that disciplined generation for whom their morning walk is a ritual as important as reading through the newspaper every morning with her favourite cup of ginger tea. My thoroughly benevolent looking Mum can be found anywhere on a water gauge with both ends marked clearly; Mother Darling and Mother Superior! What you get on a particular day or just an odd stolen moment is purely your luck.

Today was special, as somehow Mum believes that the first day of the year represents how the rest of the year would follow and nothing must go wrong. We are not allowed to pick up a fight on 1st of January, get on each other's nerves or crib about the food being served. Mum goes overboard in order to ensure everything goes well on this one day of the year.

From the comfort of my warm blanket, I heard Mum return from her morning walk and walk straight to the kitchen. Soon, wafts of warm and fragrant desi ghee[42] filled my nostrils, warmed my heart and I drooled over the thoughts of 'Maa de hath da halwa'[43]. Proper Punjabi rich and loaded halwa rather than the cholesterol and calorie-conscious halwa we get when Bhabi[44] gets her way, and she gets away with it all too often. Finally, this 3-kg overweight fat cat had something to look forward to in the New Year.

Slowly as I rose from the dead and sat up in bed with my warm feet trying to locate the truant slippers on a cold floor, Mum in one swift movement got up from the sofa and stood

---

[42] ਦੇਸੀ ਘਿਉ (Clarified butter).
[43] ਮਾਂ ਦੇ ਹੱਥ ਦਾ ਹਲਵਾ (Traditional north Indian sweet made by mother, with love).
[44] ਭਾਬੀ (Brother's wife).

right in front of me. It was a little too quick for my drowsy brain to figure out if I was going to get a hug or a clip around the ear, but with no desire to tempt my fate, I did not even look up. With Mum towering over me, I sat still, waiting for the verdict to be delivered without being given an opportunity to be heard.

As expected, Mum made her next move with no notice whatsoever. Even before I could take a long breath to brace myself, I felt Mum's arms go around me. She held me in an embrace without saying a word. Gently she planted a few kisses on my ruffled hair and gave me a little squeeze around the shoulders, carefully avoiding any pressure on my chikungunya inflamed left shoulder joint. As I put my 'good' right arm around her waist, she took a step yet closer and held my head close to her heart in a warm embrace.

This is the woman who had borne my dead weight for 9 months in her womb, without being able to keep a morsel down in her belly. This is the woman who had given birth to a breech baby, which was declared dead upon birth. This is the woman who had refused to let me go, till I was revived, long after condolences had already been offered to my father.

Feeling misty eyed, I started counting the heartbeats of this gentle soul with a spine of steel. Chikungunya be damned, I raised my barely moveable left arm to complete my circle of love around Mum. As I locked my fingers behind my mother's back to stop my left arm from falling down, Mum started tenderly running her hand from my head to my shoulders, as if blessing me silently. I felt my nightshirt getting a little wet around my shoulders. Much as I did not want this to end, Mum also held on to me, as if refusing to let go of me, yet again.

May your year be as blessed, as my mother made mine this morning. Happy New Year.

Later in the year as I was struggling to stay awake one sultry afternoon, Mum asked me when is the Mother's Day? Feeling guilty that I had done nothing for her at all, I fibbed. I said, 'Ethe da pata nahin, England te March wich hunda hai.'[45] We left the conversation at that. Mum walked out and I felt even more guilty, more than usual actually.

While oscillating between guilt and sleep, Shayda, a journalist friend popped a question on WhatsApp, which woke me up suddenly. She wanted me to share 'Maa ki seekh'[46] in two lines. Now Shayda is someone you trust implicitly. When she asks something from you, you don't even ask for her motive behind the task because you know she would present things conscientiously and with a refreshing perspective. However, you are always keen to know how she writes the story.

First thing I did when I woke up the next morning was to switch on the laptop to look up the e-paper of Dainik Bhaskar and there I found my Mom on the front page of City Life, beaming with her usual grace, sitting above Nani's quote and wearing the maang teeka[47] Nana had gifted to Mum, which she had worn on her wedding day 52 years ago. Like any child, I could not wait to see Mum's reaction when she sees herself on the front page of the newspaper.

---

[45] ਇਥੇ ਦਾ ਪਤਾ ਨਹੀਂ, ਇੰਗਲੈਂਡ ਤੇ March ਵਿਚ ਹੁੰਦਾ ਹੈ (I don't know about India but in England we celebrate Mother's Day in March.)
[46] ਮਾਂ ਕੀ ਸੀਖ (Mother's advice).
[47] ਮਾਂਗ-ਟਿੱਕਾ (A piece of jewellery worn on the forehead by women in India).

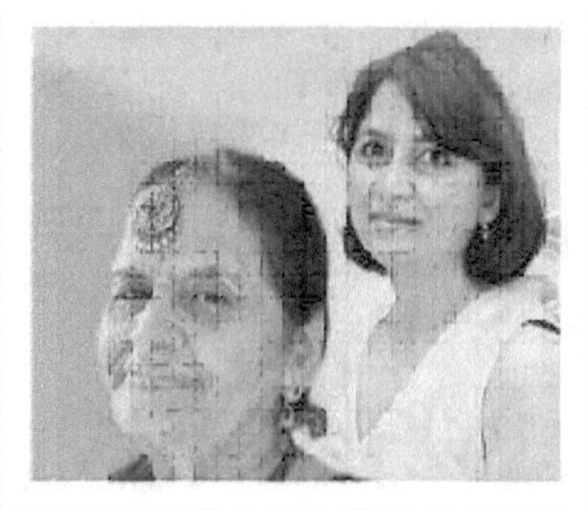

(Nani taught how to become larger than the problem,
Mother taught the magic of the spoken word)

Eventually Mum returned home from her morning walk. As she walked in, I cheerfully said 'good morning' which she merrily ignored and walked past! Then I shouted after her, 'Mumma, ethe aayo.'[48] She again ignored and went around doing her down stuff before finally emerging through the door. 'Ki chahida hai savere-savere?'[49] She almost gave me a whack when I told her to come wearing her glasses. Somehow, she mellowed, put on her glasses and stood by my bedside to look on the screen I was tapping. She broke into this huge smile and brought her face a little closer to the screen, 'Laa ditti tikke wali Ma?'[50]

As she realised that she was not looking at a random picture but that she was part of a newspaper story, she knelt down a little more to kiss my tousled hair, squeezed my shoulder and sat down quietly, very quietly. Reading the screen, tossing memories of her own beloved parents in her head, she

---

[48] Mumma ਇੱਥੇ ਆਇਓ (Mum can you please come over here?)
[49] ਕੀ ਚਾਹੀਦਾ ਹੈ ਸਵੇਰੇ-ਸਵੇਰੇ? (What do you need first thing in the morning?)
[50] ਲਾ ਦਿੱਤੀ ਟਿੱਕੇ ਵਾਲੀ ਮਾਂ? (So you got the tikka-wearing mother in the newspaper?)

pretended to prop up her face with her hand while I knew she was very delicately wiping off a tear from the corner of her eye. After reading those two lines, she hugged me tight and let her weight rest against my body. Shayda had brought three generations together in one picture you see, and ever so beautifully.

'71 saalan wich pehli vaar eho jeha Mother's Day aaya ke mera naam vi akhbaar vich aaya!'[51] Then she sat down on the sofa and said, 'Tainu pata ajj mera ki jee karda? Ke main ikk vaddhiya jeha, khasta jeha, naram jeha, aaluaan da bhareya hoya paraantha khawaan!'[52] And she manages to say all this by puckering up her nose, smacking her lips, crinkling up her eyes and rocking her head like a Russian doll, all in one go of course, 'Maawan te dhiyaan rall baithiyaan ni maaye, kardiyaan gallariyaan.'[53] How complex are Mum's moods and yet, how simple are Mum's ways to celebrate every aspect of life! Wish I imbibe some of these qualities.

My mother is fond of festivals, the whole lot of them, in fact all of them. She celebrates each one with equal aplomb, even if they keep emerging like the boxes off a production line! Her passion transcends beyond food as she puts her heart and soul into buying festival specific paraphernalia, and makes sure all 'shagun'[54] is done, as per the stated rituals. I feel somewhere this is her way of breaking the monotony of a housewife's life.

---

[51] 71 ਸਾਲਾਂ ਵਿਚ ਪਹਿਲੀ ਵਾਰ ਇਹੋ ਜੇਹਾ Mother's Day ਆਇਆ ਕੇ ਮੇਰਾ ਨਾਮ ਵੀ ਅਖਬਾਰ ਵਿਚ ਆਇਆ (It is for the first time in 71 years that my name has also been printed in the newspaper.)

[52] ਤੈਨੂੰ ਪਤਾ ਅੱਜ ਮੇਰਾ ਕੀ ਜੀ ਕਰਦਾ? ਕੇ ਮੈਂ ਇੱਕ ਵਧੀਆ ਜੇਹਾ, ਖਸਤਾ ਜੇਹਾ, ਨਰਮ ਜੇਹਾ, ਆਲੂਆਂ ਦਾ ਭਰਿਆ ਹੋਇਆ ਪਰੌਂਠਾ ਖਾਵਾਂ (Do you know what I fancy today? That I eat one nicely done, pan-fried, flaky, layered, Indian bread stuffed with savoury potatoes.)

[53] ਮਾਵਾਂ ਤੇ ਧੀਆਂ ਰੱਲ ਬੈਠੀਆਂ ਨੀ ਮਾਏ, ਕਰਦੀਆਂ ਗੱਲੜੀਆਂ (A traditional Punjabi folk song signifying the beautiful and strong relationship of mothers and daughters).

[54] ਸ਼ਗੁਨ (An act, an indication or an offering to convey best wishes or good luck).

Since the occasion was Karva Chauth[55], how can we let the sunrise without some mehandi[56] on our hands. There are four women in the house, all potential customers of mehandi, also popularly called 'henna tatto'. However, as luck would have it, both my Bhabi[57] and niece had already had the mehandi done. That left just Mum and I. Since I am not particularly fond of mehandi, Mum asked me to make some pattern on her hands to complete the 'shagun' ritual of a 'suhaagan'.[58] I protested loudly since though I can paint with oil colours on a canvas, I am hopeless in any other medium, on any other surface.

I find it absolutely impossible to control the watercolours on paper and the layer of acrylics dry even before I can make up my mind about which direction should I make the stream flow on the landscape I am trying to paint! Given this level of expertise, using a mehandi cone to thinly lace my mother's delicate hands with exquisite patterns in mehandi was a mission impossible. I offered to take Mum to a trained mehandi-wala[59] but she would have none of it. Despite my protests, Mother Darling paid no heed as she firmly believed that if one can paint a canvas and one's face, one should be able to draw mehandi patterns too!

I eventually had to call truce after Mother Darling refused to budge from her pole position. Instead of just dropping a huge blob in the middle of her palm as a sun with little dots around to make it decorative, I thought I might as well make use of my laptop a little

---

[55] ਕਰਵਾ ਚੌਥ (Karwa Chauth is an annual fast, a ritual observed primarily by married ladies to pray for good and long life of their husbands. Married women dress up in their fineries like a bride on this day and fast without food and water from dawn till the moon rises. As a thank you gesture, affectionate gifts are given by their husbands and family.)
[56] ਮਹਿੰਦੀ (Henna is considered to be pure and hence, especially used in all happy occasions.)
[57] ਭਾਬੀ (Brother's wife).
[58] ਸੁਹਾਗਣ (Married woman whose husband is alive).
[59] ਮਹਿੰਦੀ ਵਾਲਾ (The henna artist).

creatively. I searched on Google a few henna designs and zeroed in on one which I thought was decorative, and yet manageable for the artistically challenged daughter. I had to draw a roundish flower in the middle and draw fragile stems laden with leaves to run over her finger. That looked easy. Alas!

Believe me my friends, I tried my best. It wasn't mehandi but my soul which was pouring out of that henna cone and yet, despite best attempts, what I could manage was a flower with twisted petals. This flower was clearly not blooming bright on Mum's hand, but looking sorrowfully sad. It had seen better days!

Once I thought I was done, I told Mum to have a look and see if she wanted some changes to it. All chuffed, Mum reached out for her near-vision glasses with a huge smile on her face. In no time her expressions started changing. The smile turned into a blank face and then a scowl followed by an open mouth! Her head started moving from left to right, nonstop. Finally she turned to me and said every so regretfully,[60] 'Mainu bilkul vi umeed nahin si ke tu mera enna jaloos kad deingi. Tu te mainu munh chadd, kisse nu hath dikhaan jogi vi na chhadeya! Ni tu ikk vaari vi na socheya ke duniya ki kahugi?' I laughed my heart out. Mum has not spoken to me since, but I have lived to tell the tale!

On another morning Mum woke up in a contemplative mood. With the deepest of sighs I had heard in a long time, she said aloud, 'Jadd takk deh – de.'[61] Loosely translated this old Punjabi couplet means:

---

[60] ਮੈਨੂੰ ਬਿਲਕੁਲ ਵੀ ਉਮੀਦ ਨਹੀਂ ਸੀ ਕੇ ਤੂੰ ਮੇਰਾ ਇੰਨਾ ਜਲੂਸ ਕੱਢ ਦੇਂਗੀ. ਤੂੰ ਤੇ ਮੈਨੂੰ ਮੂੰਹ ਛੱਡ, ਕਿੱਸੇ ਨੂੰ ਹੱਥ ਦਿਖਾਣ ਜੋਗੀ ਨਹੀਂ ਛੱਡਿਆ! ਨੀ ਤੂੰ ਇੱਕ ਵਾਰੀ ਵੀ ਨਾ ਸੋਚਿਆ ਕੇ ਦੁਨੀਆਂ ਕੀ ਕਾਹੁਗੀ? *(Not for a minute did I think that you would create such a mess on my hand. Forget showing showing my face, I can't even show my hand to anyone in shame! Did you not think even once before messing up my hand, as to what would the world would think?)*

[61] ਜੱਦ ਤੱਕ ਦੇਹ - ਦੇ (Till you have the resources or are breathing, give/donate/offer).

Till you have the body (or being) – give/donate/offer
(Till you have the resources – give/donate/offer
OR perhaps
Till you are breathing – give/donate/offer)

I am not sure what had prompted Mum to recite this couplet. Was she wondering about the fragility of life? Was she worrying about Dad's health again? She had lost so much already, so many of her loved ones had been consigned to flames. Was she missing anyone in particular today? Why was she talking about giving away? Was she giving up on life? That was not like Mum at all. Was she worrying about what had she accumulated over her lifetime that she wanted to will away?

I shuddered. I can't even imagine my life without my mother. If anything was to happen to her, who would worry about me, fret over me, keep me on the straight and narrow? Who would pick fights with me over little things? There really is no one else who cares for me as much as Mum does. What would I do without her? Without saying a word, I rolled over a little towards her side of the sofa and let my head rest on her shoulder.

I did not want her to feel alarmed but I needed her to know that she is loved and wanted. I was desperate for her to know that she is the foundation of this household and we would all be lost without her. I didn't want her to know that I was feeling vulnerable because that would worry her even more. Seeing me broken would have made her feel like a failure as she gave her heart and soul to make both her kids strong. She underwent every hardship to ensure a brighter and better future for her kids. The mother so strong, so resilient, why was she uttering such a despondent phrase?

I held out my hand from the blanket towards my mother and said, 'chall mata de ki dena apni Munni nu.'[62] After a brief lull, Mother Superior lifted the blanket and gave me one whack around my ears. Just to make sure she had made her point, she went on to ask, 'bass ke kuchh hor vi devaan?'[63]

There are two truths which dawned upon me, pretty late I must say. First, no matter how old you become, you will always remain the little girl for your mother, the girl every mother will protect till her dying day. Second, looks can really be deceptive and we make an ass of ourselves when we make an assumption, truly proved to be an uncomfortable truth for yours truly that morning.

I had taken Mum to Fortis Hospital for her bi-annual consultation with Dr. Murlidharan, her endocrinologist. Since you are lucky to get an appointment with the most sought-after doctor of the town for diabetes and thyroid disorders once in 5 months, you make sure that you follow the instructions from the previous appointment to the tee. Though we reached in time and had the pre-appointment tests done, we were told to be prepared for an hour-long wait. Lucky enough to find two seats facing each other, I got busy with the opening ceremony of Rio Olympics on my phone and Mum started flicking through her WhatsApp messages.

Suddenly I felt a pair of 'trousered' legs stand too close to my 'dress legs'. At first I thought the owner of the legs would move out or step back, but he refused to budge. Unbeknown to me, Mother Darling sitting across me also noticed what was happening. Before I could say 'Boo to the goose', my Mum was already on her feet. Like only a blue-blooded sardarni can,

---

[62] ਚੱਲ ਮਾਤਾ ਦੇ ਕੀ ਦੇਣਾ ਆਪਣੀ ਮੁੰਨੀ ਨੂੰ (Fine Mum, now give to your daughter whatever you want to give.)
[63] ਬੱਸ ਕੇ ਕੁੱਛ ਹੋਰ ਵੀ ਦੇਵਾਂ? (Is this enough or should I give you some more?)

she went up to the young man and enquired very curtly, 'What are you looking at?' Sheepishly the man answered, 'My bottle of water is lying behind Ma'am's legs. Auntie can you please help me retrieve it?!' Mum and I burst out laughing. Once a mother, always a mother.

The other day Mother Darling came up to my bed, sat next to me and gave me an impromptu hug. Surprised I looked at her and in came a flying kiss. She was up to something but I just could not figure it out. I noticed that she was slipping her feet out of her furry winter carpet shoes so I thought perhaps she wanted to have a chat. She had just reconnected with lots of her cousins after decades, so perhaps she wanted to share her old memories with me. I suddenly felt special. This was going to be one special mommy-and-I session.

Just as I sat back in bed in preparation for a long heart-warming session with Mum and started to glow with a brush of daughter's pride, Mum said with twinkling eyes, 'Chal pher Ma di furr wali jutti paa ke dekh, kinni naram te nigghi hai.'[64] All Mum wanted to do was borrow my colourful rubber non-slip house slippers to use for her bathing session! Sab moh-maya hai.[65] As a dear friend Jagruti said something absolutely impossible to translate,

'Yeh jo moh maya ke dhaage, teri ungliyon se jaa uljhe …

Kitni khwahishon ko hain lipte, par jootiyon se gaye suljhe!'

Since newspapers either depress me or agitate me, I don't read them. I much prefer to catch up on the news on the net, choosing the sections I can digest. Mother Superior does not

---

[64] ਚੱਲ ਫੇਰ ਮਾਂ ਦੀ furr ਵਾਲੀ ਜੁੱਤੀ ਪਾ ਕੇ ਵੇਖ, ਕਿੰਨੀ ਨਰਮ ਤੇ ਨਿੱਗੀ ਹੈ (Come, wear Mum's cosy fur-laced slippers. These will keep your feet nice and snug.)
[65] ਸਬ ਮੋਹ-ਮਾਇਆ ਹੈ (The whole world is nothing but an illusion.)

like it. Being old-fashioned, she likes newspapers and believes they must be read. PERIOD. So following her morning routine, Mum makes the tea and serves it with a rusk and a newspaper. Much to her chagrin, I tend to drink the tea while catching up with work using my mobile or the laptop, completely ignoring the newspapers.

I remember a fine morning which also happened to be CATS blood donation camp no. 27, I was sipping tea and making some last-minute calls to Fortis Hospital's Blood Bank as well as sending in some text messages. While balancing her cuppa-cha in one hand and the newspaper in her other hand, Mum kept peering over her reading glasses to see what was I doing, and not doing, disapprovingly of course. Finally she slammed her cup down to get my attention and said ever so politely, 'Eh akhbaar parran layi ditte ne tainu, kambal nu niggha rakhan layi nahi ditte!'[66]

Everyday Mother Darling is slowly finding different ways to introduce me back to reading newspapers, as I continue to evade her attempts, all done surreptitiously of course. The other day Mum made the herbal tea as usual but brought along a coconut cookie. Noisily as she put the plate full of goodies down, she used her now empty hand to pat my cheek and said very endearingly, 'Chai Chai Chai Wala.'[67] Just as I warmed up to her and gave her a flying kiss, pat emerged her other hand with a fistful of newspapers, 'Dekh duniya wich kee ho reya hai.'[68] Then she went a step further and walked off with my mobile! Once a mother, always a mother! In one flick second she reduced me to the status of my teenaged nephew who is

---

[66] ਇਹ ਅਖਬਾਰ ਪੜ੍ਹਨ ਲਈ ਦਿੱਤੇ ਨੇ ਤੈਨੂੰ.. ਕੰਬਲ ਨੂੰ ਨਿੱਘਾ ਰੱਖਣ ਲਈ ਨਹੀਂ ਦਿੱਤੇ (I have given you these newspapers to read, not to warm up your blanket!)
[67] ਚਾਹ ਚਾਹ ਚਾਹਵਾਲਾ (Chai – Hot Chai … Anyone for tea?)
[68] ਦੇਖ ਦੁਨੀਆਂ ਵਿੱਚ ਕੀ ਹੋ ਰਿਹਾ ਹੈ (See what is happening outside in this world.)

randomly awarded 'gadget ban' for watching too much TV or even for not drinking eight glasses of water a day! If Mother Superior is going to toddle off with my mobile or hide my laptop, I might as well balance the loss of work with a gain on health front and go out for a walk!

As Mum kept getting regular at hiding my gadgets, I started going for my morning walk regularly. Upon my return to the house, I would pick up the papers from the gate. Allow me to share that Mum's efforts were producing results. I started to selectively browse through the papers. I skipped over the kill/steal/rape news and pour over the progressive/constructive news. I must confess that between Hansie Cronje admitting to match fixing in 2000 and tennis match-fixing scandal recently, I still don't really open the sports pages. Spending about 20 minutes on the papers was a major achievement as far as I was concerned, courtesy Mother Darling. However, she had little confidence in my newspaper reading and still eyes me suspiciously.

So this morning after we were done with the tea and I gave all the papers back to her, she grabbed my arm and made me sit next to her on the sofa. I thought Mum was in a good Sunday mood and was expecting a cuddle from her. Alas! Mum opened the city edition of a national paper and said, 'Tu akhbaar parr laye na?'[69] The Chicken answered confidently, 'Haanji'.[70] Mum marched ahead, 'Chal pher dass, Aikom da bhog kadon hai?'[71] Now I honestly dont pay attention to the obituaries as that is Dad's department. He generally looks up those 'Kaale haashiye wale frame'[72] to find out which friend or acquaintance has he lost. Hedging my bets on the assumption

---

[69] ਤੂੰ ਅਖਬਾਰ ਪੜ ਲਏ ਨਾ? (You have read the newspapers, right?)
[70] ਹਾਂਜੀ (Yes).
[71] ਚੱਲ ਫੇਰ ਦੱਸ ਏਕਮ ਦਾ ਭੋਗ ਕਦੋਂ ਹੈ? (Go on then. Tell me when are the last prayers of Ekom?)
[72] ਕਾਲੇ ਹਾਸ਼ੀਏ ਵਾਲੇ ਫਰੇਮ (The obituaries which are always written in black borders).

that bhog notifications usually appear on the same day the bhog is, I said, 'Today'. Mum gave me a look of approval and I heaved a sigh of relief. As I made a move to get away, Mum pinned me down to the sofa, giving a clear indication she is not done yet with me.

Mum turned another page of the main newspaper and asked, 'Who is Chancellor of Panjab University?' This one I knew so I promptly said, 'Vice President of India'. Mother Superior was not impressed, 'Naam Dass!!'[73] Being terrible with names, for a moment I went blank and then said, 'Mum he used to be in the Foreign Services.' Unimpressed, she started reaching out to my ear just when lightening struck and hallelujah, 'ANSARI' I shouted while pulling away from her. Fortunately, Dad walked in to ask something off Mum, enough of a diversion for the Chicken to disappear from the room altogether to save its skin on a cool Sunday morning.

Since my biggest weakness is boredom tied down with routine, I decided to alternate walking, running with cycling to break the monotony of every morning. Upon seeing the old cycle getting oiled and repaired, mother affectionately put her arm around my shoulders. I got encouraged with the huge smile on her face, thinking she was just the support I could rely on when chips would be down. Alas! Little did I know!

Even before I could respond to her deceptively benign looking smile, Mum quipped, 'Dekh cycle theek karwa rahin hain, hunn 4 din chalaa vi layeen!'[74] As I looked sheepishly at her, thinking about my last bout of fitness bug which lasted less than a week, Mum had more to add, 'Tu shayd bhull gayi

---

[73] ਨਾਮ ਦੱਸ (Tell me the name.)

[74] ਦੇਖ ਸਾਈਕਲ ਠੀਕ ਕਰਵਾ ਰਹੀ ਹੈਂ, ਹੁਣ ਚਾਰ ਦਿਨ ਚਲਾ ਵੀ ਲਈਂ! (See now that you are getting your bicycle repaired, make sure that you use it too for a few days.)

hovein, cycle sirf onni hee door chala ke jaavin, jithon wapis ghar pahunch sakein, aap cycle chala ke!'[75]

As if this was not enough, Mother Darling continued, 'Pichhali vaar di tera rasste vich lokaan to paani na mangdi vapis aayeen!'[76] Just when I thought Mum was done with me, I heard my nephew chime in, 'Grandma she did not ask for water from passersby. She actually rode into the local hospital and asked for glucose water with lemon without a penny in her pocket to pay for it!' Humm Ho! Is there any hope for me?!!

For someone who ran an adventure group, to be virtually paralysed neck down for weeks with no end to the pain in joints, was a huge shock to my body and soul. Life took on a different meaning altogether when I had virtually been grounded with chikungunya. I went to sleep feeling shivery and just could not get out of bed even to brush my teeth the following morning.

The sheer pain in every small and large joint was simply debilitating. I am not sure who was more heart broken at seeing my body in this shape: my mother or me? Mum had to help me with everything, right from lifting my non-responsive body into a sitting position and then helping me get on my feet. I literally had to drag myself to the sink to brush my teeth, only to realise that I could not even unscrew the toothpaste tube. I had to call Mum out to so do. Once the toothpaste was on the brush I realised I could not rotate the tap handle to get the water. Mum opened the tap too for me. Then I realised that my hand could not grip the toothbrush handle. I kept the toothbrush in one place and moved my head left to right to go through the motions of cleaning my mouth! I guess this should give you a fair

---

[75] ਤੂੰ ਸ਼ਾਇਦ ਭੁੱਲ ਗਈ ਹੋਵੇਂ, ਸਾਈਕਲ ਸਿਰਫ਼ ਉੱਨੀ ਦੂਰ ਹੀ ਚਲਾ ਕੇ ਜਾਵੀਂ, ਜਿਥੋਂ ਵਾਪਿਸ ਘਰ ਪਹੁੰਚ ਸਕੋ ਆਪ ਸਾਈਕਲ ਚਲਾ ਕੇ! (In case you have forgotten, cycle only as far as you can pedal back the cycle on your own.)

[76] ਪਿਛਲੀ ਵਾਰ ਦੀ ਤਰ੍ਹਾਂ ਰਸਤੇ ਵਿੱਚ ਲੋਕਾਂ ਤੋਂ ਪਾਣੀ ਨਾ ਮੰਗਦੀ ਵਾਪਿਸ ਆਈਂ! (Don't start asking for water from passers-by, as you did last time.)

idea of how bad the scenario was with me. Slowly it dawned upon us that I had turned into a chronic case of chikungunya and we made peace knowing that I would take months to recover. It was not going to be easy but was there a choice?

When this hyper-active and super-busy woman was tied to the bed, even I did not know what to do with myself to be honest. One day I got so bored of my life that I popped some painkillers and decided I deserved some fresh air. Tempted by the 'Vagina Monologues' being staged today at Tagore Theatre, I called up a dear friend who is also fond of theatre. However, since my body was functioning at a fraction of the speed of my brain, I had loads to organise. I had to forewarn my friend, gently of course, just in case she changed her mind if I told her the real situation.

Mum overheard me talking to a friend over the phone, 'If you pick me up from home, can you please ensure that you drive slowly so that you avoid braking, and avoid the potholes, and be slow when you will have to take turns at roundabouts and intersections?' The list of requests went on as every joint behaved differently with every movement. As I put the phone down after talking to a non-committal friend, Mum asked me without looking over the book she was reading, 'Dost naal setting ker rahi si ke ambulance book ker rahi si??!!!'[77]

One evening a dear client, friend and running partner, Guneet Sethi, made a very tempting offer to me. She was going to Amritsar with her daughter and invited me to join her to visit the Golden Temple. In my entire life, I have been to this holiest place for Sikhs only once, and that too because I was early for

---

[77] ਦੋਸਤ ਨਾਲ ਸੈਟਿੰਗ ਕਰ ਰਹੀ ਸੀ ਕੇ ਐਮਬੁਲੈਂਸ ਬੁੱਕ ਕਰ ਰਹੀ ਸੀ? (Were you making plans with a friend or giving instructions to an ambulance service?)

my appointment at the client's site and so we went there to pay obeisance and also went to Jallianwala Bagh.

This is the place where on 13 April 1919, troops of the British Indian Army under the command of Colonel Reginald Dyer fired bullets into a gathering of Indians protesting against the Rowlatt Commission. Rowlatt Acts, a legislation passed in February 1919 by the Imperial Legislative Council, the legislature of British India, allowed certain political cases to be tried without juries and keep suspects incarcerated without trial.

Though not religiously or politically inclined, the thought of going away for a couple of days excited me no end. I knew I would be pampered by Guneet and my partially geriatric body would be handled with care too. The temptation of world famous food and beverages of the holy city such as Amritsari kulcha, imli laddu and pere wali lassi kind of made the trip all the more irresistible.

Since Mum had been painstakingly taking care of my creaking joints for over 2 months, I thought it would be appropriate for me to run my thoughts past her. She had the right to decide whether I was road worthy or not you see. As Mum finished checking her WhatsApp messages, I asked her if I should consider this offer made by Guneet. She looked at me incredulously and retorted, 'Duniya saari challi Sirhand te Chamkor Saheb mathha tekan te tu chal Amritsar! Puthha challya ker tu sadaa!'[78] Shaheedi Jor Mel[79] is a congregation organised every year in December at Gurdwara Fatehgarh Sahib of Punjab to pay homage to the martyrdom of Zorawar

<hr>

[78] ਦੁਨੀਆਂ ਸਾਰੀ ਚੱਲੀ ਸਰਹਿੰਦ ਤੇ ਚਮਕੌਰ ਸਾਹਿਬ ਮੱਥਾ ਟੇਕਣ ਤੇ ਤੂੰ ਚੱਲ ਅੰਮ੍ਰਿਤਸਰ.. ਪੁੱਠਾ ਚੱਲਿਆ ਕਰ ਤੂੰ ਸਦਾ (The whole world is moving towards Sirhind and Chamkor Saheb and you want to go in the opposite direction towards Amritsar. Have you sworn to always go against the flow?)
[79] ਸ਼ਹੀਦੀ ਜੋੜਮੇਲਾ (This religious congregation is of immense importance in Sikh religion.)

Singh and Fateh Singh, the youngest sons of the Sikh Guru Guru Gobind Singh.

I understand her sentiments but what was my fault that Guneet chose to visit her daughter at the same time as the rest of Punjab was commemorating the matrydom? I can't get it right at all with Mum ever? Shaheedi meri free wich hundi hai,[80] regardless of what the reason might be!

Sulking, as I crawled back into my comfy blanket, I found Mum standing next to my bed. Wondering what more she had to add, I peeked a little from my lovely blanket. This was enough for Mum to throw in another shrapnel. 'Dekh Munni. Ajj mausam sardi wala ho gya. Te je mainu raati laggii dhand, main chup karke tere kambal wich aa warrna! Hunn dass ditta tainu!'[81]

Chicken meekly looks at her mother's dimensions, does a weak calculation of the spread her soft little blanket can manage for two bodies. Then takes her mother's tiny fists into account, nods gently and lets go with a deep sigh. Goodnight.

There is another issue I have with my Mother Superior. Is it just my Mum who indulges in random and often pointless interrogation, or is it a universal phenomenon? At times it leaves me wondering if this is her 'third-degree' treatment to call my bluff, in case I am fibbing for the most mundane things in life, or is it something all of us have to go through? Let me share an example to present my case.

No. 1: We have an old family friend whom we lovingly call Baby Didi and she addresses my Mum as Chachi Ji[82]. One

---

[80] ਸ਼ਹੀਦੀ ਮੇਰੀ free ਵਿੱਚ ਹੁੰਦੀ ਹੈ (I get martyred by everyone from all directions by everyone gratuity!)
[81] ਦੇਖ ਮੁੰਨੀ. ਅੱਜ ਮੌਸਮ ਸਰਦੀ ਵਾਲਾ ਹੋ ਗਿਆ. ਤੇ ਜੇ ਮੈਨੂੰ ਰਾਤੀ ਲੱਗੀ ਠੰਡ, ਮੈਂ ਚੁੱਪ ਕਰਕੇ ਤੇਰੇ ਕੰਬਲ ਵਿਚ ਆ ਵੜਨਾ! ਹੁਣ ਦੱਸ ਦਿੱਤਾ ਤੈਨੂੰ! (See kiddo. There is a little nip in the air today. If I feel a little cold, then I am going to quietly slip into you blanket at night. I am warning you beforehand.)
[82] ਚਾਚੀ ਜੀ (Paternal aunt).

evening while sitting with Mum, I told Mum that I was going to call Baby Didi as it had been a while since we met. After exchanging pleasantries and general chit-chat, Didi wanted to speak with her Chachi also, so I handed the phone to Mum sitting next to me. After yapping away with her beloved Baby for half an hour, Mum finally bade goodbye to her. Handing over the phone to me she asks, 'Tere kol number si Baby da?'[83] I mean, how else could I have called Baby Didi if I did not have her number? It is similar to the times when people call you and ask if you were sleep! Should we actually turn this interrogative habit into a national sport of mothers? Here's another one if you think I am being unnecessarily harsh on Mum.

No. 2: My mother has only one elder sister; our awe-inspiring Vaddi Massi[84]. This has been an undisputable fact ever since Mum has been born! Vaddi Massi shifted to Jagraon 25 years ago, another fact established since decades. Massi's only son got married to Leena 6 years ago. I received a call from Vaddi Massi while I was in a meeting so I could not speak with her. As soon as I reached home, I hugged Mum and told her, 'Mumma Vaddi Massi da phone aaya si. Ohna naal gall ker layo.'[85]

Mum: Vaddi Massi?

The Chicken: Haanji.[86]

Mum: Jagraon wali??[87]

The Chicken, looking at Mum a little bewildered: Haaaanji.

Mum, still not done with me as yet: Leena di Mummy?[88]

---

[83] ਤੇਰੇ ਕੋਲ ਨੰਬਰ ਸੀ ਬੇਬੀ ਦਾ? (Did you have Baby's number?)
[84] ਵੱਡੀ ਮਾਸੀ (Mum's elder sister).
[85] Mumma ਵੱਡੀ ਮਾਸੀ ਦਾ ਫੋਨ ਆਇਆ ਸੀ, ਓਹਨਾ ਨਾਲ ਗੱਲ ਕਰ ਲਏ (Mum your elder sister called for you. Please call her back.)
[86] ਹਾਂਜੀ (Yes).
[87] ਜਗਰਾਓਂ ਵਾਲੀ (The one from Jagraon city).
[88] ਲੀਨਾ ਦੀ ਮੰਮੀ (Leena's mum).

Chicken is ready to walk to the slaughterhouse to commit suicide!

Ah well. Why speak about death while Mum has been working on my joints. Having lived off the edge, both of the bed and the physical state of my being, for a year, I finally decided to take charge of the situation and joined a Zumba class held five mornings a week. Mother Darling was all too happy to see me getting back to some action, finally. She got so excited that she asked me, 'Chal changga keeta. Sawer-Shaam jaa aayi.'[89] Horrified at being made to sweat out twice a day in a high-powered Zumba class, I promptly clarified that class would be held only in the mornings. She did not seem to like it but somehow made peace, 'Chal koi na, issi bahaane kuchh taan hillengi.'[90]

Before she got some more fancy ideas, I also added that classes would be held Monday to Friday, clarifying further to register, 'five days a week'. Almost disappointed Mum walked off while gently shaking her head. Hoping that everything was clear, I got along with my day too. Mum saw me diligently getting ready every morning to go to Zumba, while she enjoyed her morning tea with the papers. As a reward, she would have fruit smoothie waiting for me upon my return from the class.

It was working out quite well, till came Saturday and I made no effort to get ready since it was my day off. Mum, of course, had forgotten the 'five days a week deal' which I gently reminded her again. Come Sunday and I left home at 5.30 am for the 'Morning with CATS' trek so she was satisfied. Being tired from the trek somehow made me oblivious to the alarm and I slept till 8 am on Monday morning. Mum was not

---

[89] ਚੱਲ ਚੰਗਾ ਕੀਤਾ ... ਸਵੇਰ-ਸ਼ਾਮ ਜਾ ਆਈ (That's neat... you can go every morning and evening).
[90] ਚੱਲ ਕੋਈ ਨਾ, ਇਸੀ ਬਹਾਨੇ ਕੁਛ ਤਾਂ ਹਿਲੇਂਗੀ (Never you mind, at least you would move your lazy bones a little!)

impressed. This was 3 days in a row that I had missed Zumba, as far as she was concerned, weekend be damned!

Finally, Tuesday morning while I was still squirming in bed around 6 am, I felt a cold tug on my ear. Though still asleep, instinctively my hand reached out towards my tender little ear to free it from whatever had landed on it. My search found my mother's cold fingers instead! Annoyed I peeked out of the blanket and before I could ask what she wanted, Mother Superior gave one more tug at the earlobe and thundered, 'Je ajj tu Zumba-jumba na gayi, taan pher teriyaan-Meriyaan gallan! Dekh pher teri shaamat kidaan aundi!'[91] Anyone heard of a ruthless matriarch?

There is one particular personality trait of my mother, which I thoroughly enjoy though. Since Mum does not go out that often, she enjoys this whole experience of picking up her clothes, perhaps choose a jewellery piece, select the footwear and pull out a matching bag. At times, she might even ask me to choose a lipstick for her when the choices become too large.

To be honest, I enjoy seeing Mum get ready for her day/hours out even more. What joy it is to watch your 71-year-old mother turn into a 17-year-old teenager, who is busy trying various combinations before she finalises on the look she wants to carry. How charmingly blessed we are.

So today Mum had an appointment for which she went through her morning routine of walk, exercise, gardening, breakfast, followed by her 'going out' routine. As luck would have it, just before we were to leave home, the appointment got postponed to next week. So what does Mum do when she is all dressed beautifully and nowhere to go? She takes selfies!

---

[91] ਜੇ ਅੱਜ ਤੂੰ Zumba-jumba ਨਾ ਗਈ, ਤਾਂ ਫੇਰ ਤੇਰੀਆਂ-ਮੇਰੀਆਂ ਗੱਲਾਂ! ਦੇਖ ਫੇਰ ਤੇਰੀ ਸ਼ਾਮਤ ਕਿੱਦਾਂ ਆਉਂਦੀ! (If today you won't go for your Zumba-jumba, I am warning you that I will take you to task for sure.)

As I sat down with my laptop to complete the paper, I heard Mum mumbling away, 'Bass? Reh gayi naahti-dhoti? Middhiyaan keetiyaan, reeban vi paaye, phull vi sajaaye. Ki faaida hoya meri loohl-karaayi da!'[92] I kept tapping away, smiling to myself, enjoying this part of the journey too.

On second thoughts, how deeply restrictive is the patriarchal system? Had Mum been allowed to learn how to ride a scooter or drive a car, I am pretty sure Mum would not have given two hoots before calling up a friend to fix up a coffee date. Damned be the doctor's appointment. Damned be her daughter's work. What do we get by limiting the opportunities to expand the horizons of our loved ones? Don't we suffer in the process too?

Karwa Chauth[93] came around again but this particular year I made sure I was nowhere to be seen or heard in the house when getting henna on the hands was being discussed. I left the women to their own devices and reached home only when I knew everything would have been sorted. Mercifully, I reached home to both the married women of our household merrily wearing bright henna on the hands.

Mum woke up at 4 am to get the morning Sarghi[94] in place for Bhabi.[95] She cooked two large aallu-paranthe,[96] boiled pheoniyaan[97] and got a large glass of milk ready for Bhabi before she embarked on her day long fast. Everyone else follows

---

[92] ਬੱਸ? ਰਹਿ ਗਈ ਨਾਹਤੀ-ਧੋਤੀ? ਮੀਢੀਆਂ ਕੀਤੀਆਂ, ਰੀਬਨ ਵੀ ਪਾਏ, ਫੁੱਲ ਵੀ ਸਜਾਏ. ਕੀ ਫਾਇਦਾ ਹੋਇਆ ਮੇਰੀ ਲੂਹਲ-ਕਰਾਈ ਦਾ? (Alas! No outing for me. I combed my hair, braided ribbons into them, decorated my hair with flowers too. What did it amount to? Here I am, sitting at home. All dressed up and nowhere to go!)

[93] ਕਰਵਾ-ਚੌਥ (Karwa Chauth is an annual fast and ritual observed by married ladies to pray for good and long life of their husbands. Married women dress up in their fineries like a bride on this day and remain without food and water from dawn till the moon rises. As a thank you gesture, their husbands and family give gifts affectionately.)

[94] ਸਰਘੀ (Pre-fast feast).

[95] ਭਾਬੀ (Brother's wife).

[96] ਆਲੂ ਪਰਾਂਠੇ (Stuffed potato Indian bread).

[97] ਫੇਯੋਨੀਆਂ (Sweet vermicelli).

the respective routine till 3.30 pm when the family is supposed to converge back at the house for the 4 pm prayers when Bhabi prays and gets to drink two large glasses of milky tea to sustain a little till the moon shines, literally.

Both Mum and Bhabi dress up like brides for this 4-pm prayer and also exchange gifts, from one bride of the house to another. It is usually quite a fun moment as we take photos of both the married couples of the house as a memory note.

After the prayers were over and the prayer tray was brought back to the kitchen, Mother Darling threw some quick instructions at me after noticing that I still had the camera in my hands. Hor kuchh aawe-na-aawe, meri mehandi te meriyaan chooriyan zaroor aan photo wich … hunn dass ditta … dhang naal lae photo.[98] I smiled inwardly, thoroughly enjoying Mum's zeal for life and took more than a few shots of her henna dyed hands.

The festive period also increases the workload for me. Since post karwa chauth I had more work to catch up on, I started returning home well past 9 pm. One night Mum caught hold of me before going to bed. Dressed to sleep she tottered towards me wearing her 'near-vision' glasses! Before I could open my mouth to enquire if all was well, Mum walked up to me and demanded that I abandon everything that I was doing on the laptop and show her all the 'karwa chauth'[99] photos. Given that she was wearing her new favourite nightsuit, I chose to indulge her.

Preening through her glasses barely 10" away from the laptop screen, she scrutinised every photo while giving me tips about how to improve my focus while framing a shot, and how

---

[98] ਹੋਰ ਕੁੱਛ ਆਵੇ ਨਾ ਆਵੇ … ਮੇਰੀ ਮਹਿੰਦੀ ਤੇ ਮੇਰੀਆਂ ਚੂੜੀਆਂ ਜ਼ਰੂਰ ਆਣ ਫੋਟੋ ਵਿੱਚ.. ਹੁਣ ਦੱਸ ਦਿੱਤਾ... ਢੰਗ ਨਾਲ ਲਈ ਫੋਟੋ
(Listen to me carefully, I want very pretty photos of my mehandi and bangles. Or else!)
[99] ਕਰਵਾ-ਚੌਥ (Karwa Chauth is an annual fast and ritual observed by married ladies to pray for good and long life of their husbands. Married women dress up in their fineries like a bride on this day and remain without food and water from dawn till the moon rises. As a thank you gesture, affectionate gifts are given by their husbands and family.)

to keep my camera straight next time. After noticing whose mouth was open and who was not sitting 'properly' for the photos, she said in a very gentle voice, 'Meri te Mona di mehndi kinni sohni aayi hai!'[100] Hallelujah, finally mother is happy. I could not help noticing that pride of a bride for another bride in Mum's voice. May God bless both the brides of our house with multiple celebrations for years to come.

Just when I reached out to take the laptop back from her, I noticed she was touching its screen randomly. I turned towards her to observe a little more and found her 'pinching' the screen by now with her thumb and index finger. Penny quickly dropped on me that Mum was confusing my laptop with iPad and does not know that my laptop screen is not 'touch sensitive'. However, before I could explain that to her, Mum exclaimed while still 'swiping' the screen, 'Tu na kuchh saambh ke rakhya! Ker leya kharaab? Ajje hunn litta si.'[101]

One summer, tired of my absolutely flat long-ish hair having lost all charm on me, I went for a haircut and asked the hair designer to 'chop it all off'. Quite chuffed with the results and feeling feather weight I bounced back home, only to be greeted by Mother Superior right in the verandah itself. Hands on her hips she mouthed off, 'Tainu te na kisse nu saboot dein di vi lorr nahin ke tu puthhi jammi si. Loki garmi wich vaal chhote rakhde ne te sardiyaan wich lambe. Tu rahi puthhi di puthhi.'[102] Yupp. I declare that I was a breech baby who was declared dead at birth. I beat all odds to survive, only to listen

---

[100] ਮੇਰੀ ਤੇ ਮੋਨਾ ਦੀ ਮਹਿੰਦੀ ਕਿੰਨੀ ਸੋਹਣੀ ਆਈ ਹੈ (See how beautiful mine and Mona's mehandi looks.)
[101] ਤੂੰ ਨਾ ਕੁਝ ਸਾਂਭ ਕੇ ਰੱਖਿਆ.. ਕਰ ਲਿਆ ਖ਼ਰਾਬ? ਅੱਜੇ ਹੁਣ ਲਿੱਤਾ ਸੀ (You just don't know how to take care of your things. It was purchased recently and you have already spoilt it!)
[102] ਤੈਨੂੰ ਤੇ ਨਾ ਕਿਸੇ ਸਬੂਤ ਦੇਣ ਦੀ ਵੀ ਲੋੜ ਨਹੀਂ ਕੇ ਤੂੰ ਪੁੱਠੀ ਜੰਮੀ ਸੀ. ਲੋਕੀ ਗਰਮੀ ਵਿਚ ਵੱਲ ਛੋਟੇ ਰੱਖਦੇ ਨੇ ਤੇ ਸਰਦੀਆਂ ਵਿਚ ਲੰਬੇ. ਤੂੰ ਰਹੀ ਪੁੱਠੀ ਦੀ ਪੁੱਠੀ *(You don't even need to provide any evidence that you are a breech baby! People keep their hair short in summers and long in winters. But no, you have to do precisely the opposite!)*

to my mother telling me off every step of the way. Wonder if it was worth all that effort!

Not feeling particularly hungry one night, I settled with a small portion of daal for dinner, which, of course, I polished off even before Mum got up to get her dinner. As she was walking towards the kitchen, I asked her if she could get me a 'gurr di bheli'[103] while returning with her dinner plate. Given the state of her hearing, I was not actually sure if she heard my request and was almost prepared to get up and get it myself.

To my pleasant surprise, Mum had not only heard me ask for 'gurr', she actually brought it along with her food. The CAT was obviously delighted. However just as I held my hand out to grab the jar of home-made gurr, she swiftly pulled her hand back and said, 'Pehlaan gaa ke suna.'[104] Now given that I am not even the bathroom singer of this household, I looked up at Mum's face curiously but she seemed quite determined. Since there was no one else in the room who had asked for gurr, she obviously was asking me to sing! Just wishing to get over and done with Mum's drama and lay my hands on a morsel of gurr she makes at home for us, I asked her as politely as I possibly could as to what she wanted me to sing. She broke into a smile and said, 'De Maayi Lohri, Jeeve teri jori.'[105] She actually made me sing it twice as the first attempt did not meet her approval. Not only she 'does it', but she 'gets away' with it.

On a balmy Sunday afternoon while I was busy making some calls to catch up with people to open doors for End Incest, Mother Darling took pity on me and meandered to her

---

[103] ਗੁੜ ਦੀ ਭੇਲੀ (A piece of jaggery).
[104] ਪਹਿਲਾਂ ਗਾ ਕੇ ਸੁਣਾ (Sing a song for me first).
[105] ਦੇ ਮਾਈ ਲੋਹੜੀ, ਜੀਵੇ ਤੇਰੀ ਜੋੜੀ (Traditional Punjabi folk song sung on the occasion of Lohri, a winter festival celebrated around a bonfire).

room to watch TV. Being hard of hearing, she puts on the TV at a little high volume, but I can live with that. Knowing that she is around, healthy and happy, flitting between news, drama, films and old songs, makes me feel suitably relieved and less guilty too as I can't be blamed for ignoring her on a day of rest. Alas! The joy did not last long!

As I was in the middle of a conversation with an Executive Director of a luxury chain, discussing an awareness and fund-raising campaign, Mum chose a channel which had a 'Hakim Saheb'[106] doling out health advice! With TV volume on full blast that of course can be heard a mile away, my ever so important conversation is competing with a patient on TV, 'Mujhe Sir piles ki problem bhi hai. Uthne baithne mein bhi dikkat hoti hai. Pareshaan hoon bahut.'[107] Just as I muttered an apology over the phone, Hakim Saheb took over, 'Achha aap da haajma kaisa hai? Gas taan nahin bann.di?'[108] If only the earth could part and the Chicken could disappear!!!

Mother Darling had once suffered from some untraceable suspected allergy or an undiagnosed irritable bowel syndrome for almost 2 years. She would have to make four to six trips to the loo, felt weak most of the time and equally importantly she was not happy with loss of glow on her face and loss of muscle tone. She was not happy that she 'looked' as old as her elder sister; elder by 2 years!

The Nushkha Queen[109] that Mum is, she finally found a 'desi'[110] remedy to cure her tummy of all ills. She chewed on

---

[106] ਹਕੀਮ ਸਾਹਿਬ (Physician practicing traditional medicine).
[107] ਮੈਨੂੰ Sir piles ਦੀ problem ਵੀ ਹੈ. ਉੱਠਣ-ਬੈਠਣ ਵਿਚ ਦਿੱਕਤ ਹੁੰਦੀ ਹੈ. ਪਰੇਸ਼ਾਨ ਹਾਂ ਬਹੁਤ (Sir I suffer from piles too. I can't even sit or stand properly. I am really upset.)
[108] ਅੱਛਾ ਆਪ ਦਾ ਹਾਜਮਾ ਕੈਸਾ ਹੈ? ਗੈਸ ਤਾਂ ਨਹੀਂ ਬਣਦੀ? (OK how is your digestion? Any problem related to flatulence?)
[109] ਨੁਸਖਾ (Some traditional remedy/solution).
[110] ਦੇਸੀ (Traditional).

a mouthful of neem+keekar+karipatta[111] leaves while she went on her morning walk. Somehow, God knows how, but this worked and Mum started blossoming soon after. Her loo trips reduced to one to two a day. Her muscle tone marginally improved, her skin started glowing, she started eating fruits again and most importantly for Mum, her elder sister began looking older to her again.

Anyone would have thought that Mother Darling would be a happy bunny with such great improvement. Alas! I found Mother Superior walking on tip toes days later with a long face. Reason dawned upon me after a little prodding. Since her gut had improved, so had her weight and she had put on 1 kilo in weight.

It was tough not to grin when Mum shared her trauma with me in miserably hushed tones, 'Tainu pata hai mera wajan 1 kilo vaddh gya? Pehlaan mein socheya aapne ghar wali machine di suyi hill gayi te main gurudware wali machine utte bhaar tolan lagg gayi. Oh 2 kilo hor faaltu dassdi hai. Pehlaan jinna hee khaandi haan pher wajan pata nahin kithhon vadhh gya. Sachhi dassaan main taan dardi hunn machine te vi nahi chhardi.'[112] Cute as hell, that is my Mother Darling. Would not exchange her for anyone in the world.

While putting one of my mornings together the other day, I told Mum that I would be leaving for Delhi for a few days. She said OK and then we both got along our respective schedules.

---

[111] ਨਿੰਮ+ਕਿੱਕਰ+ਕੜੀ ਪੱਤਾ (Leaves of Mahogany, Acacia, Murraya Koeniggi trees).
[112] ਤੈਨੂੰ ਪਤਾ ਹੈ ਮੇਰਾ ਵੱਜਨ ਕਿੱਲੋ ਵੱਧ ਗਿਆ? ਪਹਿਲਾਂ ਮੈਂ ਸੋਚਿਆ ਆਪਣੇ ਘਰ ਵਾਲੀ ਮਸ਼ੀਨ ਦੀ ਸੂਈ ਹਿਲ ਗਈ ਤੇ ਮੈਂ ਗੁਰਦੁਆਰੇ ਵਾਲੀ ਮਸ਼ੀਨ ਉੱਤੇ ਬਾਹਰ ਤੋਲਣ ਗਈ ਸੀ. ਉਹ 2 ਕਿੱਲੋ ਹੋਰ ਫਾਲਤੂ ਦੱਸਦੀ ਹੈ! ਪਹਿਲਾਂ ਜਿੰਨਾ ਹੀ ਖਾਂਦੀ ਹਾਂ ਪਰ ਵੱਜਨ ਪਤਾ ਨਹੀਂ ਕਿਥੋਂ ਵੱਧ ਗਿਆ? ਸੱਚੀ ਦੱਸਾਂ ਮੈਂ ਤਾਂ ਦਰਦੀ ਹੁਣ ਮਸ਼ੀਨ ਤੇ ਵੀ ਨਹੀਂ ਚੁੜਦੀ. *(Do you know I have put on 1 kg weight? At first I thought something has gone wrong with our weighing machine at home. So I went to the Gurudwara to check my weight there. That machine said I had put on not 1 kg but 2 kg more! Tell me what to do. My diet has not increased but the weight continues to rise up. To be honest, I am now afraid of even getting onto any weighing machine now.)*

A couple of hours later I finally went to have bath on that cold winter mid-morning. Just as I had set the water mixer temperature just right for my chattering teeth to warm up a bit and started to take the layers off to have my bath, I heard a frantic knock on my bathroom door with Mum shouting, 'Gall Sunn Chhetti.'[113]

Since Mum and I share the bathroom, I assumed Mum perhaps needed to pick up something, but couldn't she wait 15 minutes? Then suddenly a penny dropped on me. Mum had had a painful tooth issue since 7 weeks. I panicked thinking that perhaps something worse had happened in her mouth and she needed to be taken to the dentist. Puffing and panting with all kind of ideas swimming in my head, as quickly as I was delayering, I frantically put my clothes back on and opened the door.

I found Mum standing right outside with her mouth wide open and that kind of made me freeze, not because of cold of course. Before I could open my mouth to ask what had happened, Mum asked, 'So you are leaving for Delhi tomorrow or day after?!!!' Really? So this was the emergency? Can you see me rolling my eyes and frothing at the mouth after having thrown myself on that cold floor??

Mum sensed that something was out of order with me, but since she did not want to add to the distress, she left me in peace the whole day. However, as the sun went down Mum's patience deserted her. Trouble was that as her friends were over, she could not share her concern in front of everyone else. At the same time, 'mamta'[114] got the better of her or I would

---

[113] ਗੱਲ ਸੁਣ ਛੇਤੀ (Listen to me quickly).
[114] ਮਮਤਾ (Mother's love).

like to claim that the combination of my cute haircut, my pretty dress and my face full of worry lines got the better of her.

On the pretext of serving finger food to her friends, she would get up to do a round of the room with snacks tray at regular intervals. Every time she would reach me, she would use her girth to create a little visual barrier between the rest of them and us. She ruffled my hair affectionately when she brought the cookies. She caressed my cheek when she brought the cake. Once she 'needed' to bend over my head to pick up my phone from the other side and pinched my cheek with the spare hand.

Even while sitting with her friends about 10' away from me, every now and then she would hide her mouth on the pretext of wiping her mouth while she was actually throwing flying kisses at me. If this is not enough, she even winked a few times. Of course what my Mother Darling does not realise is that she ends up crinkling both her eyes rather than using just one when she believes she is winking.

After about half a dozen rounds, my cheeks were red, my dress had chocolate marks, I had 'straight out of bed' haircut and Mother Darling had unplugged my laptop as she had taken away everything else she could pick up using one excuse or another.

There can't be anyone else like a mother, can there?

'Mother's love is ever in its spring.'

- A French Proverb

The Digital Affairs

Though Mum has never been exposed to a mechanically or electronically complicated world, she has always had a knack to make things work. Dad needs Mum to change television channels, maid needs Mum to use grinder, and we all need Mum to keep us in order! Jokes aside, lately I found Mum looking longingly at mobiles phones. On an odd occasion she asked one of us about how things work on a mobile or drop a hint how she had to borrow the mobiles from strangers if she got stuck while shopping or that even maids have mobiles these days.

Like a typical Punjabi patriarch family, none paid attention to the matriarch and her dreams. Her son mulled over the expense of another monthly bill and the teenaged granddaughter questioned the very need for Grandma to have her own phone in the first place. Little did any of us know how this one little gadget would change the fabric of our family, with some thoughtfulness of a friend and, of course, the click of a button.

Mum's landmark 70th birthday was approaching and I wanted to make it a little special for her. I discussed with our dear friend Vipin about the possibility of gifting Mum a mobile phone. Given that her own mother never wanted to use one, he got excited by the idea of my mother carrying and using a 'nice' mobile phone. However, being the wise man that he was, he suggested that we buy a SIM in my name and use his spare mobile handset to gift her on her birthday. He said that if Mum gets to grips with the smartphone gadget and its technology, then we would buy a new handset to ensure Mum's mobility. This sounded like a reasonable deal and the very next day we put the SIM and the handset together for Mum to explore. To be honest, it was a joy unparalleled to see Mum so happy upon seeing her gift. She quickly sliced through the cake and told us that coffee would be served after her birthday selfie!

At first we thought Mum was joking but it turned out that she meant business. Mum literally frogmarched her flock outside and demanded that the prettiest angle be selected for the selfie. When we laughed at her antics, Mum roared, 'You can't control or laugh off my birthday memories!' I wondered if any of us would have such enthusiasm left in us for life, if and when we reach the ripe old age of 70. I also wondered how would Mum use the touchscreen mobile with her butter soft fingers as she had never used even the old Nokia phones with push-back buttons. We did not have to wait for long!

The next day I returned home to see that Mum had suddenly become the apple of everyone's eyes, everyone wanted to snuggle up to her, hugging and cuddling her. I finally figured out the reason. The home Wi-Fi had conked off! Her phone had become everyone's hotspot you see.

Balmy Sunday afternoon I climbed into bed for a well-deserved siesta. As Mother Darling saw me getting comfortable in bed, she grabbed the opportunity for a revision lesson in taking selfies! Amused, I gave her verbal instructions as she snuggled next to me in bed. Mum followed my instructions to the tee; clicked on camera button, reversed the camera for selfies, adjusted her arm and then pressed click. I thought it was a neat picture, but Mother was horrified! She sat bolt upright in bed and lost all composure. 'Haye Rubba! Eh mera nakk kinna vadda aaya photo wich!! Mera nakk koi enna vadda hai? Eh te metre lamba nakk hai. Munh te horr kuch dikhda hee nahin. Eh ghalat hai. Dubara leni main selfie.'[115]

During her panic stricken monologue Mother Superior completely forgot that if there is one thing which is common and easily recognisable amongst all her six siblings, it is their trademark razor-sharp nose, which my brother also happened to have inherited. However, to avoid entering into an argument with Mum while all I was looking for was a simple quiet nap, I offered that we could take another selfie easily. Giving me a peck on the cheek, Mum snuggled closer to me once again, I raised her selfie arm to adjust the angle of her khandaani[116] nose and told her to click the button. Voila! I got a big beary hug in return for the second attempt. Doesn't take much to make Mum happy!

Since technology can be challenging even for us, I sat down with my nephew to make the mobile 'Grandma-friendliest'. Given Mum is both short- and long-sighted but does not wear glasses all the time and yet is fond of taking pictures, we chose to keep the 'shutter sound' option ticked on her mobile's camera. Idea being that even if her eyes are unsure, the click sound of the shutter would tell her that the photo has been clicked. Kids can be quite considerate like that.

---

[115] ਹਾਏ ਰੱਬਾ! ਇਹ ਮੇਰਾ ਨੱਕ ਕਿੰਨਾ ਵੱਡਾ ਆਇਆ ਫੋਟੋ ਵਿੱਚ!! ਮੇਰਾ ਨੱਕ ਕੋਈ ਇੰਨਾ ਵੱਡਾ ਹੈ? ਇਹ ਤੇ ਮੀਟਰ ਲੰਬਾ ਨੱਕ ਹੈ. ਮੂੰਹ ਤੇ ਹੋਰ ਕੁਝ ਦਿਖਦਾ ਹੀ ਨਹੀਂ.. ਇਹ ਗ਼ਲਤ ਹੈ.. ਦੁਬਾਰਾ ਲੈਣੀ ਮੈਂ selfie. *(Oh God! How big my nose looks in the photo! My nose is certainly not THAT big! One can't see anything but my nose on the face. This is unacceptable. I want to take another selfie.)*
[116] ਖ਼ਾਨਦਾਨੀ (Hereditary inheritance).

Days later while driving to attend a wedding, you notice Mum casually reaching out to her mobile. You tease her if she was going to take selfies, not so casually of course. Dressed to the tee, she furiously shook her head in a BIG NO, 'Message check kardi ke lawaan ho gayiyaan?'[117] You smile and look out of the window. Then you hear a soft click. Mum was taking a selfie.

She does not realise that we can hear her shutter click over the sound of music in the car. From the corner of your eye you notice that Mum is not satisfied by the way her head is bobbing. Another soft click. May be this one? An even softer tch-tch followed by another soft click. Nope, this won't work either and her soft as butter fingers quickly delete some more photos. After she made compromises with me, nothing but perfection would do for my mother. Timing her selfie session with the rough and smooth patches of the highway was as difficult a task, as was to take selfies without the knowledge of her kids in the car. After about 25 minutes Mum finally succeeded in her mission. And then you raid Mum's mobile to steal her selfies, while she goes to powder her nose.

Over the years, Mum's phone had actually become a source of joy to everyone at home. As parents would occasionally frisk through their children's stuff to see what they have been up to, now grandkids had started doing the same to Mother Darling. They flicked through her mobile almost on a daily basis to see what she had been up to, and also to help her learn better way of doing things on the mobile. There was uproar in the other part of the house one day. I could hear voices, chuckles, arguments and laughter, all in the same breath.

---

[117] Message check ਕਰਦੀ ਕੇ ਲਾਵਾਂ ਹੋ ਗਾਈਆਂ? (I am just checking messages to see if the bride and the groom have exchanged marital vows in the Gurudwara yet or not.)

A few minutes later Mother Superior walked up to me with her mobile in her hand, demanding that I drop everything and tell her the meaning of a particular emoticon, which happened to be both hands with flat palms facing out. I explained to Mum that this emoticon signifies that you are having a good time or having a lot of fun as these are hands stretched upwards to celebrate. It could also stretch to mean that you are at a party, dancing wildly and friskily.

Mum suddenly turned red, snatched the phone off me and walked to her room. This obviously smelt too fishy so I followed her and asked her what exactly had happened and why was she sulking. Mum would not open her mouth. Sensing that she had obviously done something, I sat next on the bed next to her and gently put my arm around her. I kissed her on the cheek and asked, 'Dasso te sahi hoya ki?'[118] At first my septuagenarian mother kept shaking her head, refusing to open her mouth. With a little more nudging she finally disclosed, 'I thought it was a symbol of blessings!' I always knew I had a groovy mother, but this made me laugh too.

In these fast-paced, money-centric, copy-paste crazy days, it has become paramount that we become more careful about our actions! It becomes even more important when we are new to technology, just like Mother Darling is with her smartphone. From having no phone whatsoever, she suddenly had this magic weapon in her hand to connect with the world. To ensure that her world remains rather in control, I ensured that she has access only to WhatsApp on her mobile and did not even download FB, Twitter or Instagram. Can you imagine the horror I might have to deal with every day? I don't even

---

[118] ਦੱਸੋ ਤੇ ਸਹੀ ਹੋਇਆ ਕੀ? (Please share what happened.)

want to think how would I feel on seeing Mum posting pics on Insta or FB with the caption, 'Chilling out with friends in Rose Garden!'

Anyway, let's get back to reality. My all-confident Super-Mum walked up to me to show off her newly acquired WhatsApp 'copy-paste' skills. She had selected one Gurupurb[119] Greeting message which she wanted to send to her selected friends, with a single press of a button. I was super impressed with her willingness to learn new tricks and to be honest, relieved also as we could perhaps trust her to manage her 'digital' affairs a little independently.

Just as she went through the process of 'showing off' step-by-step, I realised that in her 'un-spectacled' exuberance at mastering a new trick, instead of her lovingly chosen Gurupurb Greetings to be sent, Mum had selected the following message and sent to everyone,'Kirpa ker ke mooli de paranthe kha ke line vich na kharro!'[120] For the uninitiated, mooli is white raddish which is very high in vitamin C, potassium, and phosphorus. In addition, it contains phytonutrients, which help in liver-related disorders and has several beneficial enzymes that help in digestion, which results in pungent emissions! Can you think of a damage-control exercise to recover from this position? Heaven save us!

No matter how much you love your mother, she can get on your nerves every now and then. Mine does more often than that! It was not even 10 in the morning and Mother Superior had picked three bones with me already. She misplaced my camera when I needed it the most, turned off the geyser while I

---

needed to have a shower to leave early and gave me an apple sliced with a knife which had been used for garlic and then forced me to eat it! Finally when she realised that she had argued with the Chicken on petty things, she sent a message on WhatsApp loaded with kisses and hearts. This is how she tried to make up. Per aaj hum na maaneinge. [121]

A fortnight later, tucked away in a blanket, while I was mulling over Shams' 40 rules of love, Mum walked in with two cups of tea. Just as I blew a kiss of thanks to her, she caught the kiss mid-air and air-kissed me back. Meri Rani-Ma.[122] Mum's rules of love are effectively, quite clear. She does not need Rumi.

One bitterly cold night as I was trying to make my aching joints comfortable in bed, trying to prop my left shoulder with a padding of towel rolled underneath and a round pillow underneath the right knee, I caught Mother Superior red-handed taking selfies, and how! While changing poses, when she noticed I was watching her antics with a huge grin on my face, at first she blushed a little and then regained her form, 'Maa teri main. Meri sikhaayi hoyi ethhe pahunchi hain!'[123] I smiled and turned over. I picked up my own mobile and sent a message to Vipin, 'Let's buy a mobile handset for Mum.'

One particular morning Mum noticed that I was packing my satchel for the day ahead, when she suddenly pounced upon me. The self-reliant woman that she is, Mum had actually made a diary of instructions to operate her mobile ever since I gifted one to her on her birthday. Mum had since revised all the

---

[121] ਪਰ ਅੱਜ ਹਮ ਨਾ ਮਾਨੈਂਗੇ (But I won't give in today!)

[122] ਮੇਰੀ ਰਾਣੀ ਮਾਂ (My Queen Mother).

[123] ਮਾਂ ਤੇਰੀ ਮੈਂ ... ਮੇਰੀ ਸਿਖਾਈ ਹੋਈ ਇੱਥੇ ਪਹੁੰਚੀ ਹੈਂ (I am your mother. It is my upbringing which has given you such solid standing in life.)

major commands and manages everything by herself. She was struggling with 'portrait' and 'landscape' options but that was small fry in comparison to what she had on her mind that day!

'Eh tussi saare de saare, din-raat Facebook di kitaab kholi baithe rehnde ho, mere phone utte kyun nahin hai??'[124] Now this was a serious demand. As a child I had no right to control my mother's decision in life, but Facebook? I mean, FB??!!! Can you imagine? Quel horreur! I picked up the car keys and left home swiftly by dodging her 5' frame and her demand in one swift moment, hoping that Mum would have forgotten all about FB by the time I returned home.

When suddenly your mother gets hold of your phone and manages to open your WhatsApp 'stashed photos' folder, you don't know what to expect. At first I took absolute delight in her expressions as she swiped the photos across. Then suddenly fear took over the Chicken, 'Have I left something in there which she might object to?'

As she rummaged through the photos, she kept on exclaiming with sheer delight, 'Madhvi kinni sohni laggdi payi. Eh uss naal Mr Madhvi hai?'[125] Mum was a little disappointed too, 'Monica ne mainu sirf 1 photo bheji, tere kol te 6 ne![126] Haaaw, meri chunni nahi theek laggdi payi iss photo wich. Tera naal kharre hon da ki faiyda hoya? Dass te dena si ke Maa chunni theek ker lai!'[127] Someone should get ready to be taken to task too, 'Renuka ne billiyaan kinniyaan sohniyaan bhejiaan tainu.

---

124 ਇਹ ਤੁਸੀ ਸਾਰੇ ਦੇ ਸਾਰੇ ਦਿਨ ਰਾਤ Facebook ਦੀ ਕਿਤਾਬ ਖੋਲੀ ਬੈਠੇ ਰਹਿੰਦੇ ਹੋ.. ਮੇਰੇ ਫੋਨ ਉੱਤੇ ਕਿਉਂ ਨਹੀਂ ਹੈ? *(How come all of you are always busy on Facebook, but it is not available on my phone.)*
125 ਮਾਧਵੀ ਕਿੰਨੀ ਸੋਹਣੀ ਲੱਗਦੀ ਪਈ ਹੈ ... ਇਹ ਉੱਸ ਨਾਲ ਮਿਸਟਰ ਮਾਧਵੀ ਹੈ? *(Madhvi is looking so pretty. Is it Mr Madhvi with her?)*
126 ਮੋਨਿਕਾ ਨੇ ਮੈਨੂੰ ਸਿਰਫ 1 ਫੋਟੋ ਭੇਜੀ, ਤੇਰੇ ਕੋਲ ਤੇ 6 ਨੇ *(Monica sent only one photo to me, but six to you!)*
127 ਹਾਅ, ਮੇਰੀ ਚੁੰਨੀ ਨਹੀਂ ਠੀਕ ਲੱਗਦੀ ਪਈ ਇੱਸ ਫੋਟੋ ਵਿੱਚ.. ਤੇਰੇ ਨਾਲ ਖੜੇ ਹੋਣ ਦਾ ਕੀ ਫਾਇਦਾ ਹੋਇਆ? ਦੱਸ ਤੇ ਦੇਣਾ ਸੀ ਕੇ ਮਾਂ ਚੁੰਨੀ ਠੀਕ ਕਰ ਲੈ *(Oh God! My scarf looks out of place in this photo. What was the benefit of you standing there? You could have forewarned me at least to adjust my scarf!)*

Mere kol te photo bheji nahin. Milegi taan puchhangi!'[128] Fortunately a client rang and she handed the phone back to me. The rest of you have been spared till next time! Thus far I had to sanitise the phone for the kids, guess it is time to make it Mum-proof too!

To safeguard my phone from my mother, I installed a little application called 'snoop guard'. What it does is that every time someone tries to unlock my phone by guessing the password, it quietly takes the picture of the culprit. Mum does not know this of course. This application keeps showing Mum as the snooper everyday! Glad to know that there is at least one person on this earth who still thinks I am a teenager, in my ripe old middle-age.

Mix coconut oil, baking powder and yogurt. Now massage it well into your face for 10 minutess. Now let it dry and wash your face off with mildly warm water. Do this everyday and your face would become free of facial hair within a month. Nopes. I have not gone nuts but Mother Darling discovered YouTube on her phone! Despite our best attempts, we could not keep Mum from making her own explorations on her mobile.

Since she is unaware of how Google tracks her movements, in her excitement she keeps pressing buttons. We were most amused when we saw an advertisement on her phone 'TALA Ant Egg Oil' which apparently is a hair removal cream. These silent snoopers had completely flabbergasted my novice septuagenarian mother who had fought tooth and nail to keep 'ghar di gall, ghar vich!'[129]

---

[128] ਰੇਨੁਕਾ ਨੇ ਬਿੱਲੀਆਂ ਕਿੰਨੀਆਂ ਸੋਹਣੀਆਂ ਭੇਜੀਆਂ ਤੈਨੂੰ. ਮੇਰੇ ਕੋਲ ਤੇ ਫੋਟੇ ਭੇਜੀ ਨਹੀਂ. ਮਿਲੇਗੀ ਤਾਂ ਪੁਛਾਂਗੀ (Renuka has sent such pretty cats to you. She did not send me any! I will pull her up when I meet her next!)
[129] ਘਰ ਦੀ ਗੱਲ, ਘਰ ਵਿਚ (The secret remains at home!)

Flabbergasted, she wanted to know how 'net' knows that she has been looking at videos on YouTube about facial hair removal. Worse still, how many ant eggs would they have used for a bottle of ant egg oil to produce a hair remover 'nuskha'!! [130] Sorry. After a long and exhausting day at work, the CAT just lost it with Mother Superior and couldn't care less about her ants or even aunts for that matter!!

On the other hand, when your Mother Darling realises that your chips are down, she rummages through the kitchen shelves and tosses up a salad which is a cross between bhelpuri and rabbit food. And when that does not work, she takes the help of her new friend 'YouTube' to give you soul nourishing food. May be YouTube is not that bad after all.

In the morning as I sat outside in the verandah to skim through the papers, Mother Darling's YouTube tutorial number 1 was almost ready. She declared, 'You must not waste the peels of garlic and onions while preparing your "tarka".[131] Collect them in a glass of water and cover it for 1-2 days. Leave the glass in a warm place in your house. After 2 days, sieve the water and this becomes your natural antiseptic for your plants. Sprinkle it using a little spray or just use your hands to spatter your plants.'

After demonstrating the sprinkling ritual, Mother Superior pointed towards a plant, 'Aah vekh, iss de patte kauliyaan warge ho gaye si. Hafte de andar pattalaan vaang siddhe ho gaye ne!'[132] I am suddenly worried. Mum often says to me, 'Vekh bandaa bann ja' or

---

[130] ਨੁਸਖਾ (A traditional solution or remedy).
[131] ਤੜਕਾ (Basic gravy made for most north Indian dishes).
[132] ਆਹ ਵੇਖ, ਇਸ ਦੇ ਪੱਤੇ ਕੌਲੀਆਂ ਵਰਗੇ ਸੀ. ਹਫਤੇ ਦੇ ਅੰਦਰ ਪੱਤਲਾਂ ਵਾਂਗ ਸਿੱਧੇ ਹੋ ਗਏ ਨੇ. (Just look at these leaves! They used to be curled up like soup bowls and look at them now, flat as plates they are in my garden.)

'Aa tainu siddha karaan!!!'[133] At first I laughed and then suddenly some possibilities dawned upon me, 'Is she going to start using the same anticipectic on me too?'

Mum and I went out for a little stroll through the market. Since India never really runs out of festivals to celebrate, the market was full of stalls offering rakhis in all shapes, sizes, colours and themes. It was that festival again when sisters tie a thread or a bracelet around the wrists of their brothers and their brothers pledge to protect them from all evils.

Spotting two women of varying age groups walking through, one young stall holder barely in his teens shouted out aloud to Mum, 'Aunty rahkri le lo apne bhai layi.'[134] While I smiled at the boy's marketing skills, Mum responded without batting an eyelid, 'Naa Beta. Main te WhatsApp hee ker davangi.'[135] My Mother Darling has embraced technology wholeheartedly.

The evidence that our Mother Superior has finally 'arrived' on the digital scene emerged not much afterwards. We had moved into our 'home' more than 35 years ago. As we are 'puraane baashinde'[136] of the neighbourhood, some of the families have seen two or even three generations grow up together. For example we have seen our neighbour's son fight tooth and nail for the love of his life. Thirty-one years later that son's younger daughter is 3 days away from getting married.

As is customary in our culture, my Mum, sister-in-law and I went over to our neighbour's home to congratulate the grand old lady of the house on the forthcoming wedding of her

---

[133] ਵੇਖ ਬੰਦਾ ਬਣ ਜਾ or ਆ ਤੈਨੂੰ ਸਿੱਧਾ ਕਰਾਂ (Would you behave yourself or shall I come and sort you out?)

[134] Aunty ਰੱਖੜੀ ਲੈ ਲੋ ਆਪਣੇ ਭਾਈ ਲਈ (Aunt won't you buy a rakhi for your brother?)

[135] ਨਾ ਬੇਟਾ ਮੈਂ ਤੇ WhatsApp ਹੀ ਕਰ ਦਵਾਂਗੀ! (No son. I will just WhatsApp my rakhi to my brother!)

[136] ਪੁਰਾਣੇ ਬਾਸ਼ਿੰਦੇ *(Old residents)*.

granddaughter. We sang 'sitthaniyaan'[137] at their doorstep and they duly welcomed us in with traditional 'laag and meetha'[138]. As we sat with them to discuss any pending work, the bride-to-be called from the jeweller's showroom asking her mother to click photos of her bracelet so that she could buy matching earrings. It was evident from how our 55-year-old neighbour-Bhabi[139] was messing around with her mobile that sending the photos was a challenge for her.

After a couple of minutes, my 70-year-old Mother Darling quietly took the mobile from the flustered mother-of-the-bride, clicked the photos, opened the photo gallery, 'ticked' the photos, redirected them towards WhatsApp and then asked her, 'Vaddi beti nu bhejaan ke chhotti nu?'[140] I just smiled.

On another day my mother came skipping to me with the greatest of joy. Obviously such cheerful behaviour raised my curiosity. Waiving her mobile around, she declared that finally someone had considered her worthy to be gainfully employed and sent a text message for a job. I looked at Mum enquiringly and before I could ask anything, she announced with great aplomb that she had a job offer in hand! I finally was able to persuade her to show me her 'contract' and as I went through the proposal, Mum kept blabbering on, 'Aapne na sahi, beghaane te meri kadar paunde ne! Ajj PAN card banvaaya kamm aayega!'[141]

Much as I was feeling upset about such shady employment proposals being sent by the opportunists to take advantage of

---

[137] ਸਿੱਠਣੀਆਂ (Songs sung at the time of Punjabi weddings).
[138] ਲਾਗ & ਮੀਠਾ (Gifts and present and sweets).
[139] ਭਾਬੀ (Brother's wife).
[140] ਵੱਡੀ ਬੇਟੀ ਨੂੰ ਭੇਜਾਂ ਕੇ ਛੋਟੀ ਨੂੰ? (Should I send this to your elder daughter or the younger one?)
[141] ਆਪਣੇ ਨਾ ਸਹੀ, ਬੇਗਾਨੇ ਤੇ ਮੇਰੀ ਕਦਰ ਪਾਉਂਦੇ ਨੇ? ਅੱਜ ਪੈਨ ਕਾਰਡ ਬਟਵਾਇਆ ਕੰਮ ਆਏਗਾ (Though my own don't value me enough, the outsiders appreciate my worth! Today my PAN card will come in handy!)

the innocence of the naive, Mum's optimism and sheer zest for life and learning prevented me from breaking her heart. At the same time, I could not help mulling over the injustice our previous generations had committed by consigning these spirited young ladies with dreams in their eyes to the kitchens and gardens, to be seen as only a trophy and not heard, and definitely not have any opinion of their own beyond the hearth.

As my mother has a very 'giving' soul, she wanted to be a nurse but that was not to be. Instead, she dutifully got married, bore children, served the joint family and continues to nurse the dream of having her own 'income'. Everyone gets only one life, so why was their right to live taken away in the name of family, honour, culture and tradition?

This text also told me just how easy it is to send manipulative offers to the technologically challenged elderly and defraud them! Mercifully Mum lives in a joint family and has plenty of people to ask or seek feedback, but what about the ones who are living alone while their children are making a living in far-off cities or countries? How easy is it to steal personal information from the elderly and use it not only to ascertain their family situation but also defraud them of their hard-earned money. I have heard some horror stories about endless insurances being sold to the elderly by emotionally motivating them to 'leave a legacy' for their grandkids while no one knows where the money went after the parents moved on. One grandfather had even bought shops in some mall which no one has been able to find till date.

Suddenly I became anxious about the safety of my own Mother. Had I made a mistake in buying her a mobile phone? Has this device made her vulnerable in any way? Just like we can restrict porn websites from the devices of our children, is there any way I can restrict these fraudsters accessing my mother's number and sending her mouth-watering offers? Forget the children; even our elderly are not safe anymore! I am worried. I am really really worried.

'A father's goodness is higher than the mountain,

A mother's goodness deeper than the sea.'

-Japanese Proverb

Wedded for Life

It was a rather quiet Saturday morning with barely a soul up and about. I was awake but refused to stir in case I was called to order. Ignorance is bliss you see, that too at 6 on a cold winter morning. Nicely snuggled up in my bed, I was listening to the sounds around me to figure out when would be the right time to get into action.

I heard Mum returning from her morning walk and going to her room. She sat on the bed with a thump, probably to take her shoes off when I heard Dad's voice with undertones of concern, 'Why are you all tired these days?' Mum responded quietly, 'Because I am 70 now. It is my age to get tired.' Dad continued, almost in a bewildered tone, 'But I am even older than you! Look at me. I am still more fit than you are.'

There was a heavy pause for a few seconds and then I heard Mum say, 'This body has borne two children, fell gravely ill in 84 and barely survived. Then suffered from two serious infections, which took me to ICU. This body bore everything this family went through. Anything which affected you or my children first tore through me. What more do you expect from this body?' There was complete silence for a few minutes after that. I held my breath from underneath my blanket in case it disturbed them. If Dad's concern warmed my heart, Mum's response tore me apart.

Do we realise what our parents go through for us? Do we realise that the job of being a parent begins when the first child is conceived and only doubles with the arrival of grandchildren? Do we realise that parenthood comes without retirement? There is simply no escaping! What right do we have to lay claim over every breath they take? Do we ever stop to think that they need some 'me-time' also?

As I was introspecting these intense thoughts of love and guilt as a child, suddenly I heard Mum's voice, 'Achha dasso tussi ki khayoge ajj lunch vich? Jo tussi kahoge, main ohee banawaangi.'[142] Dad, being Dad, 'Kuch vi bana layeen.'[143] Mum asked him endearingly again, 'Nahin nahin. Jo tuhaada mann karda hai, oh dasso. Main special banaawangi aap layi.'[144] Dad hesitated a little and then said, 'Chal pher mungi-masri di daal bana lae. Naale chhetti bann jayegi.'[145] Mum continued, 'Hor naal ki banaawan? Jo vi tussi khushi naal khaana pasand karoge, main ohi banaawangi.'[146] Dad insisted, 'Nahi, tu thakki hoyi hain. Sirf daal banaayi. Hor kuchh nahin.'[147]

A short while later I went to the kitchen to make tea for us. Mum was about to put 'mungi-masri di daal'[148] in the pressure

---

[142] ਅੱਛਾ ਦੱਸੋ ਤੁਸੀ ਕੀ ਖਾਓਗੇ ਅੱਜ ਲੰਚ ਵਿੱਚ. ਤੁਸੀ ਜੋ ਕਹੋਗੇ ਮੈਂ ਓਹੀ ਬਣਾਵਾਂਗੀ (Go on, tell me what would you like to have for lunch today. I will cook whatever you fancy.)

[143] ਕੁਝ ਵੀ ਬਣਾ ਲਈਂ *(Cook anything).*

[144] ਨਹੀਂ ਨਹੀਂ.. ਜੋ ਤੁਹਾਡਾ ਮੰਨ ਕਰਦਾ ਹੈ, ਉਹ ਦੱਸੋ.. ਮੈਂ ਸਪੈਸ਼ਲ ਬਣਾਵਾਂਗੀ ਆਪ ਲਈ (No. Please tell me what you fancy. I will cook whatever you would like. I will cook specially for you.)

[145] ਚੱਲ ਫੇਰ ਮੂੰਗੀ-ਮਸਰੀ ਦੀ ਦਾਲ ਬਣਾ ਲਈਂ, ਨਾਲੇ ਛੇਤੀ ਬਣ ਜਾਏਗੀ (Alright then. Cook simple lentils and it wouldn't take much time either.)

[146] ਹੋਰ ਨਾਲ ਕੀ ਬਣਾਵਾਂ? ਜੋ ਵੀ ਤੁਸੀ ਖੁਸ਼ੀ ਨਾਲ ਖਾਣਾ ਪਸੰਦ ਕਰੋਗੇ, ਮੈਂ ਓਹੀ ਬਣਾਵਾਂਗੀ *(What else shall I cook? I will cook only whatever you prefer to eat.)*

[147] ਨਹੀਂ ਤੂੰ ਥੱਕੀ ਹੋਈ ਹੈਂ. ਸਿਰਫ ਦਾਲ ਬਣਾਈ, ਹੋਰ ਕੁੱਛ ਨਹੀਂ (No, cook only the lentils since you are already so tired. Don't bother yourself too much.)

[148] ਮੂੰਗੀ ਮਸਰੀ ਦੀ ਦਾਲ *(Simple lentils).*

cooker. Ingredients to cook Dad's favourite 'aallu-gobhi di sabzi'[149] were on the shelf too. Dad loves 'makki di mooli-methi wali roti'[150], which is precisely what we got for breakfast that day. Isn't it amazing how children, and grandchildren tend to benefit from everything our parents do as a couple?

My phone was as tired as I was one night and died out by the time I woke up in the morning. Since I listen to music to keep pace during my morning walk, I took Mum's phone instead and guess what I found! Mum has the best collection of old songs on her phone. Every song flooded me with delightful memories. Another observation I made is that the camera on Mum's phone is miles better than the one I have. It was a delight to take photos of the world, as it was slowly waking up around me. The most smile-worthy observation of the day has to be that Mum has a remarkable set of tech-savvy friends who give two hoots about using the system to the hilt. Thirteen WhatsApp messages in an hour! Mum's popular I must say. And then she has complaints that I remain glued to my phone! Can you imagine if we opened an FB or Instagram account for her?

It is not just I who is noticing this change. Mum and Dad were sitting in the verandah the other day, enjoying the rain showers over a cup of tea. Mum is reading out aloud all the inspirational and motivational WhatsApp messages to Dad. Mum, 'Dekho kinna sohna message hai Hindi wich. Aap jeevan mein sarv-sresth hain. Aap ke jaisa koi nahin. Apni tullna kabhi kisi se na karein.'[151] Dad quietly responded back, 'Main te hain hee special. Taan hee te Pitaji ne tainu mere larr

---

[149] ਆਲੂ ਗੋਭੀ ਦੀ ਸਬਜ਼ੀ (Potato and cauliflower dish).

[150] ਮੱਕੀ ਦੀ ਮੂਲੀ ਵਾਲੀ ਰੋਟੀ (Maize floor Indian bread stuffed with white raddish).

[151] ਦੇਖੇ ਕਿੰਨਾ ਸੋਹਣਾ message ਹੈ ਹਿੰਦੀ ਵਿੱਚ ... ਆਪ ਜੀਵਨ ਮੇਂ ਸਰਵ-ਸ੍ਰੇਸ਼ਠ ਹੈਂ.. ਆਪ ਕੇ ਜੈਸਾ ਕੋਈ ਨਹੀਂ.. ਆਪਟੀ ਤੁਲਨਾ ਕਭੀ ਕਿਸੀ ਸੀ ਨਾ karein (See what a lovely message in Hindi? It says that you are the best in life. You are incomparable, so never compare yourself with anyone.)

laaya si!'[152] Dad later went inside the house and asked my nephew, 'Grandma nu mobile kis ne le ke ditta hai?!!'[153]

Rarely, but Mum does take Dad by surprise. Years ago my brother got into a habit of touching Mum's chin affectionately, which Mum used to hate. She stopped him often, which of course he ignored. One night Mum was making dinner while both of us were yapping away. Unbeknown to Mum, Dad entered the kitchen. He approached Mum from behind and of all things, chose to touch Mum's chin to get her attention. Enraged, Mum turned around, waiving her rolling pin and yelled, 'thehr tainu dasaan main!'[154]

My parents recently completed 50 years of their union. It was a joy to see Mum prancing around the house that day, dressed to the tee in a new suit, kundan danglers, bangles, bindi and kumkum. I am sure on her wedding day she must have behaved like a shy Punjabi bride, but on her golden wedding anniversary, she was a confident bride who gave two hoots.

One evening soon after, as I had barely walked through the door with papers and bag still occupying my hands, she put her arms around my neck and said, 'Chal mainu photos dikhaa anniversary diyaan, main pher tainu parantha banaa ke dawaangi.'[155] I told her that neither was I hungry nor did I have the camera in the car. It was in office so I would show the pictures another day. A little disappointed, her arms dropped off my shoulders and slung back to her hips, 'Sachhi-sachhi

---

[152] ਮੈਂ ਤੇ ਹੈਂ ਹੀ ਸਪੈਸ਼ਲ.. ਤਾਂ ਹੀ ਤੇ ਪਿਤਾਜੀ ਨੇ ਤੈਨੂੰ ਮੇਰੇ ਲੜ ਲਾਇਆ ਸੀ!' *(I know I am special that is why your father married you to me!)*

[153] Grandma ਨੂੰ ਮੋਬਾਈਲ ਕਿਸ ਨੇ ਲੈ ਕੇ ਦਿੱਤਾ? *(Who got the mobile phone for Grandma?)*

[154] ਠਹਿਰ ਤੈਨੂੰ ਦੱਸਾਂ ਮੈਂ! (Wait… Let me sort you out!)

[155] ਚੱਲ ਮੈਨੂੰ ਫੋਟੋ ਦਿਖਾ anniversary ਦੀਆਂ. ਮੈਂ ਫੇਰ ਤੈਨੂੰ ਪਰਾਂਠਾ ਬਣਾ ਕੇ ਦਵਾਂਗੀ. *(Show me the anniversary photos. Then I will make aallu parantha for you.)*

dass!'[156] I assured her that the camera was indeed in the office and she could ring the office boy to confirm.

Hearing this she relaxed a bit, but she still won't let me walk past. Getting hold of my cheek she asked, 'Achha chal photo kal dikha deveen, per eh taan dass teri Mumma keho jehi laggdi si uss din?'[157] I assured her that she was looking gorgeous. Looking deep into my eyes, her fingers climbed towards my ear lobe and pulling it tenderly she asked, 'Mummy daa mann rakhan layi taan nahi keh rahi?!!'[158] I dropped everything and hugged her.

The best part about this conversation was how time stands still when a woman gets dressed for an occasion. Regardless of the passage of time, she is still the bride anxious about her looks and wants to check the results of her efforts. How tender is that fleeting moment of uncertainty, the stolen moment of vanity for a bride. What can we do to preserve every happy moment for our parents? After all, they took pictures of even our snorty

---

[156] ਸੱਚੀ-ਸੱਚੀ ਦੱਸ! (Go on – tell me the truth!)

[157] ਅੱਛਾ ਚੱਲ ਫੋਟੋ ਕੱਲ ਦਿਖਾ ਦੇਵੀਂ ਪਰ ਇਹ ਤਾਂ ਦੱਸ, ਮੰਮੀ ਕਿਹੋ ਜਿਹੀ ਲੱਗਦੀ ਸੀ ਉਸ ਦਿਨ? (Fair enough. Show me the photos tomorrow but at least how did your mother look like that day.)

[158] ਮੰਮੀ ਦਾ ਮੰਨ ਰੱਖਣ ਲਈ ਤਾਂ ਨਹੀਂ ਕਹਿ ਰਹੀ ਕਿਤੇ? (Are you sure you are not saying this just to get me off your case?)

little faces and recorded videos of us taking our first baby steps, even if it looked as if a fat duck was trying to wade across an oily floor! Nopes – we would have to live 10 more lives to be half as generous as our parents.

Stressed out by things beyond my control, I treated myself to a new night suit a couple of weeks after the anniversary celebrations. I chose a soft mull fabric to kiss my exam blues away. I loved the tiny daises embroidered on the white pyjama with a lime green shirt with matching leaves embroidered on it. 'Cute as hell' as one would say. Super chuffed by my purchase I walked in to my mother's room and started twirling around, as little girls generally do to show off and win some compliments.

Mum, who was busy reading when I barged into her room, slid her reading glasses down the ridge of her 'khandaani'[159] nose, examined me from head to toe and then as I saw her reading glasses, and then as she slid the reading glasses back up her nose, I could immediately gauge a sense of disapproval rising in the room. Disappointed, but not to let the matter rest, I asked Mother Darling how I looked in my new prized possession. Nothing quite prepared me for what Mum said eventually, 'Apne peyo di dhee laggdi iss vich tu!'[160]

Alright! It is a foregone conclusion that my patriarch Dad is fashionably challenged or perhaps we can say, challengingly fashionable. However, forget about roasting me, does Mum realise that in one single breath she has equated Dad with daisies? Does Mum realise that she is scarring us both for life?

I am a product of a truly amazing combination of two people who are poles apart and got together over 50 years ago

---

[159] ਖਾਨਦਾਨੀ (Family inheritence).
[160] ਆਪਣੇ ਪੀਓ ਦੀ ਧੀ ਲੱਗਦੀ ਇਸ ਵਿੱਚ ਤੂੰ! (It reflects your father's sense of clothing.)

to tie the matrimonial knot. My mother, as you all know by now, is a cute and cuddly mass with steel hidden in her spine, someone who will try anything once, is always up for a ball. My father on the contrary is an authoritarian patriarch, old school boy who worked hard to provide for his family. He follows his daily schedule as was fixed in 1964! True to his generation, kids were to be seen and not heard and any affection to be shown towards kids or wife was considered blasphemous. If we did something remarkable then Dad would gloat, 'Vekhe mere bachhe?'[161] and if heaven forbid we messed up then Dad would thunder at Mum, 'Vekhi apni aulaad?'[162] I am sure this is something a lot of Punjabis my age would be able to recognise almost instantly.

Unlike my mother, Dad does not believe in 'trying' anything. He never has a vacation as that would involve not being able to sleep in his own bed. At night he eats at home before attending a wedding to avoid eating out. So when Mum wanted to go for higher studies, or learn to ride the bullet, or learn to drive the car, or work from home to become a 'proud working woman', every request was met with a single word – NO. True to her being, Mum bore everything with a chuckle and utmost grace. Perhaps that is where I learnt to always look for solutions rather than cry over the spilt milk.

Anyway, while Mum was crying hoarse over chilly foggy morning with temperature gauge dipping to 5 degrees, Dad was ready to leave for office and on his scooter at that! Whether kids are ready to drop him to office in car is absolutely immaterial. Whether his going to office at 7.30 am causes

---

[161] ਵੇਖੇ ਮੇਰੇ ਬੱਚੇ? (Have you seen my kids? How remarkably well they have performed?)
[162] ਵੇਖੀ ਆਪਣੀ ਔਲਾਦ? (Have you seen what your brats have done?)

hassles to the resident staff in the workshop is also immaterial. He does not think twice before ordering a communal court martial, even without holding a Court of Inquiry, in case his appointment with his daily schedule gets delayed. So while Dad was complaining to Mum about Mum's truant kids, not his of course even now, Mum threw a flying kiss in his direction and said, 'Hunn pata laggya mainu car na sikhaan da nateeja? Main kehndi rahi ke mainu car sikha deyo per tussi nahin manne. Je uddon mera kehna mannya hunda te ajj iss aulaad vall na vekhna painda!'[163] Dad walked out by pretending to be annoyed. My brother and I smiled, benignly of course.

As most of the children, I consider myself inadequate when it comes to making time for our parents. So engrossed do we become in our own lives that as family, we simply exist for our parents, taking care of their generic needs, medical attention they may need and generally keep things in order. However, any spare time of ours is for our partners/spouses, children, even pets! We use our non-work times to plan for future, use it judiciously to plan social events which are really networking opportunities to create more work opportunities, (re)build our homes, worry about our children's future and plan for their universities or careers, recharge ourselves with our friends getting sloshed or tickle ourselves with great laughter nights out. Our holiday plans also begin to exclude our parents as we convince ourselves that they are not physically strong anymore so won't be able to bear the stress of vacations.

In doing so we forget that our parents are not just getting old biologically, they are slowly becoming lonely too. After

---

163 ਹੁਣ ਪਤਾ ਲੱਗਿਆ ਮੈਨੂੰ car ਨਾ ਸਿਖਾਣ ਦਾ ਨਤੀਜਾ? ਮੈਂ ਕਹਿੰਦੀ ਰਹੀ ਕੇ ਮੈਨੂੰ car ਸਿੱਖ ਦੇਯੋ ਪਰ ਤੁਸੀ ਨਹੀਂ ਮੰਨੇ. ਜੇ ਉਦੋਂ ਮੇਰਾ ਕਹਿਣਾ ਮੰਨਿਆ ਹੁੰਦਾ ਤੇ ਅੱਜ ਇਸ ਔਲਾਦ ਵੱਲ ਨਾ ਵੇਖਣਾ ਪੈਂਦਾ! *(Now you realise the mistake you made by not letting me learn how to drive a car despite my repeated requests? If you had honoured my request then, you would not be at the mercy of your kids now!)*

retirement their network begins to shrink. With every friend or relative passing away, their circle of friendship and companionship reduces. There are less people left around them with whom they can share their joys and sorrows.

All this happens while we continue to believe that we are 'doing our best' for our parents. They are living with us, we are around them, we are living together, we meet each other daily, we are doing our duty, we are providing for them. If we miss something, they just have to ask and we would make arrangements. While our parents did everything for us joyously, why do we underline and highlight everything we do for them as our duty? Can the eye we keep on them, see beyond our inheritance or their will?

Somewhere we forget, that perhaps all our parents need is, our time. A bit of undivided attention allows for that precious parent-child bonding required to nurture their soul and bring them alive. If our kids are our only 'property' we are slogging away for, why we overlook that we are also our parents' prized treasure? In creating our kids' future, we forget that we are compromising with our parents' hitherto 'future' too.

Anyway, to redeem myself, I started taking Mum out once a week to do anything she wished to do; whether it is to take her to her friends, watch a film, go to her favourite restaurant, run any pending errands, or shopping, the idea being that for those few hours you put your work/leisure aside and give Mum your complete attention. You came off her, this is the least that you can do for your mother. However, as generally happens, these weekly windows became fortnightly doors and I am ashamed to admit, they have become monthly double doors of time out now. During one of these mini 'Mum-and-Chicken' days out I happened to bump into a work acquaintance.

After exchanging pleasantries, I told him that we can't discuss work since I am with Mum but can touch base with him later. He asked for my current contact details and for the life of me, this workaholic could not find any business card even after searching every nook and cranny of my handbag. As I was apologising profusely to the gentleman about running out of my cards, I noticed Mum opening her bag. Within seconds Mum gracefully offered my card to the gentleman and wished him well. Embarrassed at being caught off-guard in a professional position, I put my arm around my Mum to convey my gratitude to her after waving off the acquaintance.

I noticed Mum was clutching something in her fist. Curiosity killed the CAT and Mum revealed a little card holder. I found each of my business cards in that little cardholder of hers; one business card each that was ever made in my name, whether in England and now in India. My Mother had safely preserved all the time that I did not spend with her, my entire career spanning 26 years, in that tiny card holder. No client could possibly take such pride in my work as my Mother Darling, the one I sacrificed every time for everything else.

Affectionately Mum reached out to tuck away my stray hair, tweaked my ear, pulled my cheeks in the busy shopping mall. She took the cardholder back, safely slipped it away in her handbag and said, 'Chal pher Mummy nu ice cream khilaa ajj.'[164] How little you need to do for them to take such enormous pride in you? How often do we express the pride we have in our parents?

---

[164] ਚੱਲ ਫੇਰ Mumma ਨੂੰ ice cream ਖਿਲਾ ਅੱਜ (Come, take Mumma out for an ice cream today.)

Isn't it amazing how love and care can never be the same for each one of us, even if the basics remain the same over generations? It took an exceptional visitor to make us realise this simple fact of life. A name to reckon with in his field, a connoisseur of arts, master of literature, a well-travelled and an eloquent story teller came visiting. He made no demands as a guest because he said he never allowed any action of his to become a habit, or the privilege to become his identity. He ate what we offered. He drank what we suggested. He had come calling, upon our invite, for a Sunday lunch. It was a day of great learning for us.

Sitting in his chair without much movement for 6 hours, he wove a bewitching tapestry of his stories, while we sat there riveted to the patterns emerging, each pattern representing a different mood or phase of his life, shifting about in our seats every now and then of course. I was snug on a sofa while my brother and mother were perched on a delicately carved thinly upholstered one. My Bhabi kept hopping between the two while my father has taken to sitting on a high back plastic chair ever since he fell ill a couple of years ago. He somehow feels secure in that chair and he feels independent since he can move that chair around anywhere he wishes to sit. He has since fully recovered from that drug-induced illness but that chair has become his throne over the years.

The younger of the siblings, the lesser prim of the two, I, of course, started with changing postures and then began hopping seats. At one point I even kicked off my shoes and curled up on the chaise lounge. As he kept sharing stories and the dusk fell, I went off to put on a jacket. I was mulling over the thoughts of lugging in a blanket too but the looks I got from my brother sitting right opposite to me, somehow told me that it won't be a good idea. I went off to put on some warm socks and snug shoes instead. I am good at making compromises you

see. Finally this charming visitor bade goodbye at dinner time and as
we walked back into the house discussing this marathon session, our
Mother Darling had us in splits when she suddenly remarked, 'Lagge
kahaaniyan de howe! Apne daddy da socheya jehre pichhle 6 ghante
to plastic di kursi wich baithe ne!'[165]

---

[165] ਲੱਗੇ ਕਹਾਣੀਆਂ ਦੇ ਹੋਏ.. ਆਪਣੇ Daddy ਦਾ ਸੋਚਿਆ ਜਿਹੜੇ ਪਿਛਲੇ 6 ਘੰਟੇ ਤੋਂ plastic ਦੀ ਕੁਰਸੀ ਵਿੱਚ ਬੈਠੇ ਨੇ?
(Don't you have any concern for your father who had to listen to these stories for 6 hours
while sitting in a plastic chair?)

'ऐ अँधेरे! देख ले मुँह तेरा काला हो गया
माँ ने आँखें खोल दीं घर में उजाला हो गया'

- मुन्नवर राणा

The Garden Adventures

My mother is very fond of gardening. She is known to wipe every leaf clean with a duster and water down every branch with a gentle baby-shower. The nightwatchman can give evidence about Mum religiously watering her plants at midnight. The Verka milk deliveryman has seen Mum with the water hose at 2 am. In fact she takes better pictures of her plants and pots than of the two legged variety which trots around her home. So I guess it has become amply clear that the green space around the house is her pride and joy. No one dare mess around with her plants.

However, Mum also has a peculiar habit. She arranges the plants by herself and no one has a say in making even a slight physical movement of anything leafy in the house. Usually this does not cause much hassle, till the plants also connive to have a last laugh, at our expense of course!

We are all herbivores in the house and picking up herbs fresh from the garden to grind, boil or cook is pretty normal for us. The plant attacked the most by everyone in the house is the good old medicinal holy basil to give us good health etc. The trouble is, Mum has planted it next to a hedge, which has almost identical leaves to holy basil, but are of course bitter in taste and with zero medicinal value. So you can imagine the taste of our morning tea when one goes out bleary eyes on cold foggy mornings to pluck a few holy basil leaves! It really becomes a lottery of sorts.

If this is not enough, the deliciously fragrant lemon grass has been planted in a pot, which has been conveniently kept next to another identical-looking plant in an identical pot. To make life interesting, it has nothing to do with either the fragrance or any food value. In fact, of all things possible in the world, it is a mosquito-repellent plant!! To complicate things further, Mum keeps changing the position of the pots, keeping them in a pair of course. Hence our attempt to memorise them as mosquito on the left and lemon grass on the right has also failed miserably! So at times we have mosquito-repellent soup for supper while smelling lemon grass by the windowsills. Now you know from where I get my sense of adventure!

One particular winter morning brought in a tinge of chill and fog rolled together, all the more reason to stay snuggled up. Mum brought in the 'lottery' tea and from the whiff of cloud rising from the cup I had strong suspicion that it might be 'hedge' tea today again! So I rolled over to bide my time. You can't escape your fate, but at least you can try to delay it! Mum figured out my intentions but was not about to give up. I get my persistence to see things through from her you see.

After reading out all the headlines from the front page of the paper, Mum asked me to have my tea. I did not respond, pretending to be fast asleep. Mum went on to read aloud about the damage caused by Cyclone Vardah in Madras, pausing to wonder if her distant friends and relatives were safe. Since I don't have the contact numbers of any of them, I kept my trap shut. Then Punjab's amphibious bus caught her attention and she let out a chuckle, 'eh bus ghatt te botta zyaada lagdi hai!!'[166] This had me intrigued and I stirred a little. She is my mother at the end of the day and knows which buttons to press you see. Noticing the movement Mother Darling adopted her 'Devi Ma'[167] avtaar, 'Dekh, ajj kayi masaale pees ke cha banaayi hai, iss layi banda bann ke uth ke cha pee lai. Nahi taan ussi maam-jiste wich paa ke tainu peesungi!!'[168] Dare I not tow the line?

Lately a couple of my friends lost their loved ones in the last few days. Different families and different relationships, but I share a beautiful bond of affection and respect with each one of them. One of the friends is Jatin Salwan, a lawyer by profession and a poet-cum-environmentalist by passion. His zeal for gardening believes in carrying 'life' forward through planting trees.

Jatin is known to gift plants when a loved one passes on in his personal as well as professional network. He can always be found seeking permission to plant trees in public places or government buildings to commemorate all major events of his family. Jatin is well aware of my mother's fondness for plants, so he keeps gifting plants to my mother, which she cherishes.

Jatin lost both his parents within a space of three days. If we as friends were shocked out of our wits, you can just imagine what this loss would have done to Jatin and his family. As days trickled by, I thought what better way to meet Jatin after the formal condolence period was over, than with a couple of plants in the memory of his

---

[166] ਇਹ ਬੱਸ ਘੱਟ ਤੇ ਬੋਤਾ ਜ਼ਿਆਦਾ ਲੱਗਦੀ ਹੈ (This looks less like a bus and more like a camel.)

[167] ਦੇਵੀ ਮਾਂ ਅਵਤਾਰ (My mother in the avatar of a Goddess, especially the Goddess of destruction.)

[168] ਦੇਖ ਅੱਜ ਕਈ ਮਸਾਲੇ ਪੀਸ ਕੇ ਚਾਹ ਬਣਾਈ ਹੈ, ਇਸਲਈ ਬੰਦਾ ਬਣ ਕੇ ਉੱਠ ਕੇ ਚਾਹ ਪੀ ਲੈ. ਨਹੀਂ ਤਾਂ ਉੱਸੀ ਮਾਮ-ਜਿਸਤੇ ਵਿੱਚ ਪਾ ਕੇ ਤੈਨੂੰ ਪੀਸੂੰਗੀ (See I have used many spices to make today's tea. So you better get up and drink it quick. Otherwise I will use the same mortar and pestle to hammer you in!)

parents. I decided to gift him a plant or a tree that not just gives flowers but renders a lovely fragrance too.

In my humble opinion, it would be nice to walk past your front door, carrying a sweet remembrance of your loved one as you march on to meet the challenges of the day. Or perhaps come home in the evening to sit underneath a tree which one planted in the loving memory of a parent or a sibling. I was thinking along the lines of 'Raat di Rani'[169] or Frangipani and wondering if lavender would grow well in our city.

I decided to seek my Mother Darling's opinion on the choice of plants since her knowledge of plants and trees is miles better than my own. I looked across the room where Mum was pondering over the morning papers with a cup of masala-tea[170] while nursing her mild cold and stuffy nose. I gently asked Mum if she could suggest a plant, which has a lovely fragrance. Pat came the reply, 'Jawain da boota changga rehnda hai. Khushbu vi sohni, te aande-jaande pattaa torr ke munh vich paa laen naal sehat vi changgi rehndi hai!'[171]

Days later engrossed in local morning papers as they were full of festive ads and happy faces, I was enjoying my cuppa-adrak-chai[172] while letting the featherweight mood settle in my soul. I wanted to feel happy and positive and joyous. However, Mother Darling had something else on mind. She kept asking

---

[169] ਰਾਤ ਦੀ ਰਾਣੀ (Cestrum, also called carom, caraway or bishop's weed. It is the flowering tree which becomes highly fragrant during the night.)

[170] ਮਸਾਲਾ ਚਾਹ (Traditional Indian tea made with various spices).

[171] ਜਵੈਣ ਦਾ ਬੂਟਾ ਚੰਗਾ ਰਹਿੰਦਾ ਹੈ. ਖੁਸ਼ਬੂ ਵੀ ਸੋਹਣੀ ਤੇ ਆਂਦੇ-ਜਾਂਦੇ ਪੱਤਾ ਤੋੜ ਕੇ ਮੂੰਹ ਵਿੱਚ ਲੈਣ ਨਾਲ ਸਿਹਤ ਵੀ ਚੰਗੀ ਰਹਿੰਦੀ ਹੈ! (Ajwain is a useful plant. It has a good fragrance. One can always chew on a leaf or two while walking past as it keeps the health in ship-shape too! [As per Ayurveda, ajwain has medicinal value and is liberally used in hot drinks such as tea as well as general food recipes. It is also known as caraway, carum or bishop's weed.])

[172] ਅਦਰਕ-ਚਾਹ (Ginger tea).

me to go outside while I wanted to just let things be, 'enjoy the moment' kind of feeling. I refused.

As I was flitting between responding to Diwali messages on WhatsApp and papers, Mum again stuck her neck out through the door and said, 'Someone is outside and asking for you.' At first suspicious as to who would come calling at such an hour, I winked at Mum with a toss of head. Mum however assured me that someone round and short is indeed asking for me. Assuming it might be a new eduCATe Scholar with papers to submit for the scholarship, I left my tea and papers to walk out to the verandah. However, I saw none outside, neither in the verandah, nor at the gate!

Even before I could curl my lips at being cheated and frown at my septuagenarian mother for successfully making a fool of me, Mum dragged me towards a corner of the garden and merrily chirped pointing towards a lone yellow flower sprouting from a new plant gifted to her by Jatin, 'Oh vekh, kinna sohna laggda peya phull.. chaar singgh vi ugg aaye ne uss de … Dekhi meri mehnat? … Chall hunn photo khich ke bhejiye Renuka nu!'[173]

What does one do with a Mother who charms your pants off by cheating you ever so blatantly??!! Why are those born with green fingers so passionate in life? To be honest, Jatin is no better! Jatin wrote a poem using the same plant as metahor, which we had gifted to him in fond remembrance of his parents. In case you feel I am fibbing and how can a grown-up woman get so excited over a single sprout on a plant, Renuka Salwan shall stand my witness as the poor thing has been playing the

---

[173] ਓ ਵੇਖ, ਕਿੰਨਾ ਸੋਹਣਾ ਲੱਗਦਾ ਪੇਆ ਫੁੱਲ.. ਚਾਰ ਸਿੰਘ ਵੀ ਉੱਗ ਆਏ ਨੇ ਉਸ ਦੇ … ਦੇਖੀ ਮੇਰੀ ਮੇਹਨਤ? …ਚੱਲ ਹੁਣ ਫੋਟੋ ਖਿੱਚ ਕੇ ਭੇਜੀਏ ਰੇਨੁਕਾ ਨੂੰ! (See, how beautiful that flower looks? It has grown four horns also! Can you see my hard work coming to fruitition? Go, click a photograph and send it to Renuka!)

spokeswoman for Jatin since years, the husband who refuses to keep a mobile!

It is not just the flowers that my mother tends to get excited. Anything green and has a tendency to grow is her baby. What do you do with your mother who wakes you up before the dawn has cracked and demands, 'Dass mere hath wich ki??'[174] Barely can you see through your groggy eyes when cheerfully she opens her fist. The Chicken was finally able to spot some roundish things resting on Mum's palm. Perplexed, managed to mutter 'kee hai!'[175] and question 'kee hai?' in somewhat the same squeal.

Mother Darling closed her fist before the Chicken could see clearly, did a little dance, and charmingly opened her fist a little again and them clam it shut. I mean, this was happening even before I could see clearly and engage my brains?! Peeved off I wanted to turn over when she landed squarely on me, practically blocking all escape from her. Then with as much pride as a mother can muster for her newborn Mum opens up her fist one more time, 'aah dekh apne ghar di kheti. Organic aallu jehre main paal-pos ke vadde keete!'[176] Happy as much as I was for Mum, I could not figure out what would we do with these almond-sized potatoes. Mum had five miniature potatoes in her fist for seven of us fully grown family members to fight over.

However, Mother Darling needs to learn how to draw the line, or shut the windows before she starts watering her plants, which she puts in every nook and cranny of the house. I remember waking up to a truly winter morning: chilly, foggy,

---

[174] ਦੱਸ ਮੇਰੇ ਹੱਥ ਵਿੱਚ ਕੀ? (Go on.. tell me what is in my fist.)

[175] ਕੀ ਹੈ! .... ਕੀ ਹੈ?? (Muuummmm… What is it?)

[176] ਆਹ ਦੇਖ ਆਪਣੇ ਘਰ ਦੀ ਖੇਤੀ ... Organic ਅੱਲੂ ਜਿਹੜੇ ਮੈਂ ਪਾਲ-ਪੋਸ ਕੇ ਵੱਡੇ ਕੀਤੇ! (Have a look, this is home farmed produce.. Organic potatoes which I tended to have become fully grown potatoes now.)

brrrr- inducing morning with no sign of sun around. Just the kind of morning you want to play peek-a-boo with the elusive sun snuggled up from beneath the warm fluffy blankets. Thanks to my father's obsession with huge windows to ensure copious amount of sun and breeze gets to kiss every corner of the house, such mornings are particularly colder for me. My bed is parked right next to huge windows on two sides, one overlooking the open verandah and the other saddled with the garden. There are nights during the monsoons when the sudden showers will drench me even before I am able to get my act together and shut the window shutters. As you can probably imagine, the situation becomes specifically challenging during winter rains!

Nevertheless, following my Mother Darling's instructions that we must not let any pensive thoughts settle in our minds on 1st of January, the dutiful daughter that I am, I decided to cheerfully climb out of the bed thinking, 'What a befitting welcome to the New Year.' Bhabi chimed in with a 'Happy New Year' wish and Mum brought in 'Halwa',[177] which was promptly followed by a hug. Life is sorted. Though still feeling chill in the bones, I let the warmth in my heart guide me towards the bathroom to scrub down the grime of last year's trials and tribulations.

The kid in me would have loved to skip the bath but the daughter in me was too afraid to let Mother Superior pick bones with me on the first day of the year. I set the water to a temperature which was hot enough to beat the cold but would not scald the skin off my bones! With teeth chattering and muttering mildly, I slowly started delayering to get over and done with it when suddenly, I find myself getting showered in

---

[177] ਹਲਵਾ (Halva, the Indian sweet made with semolina, clarified butter and nuts).

bitterly cold water out of the blue. Getting over this extreme form of torture on a bitterly cold winter morning, I finally regain senses to find Mother Superior singing softly to herself and merrily watering her plants sitting pretty on the huge bathroom windowsill using a waterhose. Aaarrrggghhhh!

This shivering, trusting child demands to know the root cause of her parents' respective obsessions, which they persistently pursue at the expense of the safety of their unsuspecting children. Why can't they just sit down with me once and for all to confirm my long-standing suspicion of being an adopted child! I am sorry. I refuse to believe that this act of showering cold water on your unsuspecting child already struggling with a bone-chilling situation, could remotely be translated as 'showering blessings' to welcome the New Year! Je refuse!

YouTube has taken Mum's passion to a completely different level altogether. She has started making compost also using all the wet waste from the kitchen. She does not complain about us leaving stuff uneaten fruits or salads in the plate anymore as all that now gets turned into manure. Given that everything we eat goes into the manure, the same stuff grows back too wherever Mum uses that smelly organic watery plant feed as she loves to call it. People have papaya trees in the grounds and lawns, ours are growing out of pots with lemon balm mint.

It took her 6 months to grow tomato plants from the kitchen waste, but finally we do have half a dozen tomato plants waving their delicate heads in the mild breeze skimming past our garden. We did not know what to do with the three almost cherry sized tomatoes, which she harvested with such pomp and show the other day. She cut those three tomatoes into seven neat slices, one each for each family member. As I reached out to grab my slice she slammed my hand down and said, 'Say a blessing first, bless the tomatoes which have sacrificed their lives so that you may grow healthy!' How can you not love someone who wishes to experience everything so wholeheartedly?

Given that Mother Darling has green fingers, I thought I would plan a little surprise for her. Greenariums is the local 'go-to' place if you wish to buy a garden in a vase, jar, bottle or even a wine goblet. I told Mum to get ready by 10.30 am and as expected, Mother Superior demanded to know, 'Kithe Jana hai?'[178]

Not willing to let the cat out of the bag about the surprise treat for Mum, I just said, 'kuchh bagh-bageeche baare hai.'[179] Mother Darling's face lit up and immediately she asked, 'Walking Shoes paa lwaan?'[180] Still not wishing to disclose that it is indoors, I said, 'Wear something comfortable.' Mother Superior pondered for a minute and asked, 'kinni der laavnge?'[181] I told her something like 2 hours. Horror crossed her face and she asked, 'kuchh khaan nu deinge ke main karaan kuchh pack?'[182] I mean, really, don't you think my mother qualifies to be in CBI?!!! How difficult is it for my mother to just 'be surprised'??

All was forgiven after a little garden was created by my Mother Darling in a round glass bowl, all by herself. Mum's very own terranium. She bowled everyone with her knack for creativity. There is literally no age bar to learning and I do admit, I am absolutely proud of the undying zeal for life that my mother possesses. Ever since she has brought her prized

---

[178] ਕਿੱਥੇ ਜਾਣਾ ਹੈ? (Where are we going?)

[179] ਕੁਝ ਬਾਗ਼-ਬਗੀਚੇ ਬਾਰੇ ਹੈ (Not much. Something to do with gardening.)

[180] walking shoes ਪਾ ਲਵਾਂ? (Shall I put on my walking shoes?)

[181] ਕਿੰਨੀ ਦੇਰ ਲਾਵਾਂਗੇ? (How long will we take?)

[182] ਕੁਝ ਖਾਣ ਨੂੰ ਦੇਣਗੇ ਕੇ ਮੈਂ ਕਰਾਂ ਕੁਝ pack? (Would they give us something to eat or shall I pack some stuff?)

possession home, she has been using Dad's tweezers to relocate the little nest of birds and her pink rabbit. She has taken control of my old blusher brush to dust off the plants. She has forced me to buy the syringe to water the plants every 3 weeks. Thank you Greenariums for bringing the spring back in my mother's feet today. Mum continues to confirm that there really is no age for learning, even if we have to accept that the learner tends to get a little demanding as one ages!

"No matter how matured a Mother is,

she watches her middle - aged children

for signs of improvement."

- Unknown

Trials and Tribulations

When kids prepare and sit their exams, mothers have their knickers in a twist till the results are declared. They will pray for your success, be at your beck and call while you revise and feed you sweet curd before you step out to appear for the exam. One is likely to assume that things improve over the years as mothers ought to get more confident in the capabilities of their kids and become less critical of their exam results. Alas! we don't get to live in this utopia we all dream about often. As I had taken admission in Post Graduate Diploma in Human Rights & Duties at Panjab University (PU), I had to sit four papers per semester to get the coveted paper in my hands, declaring that I am a PU alumna.

If you think memorising and preparing for the exams to sit the 3- hour-long exam would have become a habit at my ripe old age, you can't be farther from truth. Revising the dates of conventions and the legal provisions was more difficult than rolling on hot coals. And if you think my mother would have been fawning all over me to ensure every facility was provided to me to prepare for the papers, you might as well take a trip to the moon! My mother really is the 'Mother of all Mothers' and she takes the biggest cookie that was ever baked.

Anyone would either be proud or take a pity on seeing a woman of my age, preparing for a series of 3-hour-long exams. Hail my mother who walks through the door, sits calmly besides me and says, 'Had you studied diligently everyday throughout, you would not have had to mug-up everything in short few days now!' I guess I can roll over and die.

On the day of the first paper, the Chicken left home an hour before the gong was to strike 2 pm to declare exam time. I wanted to ensure that I was well in time to park the car, find the examination hall and plant myself in the appointed seat to write out my first 3-hour paper in over a decade. Despite the best of revision, a clutch of pens in my zip-lock bag, I found myself way short of preparation for the exam. I had not quite rationed in the fact that this was the first time I was sitting a higher education exam in India which had its own norms.

It has been years since most of us wore a wristwatch as we just rely on our mobile phone to give us the time. Alas! I did not know that in India, the examiners ask you to deposit your mobile phones on the main table before they give you the question paper. I pleaded that I would keep my phone on the 'airplane' mode so that I could just keep an eye on the time but it was not permitted. I looked frantically around for a wall clock in the examination hall, but there was none. As the clock was ticking closer to 2 pm, I realised I had no option but to call my lifeline, my dear friend Vipin to come and give me his wristwatch.

Fortunately for me, he lived not too far from the university campus and promptly reached the examination hall. Though rules do not permit anyone not connected with the paper in progress to be allowed inside the examination building, I guess his elderly benign looks combined with white hair worked in my favour and he was allowed in to give me his wrist watch. What a pitiful look Vipin had on his face when he handed me the watch in front of the whole class though. Shaking his head, all he could muster was 'tea would be ready for you at home.' Thank God for small mercies and merciful friends.

Finally, the examination started and I started scribbling my life away for the next 3 hours. Exhausted, I drove to Vipin's house to hand over his wristwatch and for that much-needed cup of tea. Looking at my frazzled self, I was duly rewarded with a warm hug from his mother and a soul-rejuvenating tea by his wife, Smriti. We discussed the paper at length and realised that I needed to abandon my British ways of studying and 'Indianise' my paper-writing tactics. With their joint academic experience, we rehashed the exam-plan, as I was only one paper down and three more to go.

Eventually I managed to make my way home where Mum was waiting for me not at the door, but in the verandah itself. Without any formalities of hugs and kisses, she came straight to the point, 'How was the paper?' I told her, 'Mum it wasn't great since 30% of the paper was out of syllabus and I had to fluff through the answers.' Mum responded with disappointment writ large on her face, 'Basss ... Reh gayi pher?' PRICELESS![183]

In case you feel this is a one-off incident and my Mother Superior is actually harmless, allow me to share an incident which had occurred 3 years ago. As I was losing my memory more swiftly than the leaf shedding during the autumn season, I was given three options by the neurologist to salvage my grey

---

[183] ਬੱਸ ਰਹਿ ਗਈ ਫੇਰ? (Baah! So you flunked?)

cells: play chess, play Sudoku or learn a language. Since, I don't like 'playing games', chess was out. As I scored precious 36/100 in my class 10 maths final paper, Sudoku was out. I zeroed in on French as Alliance Française was not too far from my home/office commute and I loved languages anyway.

Let me tell you that I had studied French for only 3 months and given my first exam for A1 level, which is the basic primary 'A for Apple and B for Bat' level but I was progressing well. I remember sitting comfortably in my bed on a cold winter morning after the first French paper finished. Mum quietly walked up to me with her adrak-chai[184] in her hand, sat at the edge of my bed and asked me, 'So can you speak French now?' Bewildered, I gave her a blank look and replied, 'Mum it has only been three months and it takes much longer to learn language which is completely foreign to us. I have to attune my ears to the sound of the language. There is no one at home to help. It will take time.'

Just as I was feeling chuffed with myself for having given her a very holistic answer, Mother Superior's face dropped in sheer disappointment, 'Achha? Taan hunn teri French oho jehi hai jivein pind de ganvaar angrezi bolan di koshish karde ne?!'[185] Is there a grading system which is available only to the mothers, especially the ones of Punjabi descent?!

Returning to the task at hand of preparing for my fresh set of exams, I was pretty much in sync with my revision so I thought of taking a little break and make some calls related to work etc. I did not have the luxury of being a full-time student

---

[184] ਅਦਰਕ ਚਾਹ (Ginger tea)

[185] ਅੱਛਾ! ਤੇ ਫੇਰ ਹੁਣ ਤੇਰੀ ਫ੍ਰੈਂਚ ਓਹੋ ਜਿਹੀ ਹੈ ਜਿਵੇਂ ਪਿੰਡ ਦੇ ਗੰਵਾਰ ਅੰਗਰੇਜ਼ੀ ਬੋਲਣ ਦੀ ਕੋਸ਼ਿਸ਼ ਕਰਦੇ ਨੇ? (Is it? Then your French is as bad as the English spoken by the village bumpkins as they try to speak in English?)

you see. Unfortunately, that was not how my mother sees me, especially during the exams. As I was finishing the last call, I saw my brother walking past from the corner of my eye. As Mum could not say anything to me, given my mouth was already busy on the phone, she addressed my brother instead, 'Aah dekh … Hai koi teri bhaen nu khyaal, ke iss ne kal paper dena hai?'[186]

Fortunately for me, the next paper went well. I had a cup of tea with Vipin and his mother at their home and finally reached home after dark. Though Mumma was not waiting in the verandah, she certainly was holding the fort well. As I walked across the verandah to ring the doorbell, I heard her voice, 'Don't bother, the door is open.' As I pussy footed through the door, she sprang up from her 'Mommy-in-Waiting' seat and positioned her razor-sharp nose barely millimetres away from mine. This is no mean feat by the way, since she is a good 6" shy of me! 'How was the paper?' she demanded to know.

'It was good Mumma, but too long so I could not do justice to the last 8% of the paper.' I thought replying in detail would satisfy her and perhaps earn myself a hug. Alas! She relented, but just a wee-bit. With heels back on the ground and hands rolled in tiny fists on each side of her waist, 'Sach-Sach dass!'[187] Ah well! What to do eh … you can't really win!

The moment I stepped inside the house after sitting one more paper, Mother Superior literally pounced on me. 'Marjaani paper kinwein ker ke aayi ajj? Pencil Box tera table

---

[186] ਆਹ ਵੇਖ! ਹੈ ਕੋਈ ਤੇਰੀ ਭੈਣ ਨੂੰ ਖਿਆਲ ਕੇ ਇੱਸ ਨੇ ਕੱਲ ਪੇਪਰ ਦੇਣਾ ਹੈ? (Just look at your sister! Has she got any care in the world that she is to appear in an exam tomorrow?)
[187] ਸੱਚ-ਸੱਚ ਦੱਸ! (Come on now… Tell me the truth!)

te peya hai!!'[188] So you see my friends, this whittled scatter brain had left the house without any writing instrument at all. For a few minutes I got all hot and bothered at the university campus because I neither had a spare pen in the car nor had the time to run down to the nearest stationery shop at the Student Centre, nor could I risk losing my parking slot by taking the car out of the parking lot to buy the pen from the nearby market, and still be back in time to enter the examination hall.

I was literally kicking myself. How could I remember to consume my coffee, but forget the life-saving pencil box at home! Finally, it was the security guard who came to my rescue today who took pity on me and handed me his precious Rs.10/- biro-pen to write my 3-hour-long paper. Good job I carry my roll number in a separate envelope or otherwise I might not have been allowed to sit the paper altogether! Even my dear psychiatrist friend Simmi remarked when she got to know of this episode, 'Oh my God! How can I tell off my 15-year-old son after all the shenanigans you have done? No pencil box to write the paper!'

Finally, as I picked up the books for the last paper of the first semester on a rather dull, grey and windy morning, my dear mother came to my room. Snuggling up in my blanket, she handed me a cup of ginger tea and started rustling the newspapers. While reading loudly through what is ailing our city, Salman getting away with murder, Hadley turning approver, she suddenly turned her attention towards me and asked, 'Is this going to be your last paper?' I nodded in

---

[188] ਮਰਜਾਣੀ ਪੇਪਰ ਕਿੰਜ ਕਰ ਕੇ ਆਈ? ਪੈਨਸਿਲ ਬਾਕਸ ਤੇਰਾ ਟੇਬਲ ਉੱਤੇ ਪੇਆ ਹੈ (You idiot! How did you write the paper today? Your pencil box is lying on the table!)

affirmative. The Queen of one-liners, my dear Mother quipped promptly, 'Chal pher main vi Monday ganga nahaa layungi!'[189]

Going through a typical student-revision phase where despite my best intentions, I just could't get into the mood for the last paper, which by the way, happened to be on the following day, I kept my pens, my revision notes and my books all neatly next to me, in a pile! However, I went to watch that piece of news on TV (and I had stopped watching TV years ago!), just wanted to have a shower (again), or drink another glass of water (and start making fresh lime instead). Despite the greys in my hair, the excuses remain the same. I smiled when I noticed was Mum reading my course books. Seeing a raised eyebrow, my mother responded non-chalantly, 'Tu te parhna nahin, main sochya main hee parr ke kal paper de aawaan!'[190] Shamed to death, Chicken picked up the books to have one final go at the revision.

I finally figured out the reason behind such huge procrastination. A major part of this paper was about the origins and evolution of human rights in the world. Since this involves historic facts, figures, dates and names, it terrified me. Given the state of my grey cells, I was told by everyone that the best way to MEMORISE was to create connections between words, features and events. So I dutifully thought I would give it a try.

Hammurabi was the sixth king of the First Babylonian Dynasty. He had united Mesopotamia and is credited with creating the earliest surviving codes of law and initiated what we now call 'human rights'. So I knew there would be a question

---

[189] ਚੱਲ ਫੇਰ ਮੈਂ ਵੀ Monday ਗੰਗਾ ਨ੍ਹਾ ਲਵਾਂਗੀ! (Good. Then on Monday I too would go have a bath in Ganga. Having a bath in Ganga is a symbolic ritual which could mean anything from washing your sins away to signaling an end of an episode of your life, such as death.)

[190] ਤੂ ਤੇ ਪੜ੍ਹਨਾ ਨਹੀਂ ਤੇ ਮੈਂ ਸੋਚਿਆ ਮੈਂ ਹੀ ਪੜ੍ਹ ਕੇ ਕੱਲ ਪੇਪਰ ਦੇ ਆਵਾਂ! (Since you are not going to revise, I thought I might as well mug-up and write your last paper tomorrow!)

related to Hammurabi Codes and I had to memorise it somehow. Hammurabi also happens to be someone who stood up for the then 'prisoners of war' and released all the slaves. I connected him with rationalists such as Kalburgi, who stood up in the face of constipated religious ideology and lost his life recently. See, making connections does help in bringing a topic alive. I suddenly felt so much better and embarked on the last dance of revision whole heartedly.

I went to the examination hall, read the question paper, lo and behold, there was one about the origins of human rights. Without much ado I wrote all I could remember and finished the paper 20 minutes before the finishing time. I felt like a dog with two tails. Somehow, as I reached home and was having my cup of tea with Mother Darling, suddenly panic set in. What name did I write in the paper? Did I mix both the names and wrote Hummburgi? Unfortunately I expressed my fears aloud. Disappointed by my facial revelation, Mother Superior shook her head and muttered, 'Meriyaan ungliyaan reh gayiaan badaam chhilde! Dass ki faayeda hoya tainu badaam khilaan da?'[191]

After exams I wanted to chill but Mother Darling wanted to mingle. We, as a family, had a very busy social calendar and I, as usual, was reluctant to socialise. Sensing my intentions, my Mum walked up to me and addressed me with as much sincerity as her cheeky smile could manage, 'Dekh, muft di salaah na koi ajj de zamaane wich dinda hai, te na lenda hai. Per main pher vi teri bhalaayi di gall kardi haan tere naal.

---

[191] ਮੇਰੀਆਂ ਉਂਗਲੀਆਂ ਰਹਿ ਗਈਆਂ ਬਦਾਮ ਛਿਲ੍ਹਦੇ! ਦੱਸ ਕੀ ਫ਼ਾਇਦਾ ਹੋਇਆ ਤੈਨੂੰ ਬਦਾਮ ਖੁਆਨ ਦਾ? (I bruised my fingers while peeling almonds for you! You wasted all my effort and the almonds too!) [Almonds are believed to help with brain development and memory in our part of India!])

Banda bann ke uth ke tyaar ho jaa, nahi ta tere naal buri bahut honi hai ajj.'[192]

I accept that I am not the brightest of tubelights around, but I know when a threat has been served on a silver platter. Much against my wishes, I dragged myself out of bed to get dressed for the occasion. One of my eldest cousins was hosting a 'path', a religious ceremony at home to celebrate the arrival of his grandson. To be honest it was fun being there as I had not met a lot of cousins, nieces, nephews and their spouses and respective broods in a long time. Given that it all started with our paternal grandfather and grandmother deciding to marry and multiply which led to six sons marrying six daughters-in-law, followed by 17 grandchildren and a mindboggling number of great-grandchildren and whatever relationship titles follow thereafter!

It was interesting to see so many of us around, some of whom I could not even recall meeting even once. I had the same status in the family as my eldest female cousin, born just 30 years apart. I was introduced to my sons-in-law who were older than me. If this was not enough, even they had their own sons-in-law to introduce to me and this is where I lost the plot! The fresh crop of grandkids seriously questioned my position as a grandmother in their lives, and with the 'just-met' sons-in-law declaring that I neither looked nor behaved like a mother-in-law, it was quickly decided that I would be the aunt for everyone!

It was fascinating to see the whole clan party together. My septuagenarian cousins were busy taking selfies, the middle-aged ones were lining up for group photos, little kids were

---

[192] ਦੇਖ ਮੁਫ਼ਤ ਦੀ ਸਲਾਹ ਨਾ ਕੋਈ ਅੱਜ ਦੇ ਜ਼ਮਾਨੇ ਵਿੱਚ ਦਿੰਦਾ ਹੈ ਤੇ ਨਾ ਕੋਈ ਲੈਂਦਾ ਹੈ. ਪਰ ਮੈਂ ਫੇਰ ਵੀ ਤੇਰੀ ਭਲਾਈ ਦੀ ਗੱਲ ਕਰਦੀ ਹਾਂ ਤੇਰੇ ਨਾਲ. ਬੰਦਾ ਬਣ ਕੇ ਉੱਠ ਕੇ ਤਿਆਰ ਹੋ ਜਾ ਨਹੀਂ ਤਾਂ ਤੇਰੇ ਨਾਲ ਬੁਰੀ ਬਹੁਤ ਹੋਣੀ ਹੈ ਅੱਜ! *(Listen, nowadays, neither anyone gives free advice, nor accepts the same. However, thinking about your own well-being I am giving you free advice. So, you better get ready for the day quickly little one or I assure you of some pretty tough time ahead today!)*

howling around and as this rather nice lazy lunch was coming to a closure and it was time to say goodbyes, the same one for which my mother had given me the veiled advice earlier in the morning, I was dragged into a corner for some clarification.

A little stunned I was presented to a young girl who asked me point blank if I was doing a Post Graduate Diploma in Human Rights & Duties at the PU. A little perturbed to share my life's details with someone I had never met, I rolled my head in that typical 'South Indian' way, which leaves all North Indians confused to figure out if it was a 'yeah' or a 'neah'. A stout lady whom I did not recognise, introduced herself as the girl's mother and said, 'I am sorry but ever since she has arrived at this lunch, she has been telling us that you are her friend/classmate and I have been telling her that you are too old to be her classmate!' The defiant little girl completely ignored her mother to address me again, 'But I was there in the classes you attended and I used to sit right behind you in the examination hall too.'

By this time I realised I could not continue to play silly buggers, despite the barb from her mother. I asked her to tell me more about her young charming self. It turned out that not only was she indeed my classmate, but I was also her father's youngest cousin and I would leave it all to you to make the calculations! She also told me with subtle pride that she was actually perusing Doctorate at PU. I congratulated her for her academic endeavours and gave her one big tight hug too.

Feeling chuffed about meeting my well-educated, well-presented and well-behaved niece, I bragged at home that we were classmates. Everyone felt very proud of the girl's academic focus in life. Then suddenly a cloud of darkness crossed my mother's face, 'Tu kitae fail taa nahin ho jaayeingi na??!!!'[193]

Finally, the result of first-semester exams was declared. Encouraged by everyone, I thought I would gently break the news to Mum. I mean, 'nearly' 70% at 'my age' surely is not a bad score for a 'non-practical' and descriptive subject. After Mum was done with dinner, I politely asked her to come over to me where I had the exam score up on the screen. I gingerly broached the subject, 'Mumma result aa gya. Aap di Munni de 69.5% number aaye ne.'[194] Mum responded with a blank face, 'Hain? 70% vi nahin le ke aayi?'[195] Quietly I added, 'Mumma Masters level'. Mother India did not seem moved. She was obviously not done with me either as yet. With one hand on her hip she fired off, 'Achha number te jinne aaye, eh dass class wich position ki aayi?'[196]

Thinking this might buy some brownie points, I quickly responded, 'Mumma 47 students si. Despite being the oldest in the class, I stood 6th!!!' There I had dug the hole even deeper for myself![197]

'Haye Rubba! first na sahi, second ya third hee le aandi … sixth nu kaun puchhda hai?'[198] She toddled off adding, 'Hunn Aman nu ki dasaangi ke ki ker ke aayi hai Bua!!!'[199]

---

[193] ਤੂੰ ਕਿਤੇ ਫੇਲ ਤਾਂ ਨਹੀਂ ਹੋ ਜਾਏੰਗੀ ਨਾ? *(I hope you won't flunk your exams?)*

[194] ਮੰਮਾ ਰਿਜ਼ਲਟ ਆ ਗਿਆ. ਆਪ ਦੀ ਮੁੰਨੀ ਦੇ 69.5% ਨੰਬਰ ਆਏ ਨੇ (Mumma result has been declared. Your daughter has scored 69.5% marks.)

[195] ਹੈਂ? 70% ਵੀ ਨਹੀਂ ਲੈ ਕੇ ਆਈ? (What? You could not get even 70%?)

[196] ਅੱਛਾ ਨੰਬਰ ਤੇ ਜਿੰਨੇ ਆਏ, ਇਹ ਦੱਸ ਕਲਾਸ ਵਿੱਚ position ਕੀ ਆਈ? (Alright. Forget the marks. What position have you secured in the class?)

[197] ਮੰਮਾ 47 students ਸੀ (Mum there were 47 students.)

[198] ਹਾਏ ਰੱਬਾ! 1 ਨੇ ਸਹੀ, 2 ਯਾ 3 ਹੀ ਲੈ ਆਂਦੀ… 6 ਨੂੰ ਕੌਣ ਪੁੱਛਦਾ ਹੈ? (My God! If you could not be first, you could have at least tried to be second or third. Who cares about sixth position?)

[199] ਹੁਣ ਅਮਨ ਨੂੰ ਕੀ ਦੱਸਾਂਗੀ ਕੇ ਕੀ ਕਰ ਕੇ ਆਈ ਹੈ ਤੇਰੀ ਬੁਆ? *(What a failure! Now how would I tell this to Aman?)*

Second semester was less of paperwork but had far more emphasis on research. Since I was least interested in run-of-the-mill topics, I chose incest abuse primarily because no one talked about it. Hence, despite everyone telling me to choose something from as mundane as 'eve teasing' to as old as 'preference for male child', I wanted to establish the prevalence of incest, that is, sexual abuse within families. I submitted the assignments, revised for the papers, prepared my thesis and appeared for the viva voce also. Mum was aware that all was done and dusted as far as this course is concerned, but was keen to know how her overgrown baby girl had faired in the second-semester papers.

As much as I tried to ignore her looming shadow, one day Mum caught hold of me the moment I put my feet up after a long day. When I saw a softer look on her face, I melted and raised an eyebrow as only a daughter can with a mother. Quietly she asked me about the results of my second-semester exams, 'Tu dassya ni ki tere result da ki baneya?'[200] Since it was turning out to be a rather genial conversation, smilingly I told her, 'Mumma ajje result aya nahin.'[201] As expected, the response did not convince her and she took a couple of steps closer in my direction, making me squirm a little. Mothers can make a move in any direction you see. Indulgingly she asked me, 'Ki gal? Number changge nahi aaye?'[202] When I nodded in the negative, she again asked, 'Kitae fail taan nahin ho gayi?'[203]

When I tried to assure her that the results were indeed yet to be declared, she thought for a moment and then gave me a little hug, 'Chal koi na, Ma hain main teri. Mainu te dass

---

[200] ਤੂ ਦੱਸਿਆ ਨਹੀਂ ਕੇ ਤੇਰੇ ਰਿਜ਼ਲਟ ਦਾ ਕੀ ਬਣਿਆ? (Look you have not told me about your exam results.)

[201] ਮੰਮਾ ਅੱਜੇ ਰਿਜ਼ਲਟ ਆਯਾ ਨਹੀਂ. (Mum I have not had the result as yet.)

[202] ਕੀ ਗੱਲ? ਨੰਬਰ ਚੰਗੇ ਨਹੀਂ ਆਏ? (What happened? You did not get good marks?)

[203] ਕਿਤੇ ਫੇਲ ਤਾਂ ਨਹੀਂ ਹੋ ਗਈ? (Are you sure you have not failed?)

de!'[204] Her indulgence made me giggle and before I could say anything in response, suddenly she stepped back and found her old self. With her hand on her hip and a determination in her voice she said, 'Bua-Bhateeji ne ikko waqt paper ditte si. Oh college jaan lagg payi te tu kehndi hain ke result nahi aaya? Iss umr wich vi eh haal?!'[205] Whoever said my mother was easy?!!

Days later as I was running through the day's list in my head while getting ready in the morning, Mother Darling chimed in looking bright and her best behaviour, 'Chal pher ajj kitae ghumaa ke leya ... Mumma ne nawaan suit paaya ajj.'[206] Because this was a full working day with back to back meetings, I refused point blank. Mum pounced upon me and we both landed on the bed with a thud, but I refused to budge. 'No means No' and about time that Mother Superior understood this. No is non-negotiable. I pursed my lips and kept tapping away on my laptop before I packed for the day and left home for work.

As time was ticking away, my tapping became more furious and I was almost on the edge of falling apart as it was an important meeting lined up and I was not yet done with my proposal. Somehow Mum also realised the pressure I was under and instead of pouting and moaning about not being taken out for a ride in town, she simply brought me a cup of tea with rusk. She knows when to put her foot down and also when to silently support me. No battle can be won on empty stomach

---

[204] ਚੱਲ ਕੋਈ ਨਾ .... ਮਾਂ ਹੈਂ ਮੈਂ ਤੇਰੀ. ਮੈਨੂੰ ਤੇ ਦੱਸ ਦੇ! (Never mind. I am your mother. At least tell me what has transpired.)

[205] ਬੁਆ - ਭਤੀਜੀ ਨੇ ਇੱਕੋ ਵਕਤ ਪੇਪਰ ਦਿੱਤੇ ਸੀ. ਉਹ ਕਾਲਜ ਜਾਣ ਲੱਗ ਪਈ ਤੇ ਤੂੰ ਕਹਿੰਦੀ ਹੈਂ ਕੇ ਰਿਜ਼ਲਟ ਨਹੀਂ ਆਇਆ! ਇਸ ਉਮਰ ਵਿੱਚ ਵੀ ਇਹ ਹਾਲ? (Both of you aunt and niece took the exams at the same time. She has restarted going to the college while you continue to claim that your result has not been declared as yet! Is this the way to behave at this age?)

[206] ਚੱਲ ਫੇਰ ਅੱਜ ਕਿਤੇ ਘੁੰਮਾ ਕੇ ਲਿਆ .. ਮੈਮਾ ਨੇ ਨਵਾਂ ਸੂਟ ਪਾਇਆ ਹੈ! (Come take me out for a spin. Don't you see Mum has put on a new dress today?)

is what my Nani's half-sister used to say. There are some human qualities which don't skip for generations you see.

Just when I thought the matter was settled, the doorbell rang. Mum went out and came back with a registered envelope from Panjab Uuniversity, in the name of Supreet Dhiman. Suddenly both my mother and my Bhabi[207] got excited while I got my knickers in a further and even more tighter twist. It contained my exam result! Mum and Bhabi wanted me to open the envelope, while I pretended to suddenly need to drink my tea first. Mum was having none of it.

Turning towards my Bhabi Mother Superior chuckled, 'Ja iss di cha thandi ker leya!'[208] Unfortunately for me, I had scored even less than the first semester. Can you imagine? I almost got disowned, yet again. Fortunately for me, though it also meant that Mum would not ask for a shopping trip for a few days, and I could continue working on the project without any distractions. Unfair – I know, but so is life.

About a month after that horrid brown envelope arrived, a crumpled piece of thick paper convinced my Mother Superior that I have not been such a waste of time, space and effort after all. Reading through the paper, I could see her expressions go through a range of emotions in a very short duration of time.

Mum took the paper nonchalantly from me as I was intruding into her TV time. She was indifferent even when I handed over her reading glasses. She seemed cheesed off at having to change her posture and glasses while she was almost snoozing off. The 'official' look of the paper made her sit

---

207 ਭਾਬੀ (Brother's wife).
208 ਜਾ ਇੱਸ ਦੀ ਚਾਹ ਠੰਡੀ ਕਰ ਕੇ ਲਿਆ! (Go tackle her cup of tea. Let's not give her any excuse to share her exam results, on account of her tea being too hot to drink.)

upright. Running her podgy hand over the golden logo softened her face a little. Reading it out aloud, coming across my full name made her a little attentive. Reading Dad's full name made her halt a little as she realised this must be an official document. She stopped point blank when she read her own name written on the paper. She looked up at me and started reading the paper haltingly, in a chocked voice by now. It is not every day that an official document in India, specifically mentions mother's name you see. Regardless of the age, I guess it does feel good to be given a place of pride, respectfully, even if it still comes after the father's name and little too late in life. My country is evolving.

She blew a kiss in my direction while joyfully tossing her head like a Russian doll, when she read the title 'Human Rights & Duties'. I smiled back. As she read FIRST DIVISION, she dropped the paper and flung her arms open as wide as her chubby skeleton could throw them open to embrace me in the warmest of hugs she could muster. Saat khoon muaaf![209] All was forgotten about my missing the 70% mark in the first semester as I had scored 69.5% and having scored a sad 66% in the second one. Feeling light as a feather, all 66 kg of her wrapped up in a 5' frame, Mum said after re-reading the paper, 'Ajj tu mainu bahut saari khushi ditti hai. Eh tu nahin, main paas hoyi haan. Saare badaam khilaaye kamm aa gaye!'[210]

[209] ਸਾਤ ਖ਼ੂਨ ਮੁਆਫ਼ (All sins forgiven.)
[210] ਅੱਜ ਤੂੰ ਮੈਨੂੰ ਬਹੁਤ ਸਾਰੀ ਖ਼ੁਸ਼ੀ ਦਿੱਤੀ ਹੈ. ਇਹ ਤੂੰ ਨਹੀਂ, ਮੈਂ ਪਾਸ ਹੋਈ ਹਾਂ. ਸਾਰੇ ਬਦਾਮ ਖਿਲਾਏ ਕੰਮ ਆ ਗਏ (Today you have given me immense joy. This is not you, but I who has qualified. The almonds have proved their worth!)

ਕੱਚ ਦਾ ਗਿਲਾਸ

ਆਹ ਲੈ ਨੀ ਧੀਏ ਕੱਚ ਦਾ ਗਿਲਾਸ
ਇਹਦੇ ਵਿੱਚ ਭਰ ਲੈ ਚੁੱਲ੍ਹੇ ਦੀ ਲਾਟ
ਰੱਖ ਲੈ ਘੁੱਟ ਕੇ ਜ਼ਿੰਦੜੀ ਦੇ ਪਾਸ
ਕੱਚ ਦਾ ਗਿਲਾਸ

ਸ਼ੀਸ਼ੇ ਚੋਂ ਸਿੰਮੇ ਭਾਂਵੇ ਏਸ ਦਾ ਚਾਨਣਾ
ਇਹ ਦੀ ਕਰਾਈਂ ਕਿਸੇ ਨਾਲ ਪਹਿਚਾਣ ਨਾ
ਸ਼ੀਸ਼ਾ ਨਾ ਤਿੜਕੇ
ਤੇਰੀ ਚਾਲ ਨਾ ਥਿੜਕੇ
ਨੱਕੋ-ਨੱਕ ਭਰਿਆ ਕਿਤੇ ਛੱਲਕ ਨਾ ਜਾਵੇ
ਡੁੱਲ੍ਹ ਨਾ ਜਾਵੇ
ਤੇਰੀ ਪਿਆਸ
ਕੱਚ ਦਾ ਗਿਲਾਸ

- ਹਰਿਭਜਨ ਸਿੰਘ

The Food Trail

That typical kid-proud mommy, she always says with such pride, 'Soch samajh ke punga laina mere naal. Main parrhe-likhyaan di ma haan!'[211] This pride has a filter in her being in multiple other ways. One being that she would drop hints rather than demand clearly what is on her mind. This is an annoying habit as you are always guessing or missing her hints, and risk being at the receiving end of her moods. However, it also gives us a clear escape route to plead ignorance if we can't cater to her incomprehensible wishes.

Mother Darling is particularly fond of cakes. In fact, I remember she encouraged me to learn to bake cakes in a pressure cooker on a hot bed of sand when we did not have a proper oven. I also remember that she would polish off half the cake even before the poor cake had had a chance to cool off on the rack. It happened not necessarily because of sheer greed on her part to get all her sweet teeth sink deep into a 'phoren' delicacy, but more because there was not much baking done at either our nana's house or our dada's house. So when I was old

---

211 ਸੋਚ ਸਮਝ ਕੇ ਪੰਗਾ ਲੈਣਾ ਮੇਰੇ ਨਾਲ. ਮੈਂ ਪੜ੍ਹੇ - ਲਿਖੀਆਂ ਦੀ ਮਾਂ ਹਾਂ! (You better think before you mess around with me. I am the mother of educated kids.) [This was her way to brag about her kids as well as throw her weight around!])

enough to experiment in the kitchen, learning to boil rice was quickly followed by learning to bake cakes. Nonetheless, true to her being, Mum would never ask me to bake one. She would drop hints and would just pretend that it was my idea to bake a cake. She has this innate ability to even drop hints about the kind of cake she wants to eat, without saying a word.

Let me share an example. She knows that I bake cakes only with fresh butter. So the day she wants to enjoy a warm slice of cake with her coffee in the evening, she whips up some fresh butter and leaves it on the kitchen shelf, right next to my bottle of cucumber/lime/mint water. Subtle as a brick that my mother is, no demand made you see, just a hint. I would usually find a basket of apples if she wants to have the apple-cinnamon cake or I would find a tin of pineapple rings if it is the pineapple upside down cake she wants. She does not spare the vegetables either as I can bake a mean bread out of gourds.

One morning when I went to brew coffee for my breakfast, I noticed Mother Darling had left a bowl of freshly beaten butter with fresh oranges close to where the coffee machine is lying in the kitchen. As I did not have an urgent appointment to serve, without saying a word to Mum I whipped up an aromatic spicy orange ginger cake. Thinking that this would be such a perfect day with no demands on my time, I left home but luck was not on my side it seems.

In the afternoon a classmate sent a message saying the result of the recently held examination was out and that we had failed! FAILED and that too at my age! I didn't know where to dig a hole to disappear. I could not even call anyone at the university to cross-check the results. What if I had really failed? But how could I fail? I accept that my memory would have faltered on more than a few occasions but surely even the eminent scholar and rationalist Mr. M.M. Kalburgi, whose name I perpetually kept confusing with King Hammubari from the Babylonian empire, would have had mercy on me and ensured that I passed.

For goodness sake, look at my age! How could anyone be so cruel and fail me in the exam? Oh Lord! With such thoughts running amok in my mind, I had lost all appetite for lunch. The office staff could see the dark clouds of stress and worry hovering around my shoulders, but what could I tell them? 'Folks, I have failed'. This would surely raise my rank a notch in their eyes! I had already lost the marks in the paper, I might as well hold on to my mark in the office. Aghast, I switched my phone off and went to lie down on the sofa, under the pretext of suffering from a headache.

As I was struggling with my emotions at work, the office landline started ringing away. Initially I ignored it but given the person at the other end was not giving up, I finally dragged myself from the sofa to see who needed our services so urgently! It was my classmate on the other end. It seems he was concerned about my well-being and finding my mobile phone switched off, he located our office landline from the Google Baba and called up. My classmate told me that he was playing pranks on all the classmates. Relieved sure I was, but equally angry too with my classmate. If technology allowed, I would have transported myself through the phone line, emerged out of the other end and strangled him by the phone cord itself! However, as they say, all is well that ends well.

I had barely recovered from this shock that there was another one in store for me. I reached home late in the evening after serving an outstation client who came visiting without an appointment. As I parked up, I saw that Mother Darling was waiting for me in the verandah. I winced as I was certain I would be court marshalled for something, again. Perhaps the cake sank rather than rise. Did I put twice the quantity of cinnamon and made the cake too bitter? Or was it not sweat enough for mother's liking? Or were the oranges too bitter? My heart skipped a beat as I walked closer to her because I had had enough stress for a day already. I just wanted to jump into my bed and sleep. Instead, Mum suddenly put her arms around me and said, 'I give you 200% marks for the cake you baked this morning.' Maa ek, Rang anek.[212]

Life moved on. I returned home after a short vacation to Agra and walked straight on to the dinner table. While there was a hand shake, a high five or an odd hug with other family members having dinner, I got a kiss and a cuddle from Mum in the bed itself. We had dinner while chatting about the trip and as we finished with food, I remembered that I had saved a little pot of 'pateesa'[213] from the train. Since my mother and nephew are really fond of sweets, I went to fetch it from my bag promptly. I made a 'grand and fake' announcement that I had brought the famous Petha[214] from Agra for everyone.

Mum immediately flung away the blanket and sat up straight in bed, with a look that screamed, 'CAT has seen the cream'! I know exactly where I stand in terms of preferences in the eyes of my mother. We all fell apart laughing. A damning case of Sweet v/s Supreet! We know (sweet) food is more

---

[212] ਮਾਂ ਇਕ ਰੂਪ ਅਨੇਕ (My multi-faceted mother).

[213] ਪਤੀਸਾ (An Indian sugar-based sweet which is feathery to touch and melts in your mouth).

[214] ਪੇਠਾ (Another traditional vegetable-based Indian sweet which though is made in most Indian cities, yet the one from the city of Agra remain most sought after.)

important than kids for Mum. She can never really have enough of anything buttery, sugary and syrupy.

When you tell the chaat-wala that you want 'Tikki Chaat'[215], you get a plate of two hot potato patties with the rest of the adornments. When you tell your Bhabi that you want 'Tikki Chaat', you get a plate of one or two hot potato patties with the rest of the adornments. If you happen to get a call from your Mother Darling out on a spin around town with family, asking if you want something from sector 23, you know she is standing at the most popular and oldest chaat-wala[216] of your city. Without thinking twice, you tell her quite clearly that you want 'Tikki Chaat'. What you get instead is a mountain of 'Paapri Chaat with Bhalla'[217] along with the usual assorted toppings in a plate!

Reasoning with your broken heart that mother probably did not hear your request over the noise in the shopping centre, you quietly work through the 'Paapri Chaat'. So what if your heart was set for a plate of hot fried tikki on a cold winter evening and your tongue was drooling aptly over the impending burst of flavours in your mouth associated with tikki? Like an obedient daughter you finish the cold wafery chaat as you don't want to break Mum's heart over her 'bad' ear.

The moment you put down the plate of the 'Paapri Chaat', which you did not really want to eat, Mother Superior appears with a plate of two hot potato patties with the rest of the

---

[215] ਟਿੱਕੀ ਚਾਟ (*Tikki Chaat* fried potato patties are topped with a tangy sweet tamarind chutney and spicy green chutney along with yogurt.)

[216] ਚਾਟ ਵਾਲਾ (The chap who sells chat).

[217] ਪਾਪੜੀ ਚਾਟ with ਭੱਲਾ (*Papri* is traditionally prepared using crisp fried dough wafers made from white flour. Green bean paste is added with spices, which is then deep fried to make croquets, called bhalla in India. On a bed of papri and bhalla, layers of yogurt, tamarind sauce and spices are added to make this snack.)

adornments!! Only a Punjabi mother could possibly decipher 'Tikki Chaat' as 'TIKKI wali Chaat and Paapri Bhalla Chaat'. There goes your dinner and your diet plan!

The morning cup of tea came with a monsoon-peppered soggy rusk. It also happened to be CATS' 11th Birthday. It also happened to be a super-busy day as we had the first and formal 'Orientation Day' for our eduCATe Scholars, a flagship project of Can & Will Foundation which emerged out of CATS to manage the philanthropic activities of the group. Hence I had been busy connecting the dots, carving out last-minute links and going through my 'things-to-do' list over and over again, only like a mad and fat CAT can do. With cake to buy, BINGO sheets to print, camera to charge, and making calls all morning, Mother Darling while reading her papers and sipping her masala chai had been calmly noticing the dance of the CAT on a hot tin roof. Being a supportive Mum, she says nothing. She lets me be.

Finally, as I finished one more call by saying, 'Awight then, you take care,' Mum got her cue and she looked up straight at me by sliding her reading glasses a little down her razor-sharp nose pointing right in my direction. 'Eh cha nu vi TAKE CARE ker lae hunn.'[218] Reham naam di cheez taan kismat vich hee nahin![219]

Then you have had a busy stressful day trying to keep pace with work demands, meeting Scholars and their parents over a quick bite or a cuppa in between the formal sessions for a few snatched moments. As you can imagine, during these kind of days, the lovingly packed lunch returns home, untouched,

---

[218] ਇਹ ਚਾਹ ਨੂੰ ਵੀ TAKE CARE ਕਰ ਲੈ ਹੁਣ. *(Please take care of the tea also!)*

[219] ਰਹਿਮ ਨਾਮ ਦੀ ਚੀਜ਼ ਤੇ ਕਿਸਮਤ ਵਿੱਚ ਹੀ ਨਹੀਂ *(Nothing called mercy in my fate!)*

before you get home. As I stepped onto the verandah, I found Mother Superior standing right there, I mean literally right there with her soft hands curled into tight fists resting on her generously proportioned non-existent waist. The Chicken knew there was no escape from the lashing!

'Dekh, ikk gall sunn le tu kann khol ke. Eh tera England-Amreeka nahin hai jithe 24 ghante wich ikk vaari roti mildi hai. Eh India hai, Maa da ghar. Ethhe 24 ghante wich 3 vaari roti mildi hai, te khaani hundi hai.'[220] How absolutely adorable. I did not tell her that of course! If you think this love for food is meant only for herself or the family members, please don't be mistaken. I offered the leftover slice of a pistachio cake from the CATS birthday celebrations to buy peace for the night.

It is not every day you get to meet people who are at the same wavelength as you are. When you get an opportunity to interact with them further, you come to respect them for their inherent value system. When you get to know them beyond their personality, perhaps after indulging in multiple rounds of discussions, that is when you begin to cherish them. One of the few whom I cherish, Savita Mahajan, had moved out of the city few years ago. I was absolutely delighted when she called one morning to say that she was in town, but for only 2 days. In the same breath, she added that she fancied 'saag with makki di roti'[221] for lunch. Since I had seen 'saag' bubbling away in the cooker before I left home in the morning, I immediately offered home-cooked lunch. Savita readily

---

[220] ਦੇਖ ਇੱਕ ਗੱਲ ਸੁਣ ਲੈ ਤੂੰ ਕੰਨ ਖੋਲ ਕੇ.. ਇਹ ਤੇਰਾ ਇੰਗਲੈਂਡ-ਅਮਰੀਕਾ ਨਹੀਂ ਹੈ ਜਿਥੇ 24 ਘੰਟੇ ਵਿਚ ਇੱਕ ਵਾਰੀ ਰੋਟੀ ਮਿਲਦੀ ਹੈ. ਇਹ ਇੰਡੀਆ ਹੈ, ਮਾਂ ਦਾ ਘਰ. ਏਥੇ 24 ਘੰਟੇ ਵਿਚ 3 ਵਾਰੀ ਰੋਟੀ ਮਿਲਦੀ ਹੈ, ਤੇ ਖਾਣੀ ਹੁੰਦੀ ਹੈ *(You listen to me carefully. This is not your England or America where you get to eat only once in 24 hours. This is India and your mother's home. Here you get to eat three proper meals a day, and there is no escaping from food!)*

[221] ਸਾਗ with ਮੱਕੀ ਦੀ ਰੋਟੀ (Saag is a mustard and spinach leaf-based dish eaten in the Indian subcontinent in the winters. It is usually eaten with roti, i.e., Indian pancakes made of wheat or maize flour.)

accepted as it would give her an opportunity to meet with Mum too. I did have an odd misgiving but then, hey my Mum is generally a well-behaved baby. Chill girl.

Running late, we finally reached home for lunch at 4 pm. Mum opened the door and I introduced the two graceful ladies to each other. As we were famished, lunch was quickly laid without much ado. All of us noticed that our dear heart was a little hesitant with 'saag' as she served only a couple of spoonful from the bowl. Now, THAT does not happen in a Punjabi home. Butter loaded saag is to be eaten 'ladelful' and not 'spoonful'.

Multiple reservations seized us at once! Is the saag the wrong colour? Has Bhabi put more white butter than Savita prefers in her saag? Is makki di roti too thick or too big for her liking? Perhaps she likes her saag in tomato gravy? Given that nothing could be done to the saag at this stage, all of us tried to encourage her to partake more but she remained steadfast. Before any of us could think of an alternative rescue plan, Mum, who had been quietly sitting on the sofa till then, swiftly walked up to our cherished friend and said in no uncertain terms, 'eh saag di katori mainu khaali chahidee hai.'[222] Five or 50, age is just a number for my dear mother, who had met Savita for the first time, literally 10 minutes ago!

I returned home knackered after putting in long hours to get a few things done and I found Mother Superior right in the verandah itself. Hoping to get a hug and a kiss from her to wash off the day's stress, I stretched my arm towards her but she was in no mood for pleasantries. With her hands on her

---

[222] ਇਹ ਸਾਗ ਦੀ ਕਟੋਰੀ ਮੈਨੂੰ ਖਾਲੀ ਚਾਹੀਦੀ ਹੈ (You better finish this bowl of saag, or else!)

hips she thundered, '11 ghante Maa di yaad ni aayi te hunn Maa-Mashkariyaan bhaaldi hain??!!'[223]

Like a dog with tail between the legs, I stepped back disappointed and presented my defence, 'Mumma I was busy all day.' Pat came another question, 'Too busy to call Mum??!!' Knowing I was up against a merciless wall, I quietly went inside the house. Since it had been a hot muggy day which needed standing at site for long stretches, I headed straight to have a shower. Feeling a little better, I finally put my feet up to call it a day. Just as I was stretching my legs, Mum appeared out of nowhere with a little plate in her hand. 'Aah lai, hunne garam-garam ghee wich shakkar pa ke choori banaayi tere layi. Ki yaad rakheingi tu vee!'[224]

Chicken floored. Saat khoon muaaf.[225]

Mother Darling loves the rains for two reasons. Firstly, she does not need to water her 'green babies' and secondly, she gets to enjoy her 'watering-free' time over chai served with hot pakoras[226] and lip-smacking jalebi[227]. This is almost a staple diet for the Punjabis to enjoy the monsoons! You can't really complain about Mum loving the rains, especially during the summer monsoons when rain actually brings in huge respite from the sultry weather. It had rained heavily one day and Mother Superior, in anticipation of the pakora/jalebi combo,

---

[223] 11 ਘੰਟੇ ਮਾਂ ਦੀ ਯਾਦ ਨਹੀਂ ਆਈ ਤੇ ਹੁਣ ਮਾਂ-ਮਸ਼ਕਰੀਆਂ ਭਾਲਦੀ ਹੈਂ? (For 11 hours you did not think of your mother even once, and now suddenly you are overflowing with love for your old mother?)

[224] ਆਹ ਲੈ, ਹੁਣੇ ਗਰਮ-ਗਰਮ ਘਿਉ ਵਿੱਚ ਸ਼ੱਕਰ ਪਾ ਕੇ ਚੂਰੀ ਬਟਾਈ ਹੈ ਤੇਰੇ ਲਈ. ਕਿ ਯਾਦ ਰੱਖੇਗੀ ਤੂੰ ਵੀ! (Here, just made this choori for you. [Choori is a traditional Punjabi sweet made at home by mixing stale bread, sugar and clarified butter. It is then kneaded into tiny balls to be eaten as a desert or a filler while travelling.])

[225] ਸਾਤ ਖੂਨ ਮੁਆਫ (All sins forgiven).

[226] ਪਕੌੜਾ (Vegetable fritters).

[227] ਜਲੇਬੀ (Indian sweet made by frying batter in the shape of a thick coil and then dunking in thick sugar syrup.)

was hopping around the house with joy. Once the tea party was over and rain had reduced to a drizzle, Mum went out to inspect her freshly bathed green babies. Lo and behold, in no time Mum returned back to my room, horrified.

Apparently one of her baby plants which she had been nurturing since a year needs very little water and thrives on only a touch of sun. Hence Mum had kept this high-maintenance plant at the edge of the verandah to catch a few kisses of the dying sun. Of course she forgot to retrieve it when it started raining cats and dogs, as all she could think of at that time was a plateful of pakoras and a bowl of jalebis. The poor plant experienced third- degree negligence, caught cold and rain instead of the sun! With ashen face Mum cried out, 'Mera nikka jeha plant. Nikke jeha si te kinni mushkil naal paal-poas ke vadda keeta si. Gamla paani vich dubbya peya hai. Eh taan nahin bachda hunn!'[228] I sympathised with Mum but perhaps, not as dramatically as Mum had expected. Hence she again lamented, 'Hai koi ilaaj tere kol?'[229] I, on the other hand, wasn't hugely affected by a bowlful of water floating in the ceramic pot, which was the home of this plant in question. Worst still, I did not engage my brains before opening my mouth and my suggestion to her question vocalised my thoughts! 'Mumma, hair-dryer le ke aawaan?'[230]

My response suddenly shook Mum out of her mourning. What I had said finally sunk-in. Mother Superior darted towards me and before I could dodge her, her soft pudgy hand

---

[228] ਮੇਰਾ ਨਿੱਕਾ ਜੇਹਾ plant ਨਿੱਕਾ ਜੇਹਾ ਸੀ ਤੇ ਕਿੰਨੀ ਮੁਸ਼ਕਿਲ ਨਾਲ ਪਾਲ-ਪੋਸ ਕੇ ਵੱਡਾ ਕੀਤਾ ਸੀ. ਗਮਲਾ ਪਾਣੀ ਵਿਚ ਡੁੱਬਿਆ ਪਿਆ ਹੈ. ਇਹ ਤਾਂ ਨਹੀਂ ਬੱਚਦਾ ਹੁਣ! *(My tiny plant – I raised it from a sapling with such love and now it is lying drowned in the pot. It is just going to die on me now!)*
[229] ਹੈ ਕੋਈ ਇਲਾਜ ਤੇਰੇ ਕੋਲ? (Do you have a solution?)
[230] Mumma hair dryer ਲੈ ਕੇ ਆਵਾਂ? (Mum shall I get hair dryer to dry out the water?)

had made contact with my equally soft but fragile ear! 'Ikk kuri layi si rabb ton mang ke ... Aah piece palle pae gya!'[231]

The benefit of being born in a huge extended family is that all tasks get divided, even if the volume of production remains high! So for example almost an entire push-cart worth of 'saag'[232] would be bought to cater to the khandaan[233], whether living under the same roof or not. Similarly, winter delicacies were also divided between all the 'devranis and jethanis'[234]. Mum was known for her punjeeri, vaddi Bebe for maal-puye[235], chhotti Bebe for talluyein[236] (till ke laddu) and chhotti Tayi for khoye de pere[237]. As happens, slowly they all bade their goodbyes and the home-made winter delicacies starting reducing. One fine day Mother Darling got into her never-say-die spirit and quickly made some talluyein for the first time in her life.

Delicious as hell but THIS is what they look like! Instead of soft aromatic, delicious with a bite and most importantly round laddu, Mum appeared with a thali of soft aromatic delicious with a bite but flat as cow pat 'something'. Trust me, had this Chicken made anything which resulted in remotely LOOKING like this, I would have been fired from the kitchen and probably disowned by Mother Superior. 'Eh Kuri? Naa ji. Meri Nahin Hain!'[238]

---

231 ਇੱਕ ਕੁੜੀ ਲਈ ਸੀ ਰੱਬ ਤੋਂ ਮੰਗ ਕੇ ... ਆਹ piece ਪੱਲੇ ਪੈ ਗਿਆ! (Good grief! I had begged for a daughter from God when I was carrying you... How was I to know that this is the piece God had in mind for me!)

232 ਸਾਗ (A leaf-based Punjabi dish made with mustard and spinach leaves).

233 ਖਾਨਦਾਨ (Family/clan).

234 ਦੇਵਰਾਨੀ and ਜੇਠਾਣੀ (Sisters-in-law, wives of older brother and younger brother).

235 ਵੱਡੀ ਵਾਲੀ ਬੇਬੇ for ਮਾਲ ਪੁਏ (Elder Bebe was known for pancakes. [Bebe is the wife of Dad's older brother.])

236 ਛੋਟੀ ਵਾਲੀ ਬੇਬੇ for ਤੱਲੁਏਂ (Younger Bebe was popular for her seasame seed balls.)

237 ਛੋਟੀ ਤਾਈਂ for ਖੋਏ ਦੇ ਪੇੜੇ (Younger aunt for sweets made with condensed milk and sugar).

238 ਇਹ ਕੁੜੀ? ਨਾ ਜੀ. ਮੇਰੀ ਨਹੀਂ ਹੈ! (This girl? Nopes! She is not mine!)

Cricket and 'Prashad'[239] have an old connection in our household. Every time there is a cricket match between the arch-rivals India and Pakistan, and India wins, the victory is sealed with a bit of home-made grease. It was a day-night 20-20 series match again between the two countries and not just the country, but even our little household was on tenterhooks too. Given that the match also was extremely exciting, with each over changing fortunes for both the teams, many of us were losing our nails. As the rest of us were sitting on the edge of the bed in anxiety, Mum was too tired tonight and was already in bed. However, every now and then I would hear her ask her grandson in a muffled voice, 'Aman ki lagdaa hai? Mainu utthna payega parshad banaan layi?!!!'[240] All is fair in love, war and cricket in the subcontinent and in our household!

Mum does not get it right all the time though. I remember one particular day as joint pains flared up in hitherto normal joints too. Consequently, while cursing the lone mosquito which bit me and led to this pathetic state of affairs for me, I spent most of the day drenched in oil rubbed to my bones. Every moving joint was tied-up to the hilt using crepe bandages and I spent most of the day snoozing off on painkillers.

Taking pity on me, Mother Darling walked past around 4 pm and asked if I would be interested in some spicy tea to warm up the bones? What more could I ask for after a day of misery. Of course, I merrily agreed. She took two steps towards the kitchen, looked at me thoughtfully and asked, 'Cake khayengi naal?'[241] Since I knew there was some cake left over

---

[239] ਪ੍ਰਸਾਦ (Parshad is a sacred offering made on all auspicious and/or happy occasions.)

[240] ਅਮਨ ਕੀ ਲੱਗਦਾ ਹੈ? ਮੈਨੂੰ ਉੱਠਣਾ ਪਏਗਾ ਪ੍ਰਸਾਦ ਬਨਾਣ ਲਈ? (Aman how do you foresee the result? Would I have to get up to make Prashad?)

[241] Cake ਖਾਏਂਗੀ ਨਾਲ? (Will you have cake with it?)

from my brother's anniversary, and I had not eaten much all day, I salivated at the thought of a nourishing high tea. What Mum left by my bedside table has no resemblance to the promise made!!! Tea with roasted diet chevra[242]. Any wonder that even my otherwise reticent brother asked if I would consider a show-cause notice to be issued to Mum!

Exhausted from my evening walk, I was dying to have something cold. Torn between something firangi or desi, I let desi win. Immediately upon reaching home I asked Mum if she wanted some golgappe[243]. 'Naaah! My tummy is a little upset.' With some cash clutched in my fist, I asked Mum if she would like something else. Without batting an eyelid for even a second Mother Darling jumped off the sofa and said, 'Chal pher nehra ho gya baahar, tu kalli ki jaana hunn. Main vi tikki kha aayungi.'[244] This has to be the quickest ever recovery from a bad tummy in history!

When Mother Darling gets charge of the kitchen, you get gajrela[245] ... Not just any other gajrela but the one from a recipe she watched on YouTube at the age of 73! All chuffed, Mum asks, 'Das pher, Ma pass ya fail?'[246] Meri majaal main meow bhi karun?[247] Mother Darling was hustling around in the kitchen one morning to get her brood fed and kicked out of the house to get on with our respective work. She cooked three

---

[242] ਚੇਵੜਾ (Puffed rice with peanuts etc.)

[243] ਗੋਲਗੱਪੇ (A popular Indian snack made with puffed fried wheat balls filled with spicy water).

[244] ਚੱਲ ਫੇਰ ਨੇਹਰਾ ਹੋ ਗਿਆ ਬਾਹਰ. ਤੂੰ ਇਕੱਲੀ ਕੀ ਜਾਣਾ ਹੁਣ. ਮੈਂ ਵੀ ਟਿੱਕੀ ਖਾ ਆਉਂਗੀ (It has gone dark outside and you should not be going out alone at this hour. I will come with you, and since I am coming along, I might as well have tikki chaat. [Tikki chaat is made with fried potato patties topped with a tangy sweet tamarind chutney and spicy green chutney along with yogurt.])

[245] ਗਜਰੇਲਾ (An Indian sweet dish made with carrots and milk).

[246] ਦੱਸ ਫੇਰ ਮਾਂ ਪਾਸ ਯਾ ਫੇਲ? (Tell me then... Is Mum pass or fail in her attempt?)

[247] ਮੇਰੀ ਮਜਾਲ ਮੈਂ MEOW ਵੀ ਕਰਾਂ! (Dare I say even MEOW in response to Mum?)

different types of rotis[248] and paranthas, two different types of milk and a pateela of adrak/tulsi/ilaichi chai[249] for all. Just as she managed to get things under control, I showed up and she gave me my tray of adrak-ilaichi milk with a rusk. As I poured over the newspaper while sipping the milk, my brother showed up and Mum went to him to give him his chopped garlic with warm honey water.

Barely had she returned to sit with me that Mum's firstborn showed at the doorstep, screwing up his nose and pulling up his handsome face in impossible directions as he probably would have done as a toddler, yelling, 'Mummmyyyy, tussi mainu adrak de ditta???!!!'[250] While Mother Darling was still processing the information through her bad ears, I had figured out what had happened, but I just let the mother and son be.

What probably would have happened is that in a rush, Mum would have first peeled the adrak for tea and then used the same knife, without realising that she had not washed it, to chop the garlic for her dear son. So there, brother got two for the price of one. As I kept my eyes glued to the papers I was reading, I could actually hear the penny drop in Mum's head a few seconds later. Without fumbling her words she addressed her firstborn, 'Pher ki hoya, adrak kinna changga hunda hai sehat layi.'[251]

Working on incest is pretty nerve wracking. We were doing something for the first time and yet there was no room for error per se. Hence I had barely been home to see what Mum had

---

[248] ਰੋਟੀ & ਪਰਾਂਠਾ (Flat Indian bread and stuffed pan-fried Indian bread).

[249] ਪਤੀਲਾ of ਅਦਰਕ/ਤੁਲਸੀ ਇਲਾਇਚੀ ਚਾਹ (Pan of ginger/basil cardamom tea).

[250] Mummmy ਤੁਸੀ ਮੈਨੂੰ ਅਦਰਕ ਦੇ ਦਿੱਤਾ??!!!! *(Mum you gave me ginger instead!)*

[251] ਫੇਰ ਵੀ ਹੋਇਆ, ਅਦਰਕ ਕਿੰਨਾ ਚੰਗਾ ਹੁੰਦਾ ਹੈ ਸਿਹਤ ਲਈ! (What's the big deal? Ginger is also very good for health!)

been up to. Finally, the team anchored on Saturday night and I breathed a sigh of relief. The only thing I did the next day was to sleep till the cows came home! When I eventually sauntered into the kitchen in the evening to get my bottle of water, Mum smiled at me with her most charming of expressions. The kind of look she had on her face meant that she had done something with some disastrous results and now she was trying to find her victims to palm it off. 'Dekh kinni thakki hoyi hain tu … kinna kamm keeta saara hafta … Chall ajj tainu main dand-karaaka khilaanwan!'[252]

Dand-Karaaka? [253] Really? Something I never really liked as a kid and here was Mum insisting that I eat that rock-hard toffee-thingie with my middle-aged teeth? One look at what she was offering and I simply refused! But of course, when has Mother Superior taken no for an answer. She managed to push the 5'6" of me, with the 5' nothing of her might against the wall. With no room left for escape, I took the tiniest of pieces I could manage. One bite into this 'dand-karaaka' and I nearly lost my tooth! Not only was it rock-hard but it was also extremely bitter. Mum's face melted a little when she saw my face contorting into different directions.

She finally admitted, 'Oh na gurr hai nahin si te main socheya shakkar vich hee jwain pa lawaan. Shakkar shayd thorri reh gayi iss ker ke jwain zyaada laggdi payi. Pher teri Vaddi Mami da phone aa gya si te mainu laggda noon vi do vaari pae gya. Oh gall thorri jehi lambi ho gayi te main shakkar

---

[252] ਦੇਖ ਕਿੰਨੀ ਥੱਕੀ ਹੋਈ ਹੈਂ ਤੂੰ.. ਕਿੰਨਾ ਕੰਮ ਕੀਤਾ ਸਾਰਾ ਹਫਤਾ.. ਚੱਲ ਅੱਜ ਤੈਨੂੰ ਮੈਂ ਦੰਦ-ਕੜਾਕਾ ਖਿਲਾਵਾਂ (Just see how tired you are… you have been working so hard all week. Come, let me treat you to a sweet-meat.)

[253] ਦੰਦ-ਕੜਾਕਾ (Sticky toffee made with jaggery).

bhull gayi chulhe utte!'[254] As I opened my mouth to spit out this nearly poisonous rock scraping my gums, Mum put another piece in my mouth, 'Chal koi na, mithha vaise vi ghatt hee khaana chahida hai.. naale noon-jwain vi donve changiaan ne paet layi … gas nahin hundi.'[255] God save me from my Mother!

You know your day is made when your mother goes for her morning walk and orders flowers for you enroute, which are delivered before she makes her way back home. If this is not enough, when she returns home, she heads straight to the kitchen to make lip-smacking halwa[256]. As dear friend Madhvi Kataria said, 'May your day be sweet like Maa ke haath da halwa and frangrant like maan ke chuney hue phull![257] Cheers!!'

Just when you think your birthday celebrations are over, Mother Darling walked up to me around midday and thrust some old photos in my hand. I laughed looking at my mini-self in that terrible 'Sadhna cut' wearing that brightly coloured orange flowered skirt I still remember so vividly. Mum gave me one tight hug and asked, 'Hunn frock vi kadd ke

---

[254] ਉਹ ਨਾ ਗੁੜ ਹੈ ਨਹੀਂ ਸੀ ਤੇ ਮੈਂ ਸੋਚਿਆ ਸ਼ੱਕਰ ਵਿਚ ਹੀ ਜਵੈਣ ਪਾ ਲਵਾਂ. ਸ਼ੱਕਰ ਸ਼ਾਇਦ ਥੋੜੀ ਰਹਿ ਗਈ ਇਸ ਕਰ ਕੇ ਜਵੈਣ ਜ਼ਜਾਦਾ ਲੱਗਦੀ ਪਈ. ਫੇਰ ਤੇਰੀ ਵੱਡੀ ਮਾਮੀ ਦਾ ਫੋਨ ਆ ਗਿਆ ਸੀ ਤੇ ਮੈਨੂੰ ਲੱਗਦਾ ਨੂਣ ਵੀ ਦੋ ਵਾਰੀ ਪੈ ਗਿਆ. ਉਹ ਗੱਲ ਥੋੜੀ ਜਿਹੀ ਲੰਬੀ ਹੋ ਗਈ ਤੇ ਮੈਂ ਸ਼ੱਕਰ ਭੁੱਲ ਗਈ ਚੁੱਲ੍ਹੇ ਉੱਤੇ! *(Ah well – I did not have the jaggery so I thought I would use its powdery version shakkar instead. I think I used a little lesser than required quantity of shakkar; hence, full quantity of carom seeds has made it a little bitter. Then your maternal aunt called up and I think in the confusion I added salt twice! The telephone conversation went a little longer than expected and I forgot about the concoction on the stove altogether!)*

[255] ਚੱਲ ਕੋਈ ਨਾ.. ਮਿੱਠਾ ਵੈਸੇ ਵੀ ਘੱਟ ਹੀ ਖਾਣਾ ਚਾਹੀਦਾ ਹੈ.. ਨਾਲੇ ਨੂਣ-ਜਵੈਣ ਵੀ ਦੋੱਵੇ ਚੰਗੀਆਂ ਨੇ ਪੇਟ ਲਈ.. ਗੈਸ ਨਹੀਂ ਹੁੰਦੀ (Baah… Don't you worry.. One should consume less sugar as it is. Salt and carom seeds are good for the stomach also. Takes care of the flatulence you see!)

[256] ਹਲਵਾ (An Indian sweet made with semolina and clarified butter with a heavy helping of nuts and dryfruits).

[257] ਮਾਂ ਦੇ ਹੱਥ ਦਾ ਹਲਵਾ ਤੇ ਮਾਂ ਦੇ ਚੁਣੇ ਹੋਏ ਫੁੱਲ (Halva made affectionately by Mum and flowers carefully selected by her).

dikhawaan?'[258] Only mothers can safe keep your treasures even when you have long consigned them to memories. Thank you Mum! My birthday was truly made. As I prepared to set myself up for the 'night shift', Mother Darling walked up to me and said, 'Ikk gall mannengi meri?'[259] A little unsure of what might follow, I gingerly shifted about while looking at her enquiringly. Breaking into a genial smile she said, 'Chall pher chocolate khila Mumma nu ajj.'[260] Phew! That was easy. I quickly ran out to buy a couple, before the things got a little more complicated. How can a birthday be over without a return gift of course?

---

[258] ਹੂਟ ਫਰਾਕ ਵੀ ਕੱਢ ਕੇ ਦਿਖਾਵਾਂ? (Shall I show you the frock also from my trunk?)
[259] ਇੱਕ ਗੱਲ ਮੰਨੇਗੀ ਮੇਰੀ? (Will you do something for me?)
[260] ਚੱਲ ਫੇਰ ਚੋਕਲੇਟ ਖਿਲਾ ਮੰਮਾ ਨੂੰ ਅੱਜ! (Come on, get your Mum a chocolate today!)

'There is nothing more powerful than a mother's love,
And nothing more healing than a child's soul.'

\- Unknown

The Family Ties

My dear brother is known to be an intelligent, soft spoken, witty, precise and a very handsome sardar. My mother is quite proud of her first born. He is also known to subscribe to 'lastminute.com' at the best of times, which does not go amiss even in Mum's eyes, generally twinkling with pride.

Mum and I were pouring over our morning papers when we heard my brother shuffling about, ready to leave the house much earlier than his usual stipulated time. He also happened to be on the phone to someone, who was obviously waiting for him, since long! As my brother reached out to fetch his car keys, we overheard him say, 'Haanji haanji. Main rasste wich haan ji. Bas main pahuncheya!'[261] Without battling an eyelid, trust Mum to have the final say, 'Haanji haanji. Main bedroom ton nikkal ke drawing room tak pahunch gya!'[262] The pair of us just smiled, one sheepishly and the other mockingly.

Next day brought in familiar scenes. The entire household was busy on this cold winter morning. Dad had already left for

---

[261] ਹਾਂਜੀ ਹਾਂਜੀ - ਮੈਂ ਰੱਸਤੇ ਵਿੱਚ ਹਾਂ ਜੀ ... ਬੱਸ ਹੁਣੇ ਪਹੁੰਚਿਆ *(Yes. Yes. I am on my way. I am just about to reach.)*

[262] ਹਾਂਜੀ ਹਾਂਜੀ - ਮੈਂ ਬੈੱਡਰੂਮ ਤੋਂ ਨਿਕਲ ਕੇ ਡਰਾਇੰਗ ਰੂਮ ਤੱਕ ਪਹੁੰਚ ਗਿਆ ਜੀ *(Yes Yes – I have left the bedroom and reached the drawing room!)*

office while kids were asleep. My brother left home uncharacteristically early, dressed in formals. I was poring over the papers in bed and Mum, as expected, was watering her plants. As I was shaking my head in disbelief over the loss of 31 lives in Mexico's fireworks market, I was painfully reminded of a similar tragedy in South India not long ago. It is such a waste of money and life itself at times, but we refuse to let go of our fascination for the fireworks across the world.

Just as I was reminiscing over the strict safety precautions taken by the organisers during each Guy Fawkes Night in England, which I used to attend religiously every year, Mum suddenly walked in, all fluffed up in great pride. At first I thought a new flower would have blossomed and she was about to frogmarch this snug CAT into the garden in this cold to appropriately fawn over the new flower which had taken birth overnight. As I was bracing for the sudden chill which was about to hit me as I was to be dragged through the front door, Mum made me fall in love with her all over again. 'Puttar dekhya mera ajj? Kinna sohna laggda si. Ajj nazar laggi ke laggi mere kapatte nu!'[263]

Shifting my thoughts from the tragedy of fireworks in Mexico to the joyous fireworks of motherhood bursting bright in our house, Mum had saved her best for the last. 'Naale dekh, waqt sir tyaar ho ke gya ajj. Kisse da phone nahi aaya!!'[264] Mother's pride eh!

Weeks later an elder cousin came visiting. A little rough on the edges but full of self-respect, this hardworking man is

---

[263] ਪੁੱਤਰ ਵੇਖਿਆ ਮੇਰਾ ਅੱਜ? ਕਿੰਨਾ ਸੋਹਣਾ ਲੱਗਦਾ ਸੀ. ਅੱਜ ਨਜ਼ਰ ਲੱਗੀ ਕੇ ਲੱਗੀ ਮੇਰੇ ਕਪੱਤੇ ਨੂੰ! (Did you see my son today? How handsome he looked! Hope he does not come under the influence of a jealous evil eye!)

[264] ਨਾਲੇ ਵੇਖ, ਵਕ੍ਤ ਸਿਰ ਤਿਆਰ ਹੋ ਕੇ ਗਿਆ ਅੱਜ. ਕਿੱਸੇ ਦਾ ਫੋਨ ਨਹੀਂ ਆਇਆ (Did you notice he got ready in time today? No one had to make a reminder call to him.)

compassionate to the core. Despite being short on resources at times, he has ensured both his kids are well educated. A post-graduate with a reasonable job, his daughter can charm the pants of everyone with her confidence and intelligence, while his son has his nose in his college books.

I still remember the last meal his mother had cooked for us, decades ago. It was a day after Diwali and I was wearing a bright puff-sleeved frock with my hair done in two tight plaits. My aunt was a beautiful and graceful lady, who cooked lip-smacking food. It was delicious 'haare di daal with makki di roti',[265] traditional meal which is cooked by the mothers a day after Diwali in our part of the world. She passed away that night. Since then he treats Mum with greatest of respect. He ensures that he touches Mum's feet and Mum blesses him wholeheartedly. He remains a loving brat son to Mum and our Mum, a caring mother in lieu for him.

As it was pretty cold when my cousin arrived, we all settled for hot milk with home-made pinni[266]. As usual, he, my mother, my brother and I caught up over endless family gossip. Who has picked up an argument with whom? Who is getting along well with whom and whom to avoid these days sort of stuff. Suddenly my niece appeared in the room and he asked which subjects was she studying at the college. Psychology did not make much sense to him so he demanded to know what is it called in Punjabi. With a noticeable handicap in what is supposed to be her mother tongue, my niece flustered at her inability to give the answer and pleaded that she was getting

---

[265] ਹਾਰੇ ਦੀ ਦਾਲ ਤੇ ਮੱਕੀ ਦੀ ਰੋਟੀ (Lentils cooked on slow fire mud stove and maize roti or pancake).

[266] ਪਿੰਨੀ (A north Indian sweet made of milk, sugar and roasted nuts, mostly eaten in winters).

late for college. He let her go only on one condition that she would ask her professors in the college to tell her what psychology means in Punjabi.

Just as my niece bailed herself out, Mum arched her eyebrow at her own two post-graduate productions. Both my brother and I squirmed in embarrassment under the scrutiny of the two 'elders' in the room. Despite having a good command over our mother tongue and not to mention six professional degrees between the pair of us, we struggled to find even a single word, which would marginally pass off as psychology in Punjabi. If our niece was skinned, both of us were roasted, psychologically of course. 'MANUVIGYAAN'[267], Mum answered and then turned to our cousin, 'Dass, kinne paise kharaab keete ehna di paraahi utte!'[268]

Our mother is deceptively ahead of her times, even though she did not have much opportunity to undertake formal education herself beyond high school. She knows how to keep her flock together and how to protect it from unwanted attention. With elections fever in the air, the campaign team of a 'particular' party chose the time to descend upon our house, when usually our Mum soaks the morning sun in the verandah itself. So there was literally no need to even bell the cat, so to speak! The said candidate's wife hugged Mum and the son touched Mum's feet, thinking they had won over the Mother Superior of the household. Alas, little did they know the fire this pint-sized Punjabi matriarch carries in her heart. After the formality of tea was over, Mum smiled and took charge of the

---

[267] ਮਨੋਵਿਗਿਆਨ (Psychology).

[268] ਦੱਸ ਕਿੰਨੇ ਪੈਸੇ ਪਰਾਬ ਕੀਤੇ ਇਹਨਾਂ ਦੀ ਪੜ੍ਹਾਈ ਉੱਤੇ (See how much money I wasted on their education!)

audience as a dozen of their supporters stood witness with folded hands.

Mum: Dekho ji saada kisse nu vi vote dein da mann nahin hai.[269]

Aghast, the wifey asked: Didi tussi enna mann kharaab na karo. Assi aap de saare kamm karaange.[270]

Mum immediately laid the trap: Chal kaka, pher list banaa![271] Not knowing which way to escape, the son meekly took out a note pad and started taking the dictation.

Mum warmed up: 'Bin-Malik phirdiyaan gaavan mere saare plant kha jaandiyaan ne. Sarkari perran nu kattan koi nahi aanda. Pher, stray dogs di problem enni vaddi hai per tussi lok kuchh nahi karde. Roz savere ik-adhe buzurg nu vaddh lende ne!'[272] When the son feigned ignorance, Mum asked him a simple question, 'Kade savere paanch waje morning walk keeti hai?'[273] Stumped, he tried to divert Mum's attention to bigger matters affecting our lives. He had no idea that this is precisely the trap Mum had laid out for him.

Mum shifted gears: 'Vaddi layo Kakaji. Pehlaan te saadi maid layi sarkari room/flat allot karwayo. Eh vidhwa hai te koi agge-pichhe nahin hai.'[274] Completely bewildered, they looked at each other. They had come asking for a vote and Mum was

---

[269] ਦੇਖੋ ਜੀ ਸਾਡਾ ਕਿਸੇ ਨੂੰ ਵੀ ਵੋਟ ਦੇਣ ਦਾ ਮੰਨ ਨਹੀਂ ਹੈ (You see, we don't fancy giving our vote to anyone.)

[270] ਦੀਦੀ ਤੁਸੀ ਇੰਨਾ ਮੰਨ ਖ਼ਰਾਬ ਨਾ ਕਰੋ, ਅੱਸੀ ਆਪ ਦੇ ਸਾਰੇ ਕੰਮ ਕਰਾਂਗੇ (Sister, please don't be so disheartened. We will ensure that all your needs are fulfilled.)

[271] ਚੱਲ ਕਾਕਾ ਫੇਰ ਲਿਸਟ ਬਣਾ (Son, you better start making the list.)

[272] ਬਿਨ-ਮਾਲਿਕ ਫਿਰਦੀਆਂ ਗਾਵਾਂ ਮੇਰੇ ਸਾਰੇ ਪਲਾਂਟ ਖਾ ਜਾਂਦੀਆਂ ਨੇ.. ਸਰਕਾਰੀ ਪੇੜਾਂ ਨੂੰ ਕੱਟਣ ਕੋਈ ਨਹੀਂ ਆਉਂਦਾ. ਫੇਰ ਅਵਾਰਾ ਕੁੱਤਿਆਂ ਦੀ ਪ੍ਰੋਬਲਮ ਇੰਨੀ ਵੱਡੀ ਹੈ ਪਰ ਤੁਸੀ ਲੋਗ ਕੁਝ ਨਹੀਂ ਕਰਦੇ. ਰੋਜ਼ ਸਵੇਰੇ ਇਕ-ਅੱਧੇ ਬੁਜ਼ੁਰਗ ਨੂੰ ਵੱਢ ਲੈਂਦੇ ਨੇ. (Stray cows feast on my garden plants. Municipal Committee does not prune the trees. The problem of stray dogs too big but you don't do anything. Every morning an odd senior citizen gets bitten by a stray.)

[273] ਕਦੇ ਸਵੇਰੇ ੫ ਵਜੇ ਮੋਰਨਿੰਗ ਵਾਕ ਕੀਤੀ ਹੈ? (Have you ever been for a walk at 5 am in the morning?)

[274] ਵੱਡੀ ਲਿਖੋ ਕਾਕਾ ਜੀ. ਪਹਿਲਾਂ ਤੇ ਸਾਡੀ maid ਲਈ ਸਰਕਾਰੀ ਕਮਰਾ ਯਾ ਫਲੈਟ ਅਲਾਟ ਕਾਰਵਾਯੋ. ਇਹ ਵਿਧਵਾ ਹੈ ਤੇ ਕੋਈ ਅੱਗੇ-ਪਿੱਛੇ ਨਹੀਂ ਹੈ. (Alright, have a bigger problem to resolve then! Get a room or a flat allotted for our maid. She is an issueless widow and has no family to take care of her.)

demanding a one- room government's low-income group flat for the maid in return!

Stung, the son suggested if Mum could lower her demands a little, promptly Mum retorted: 'Chal Kaka tu chhota kamm hee ker de mera. Apne hee ghar aan/jaan layi saanu 10 minute lagg jaande ne. Police wale challan nahin issue karde "wrongful parking" layi kisse nu vi. Ethe double yellow line lagwa deyo te police nu kaho ghalat kharri car nu "tow" karwa deyo.' [275] Shocked at Mum's knowledge of double yellow line, the son looked up at Mum but sensing that Mum was in for a long inning, the son quickly touched Mum's feet and promised to sort out all the problems from the list, provided the entire household votes for the said candidate. After they left, Mum looked around to see Bhabi and I laughing our heads off through the living room window. Mum grinned triumphantly, 'Hunn ni koi tang karda aapaan nu!'[276] Word spread fast and honestly speaking, our house was given a clear miss by almost all other candidates for rest of the campaigning period.

However that does not mean that we were untouched by the election fever. The whole household was full of excitement on the day of the elections. Dad was all for change but Mum had no faith in anyone and was occupying herself with the newspapers. Tinkering her college timetable and voting timings, my niece was like a dog with two tails. She was finally 'baalig'[277] enough and getting to cast a vote for the first time in her life. My nephew was feeling a little left out, though he was keeping his chin up. He was claiming to be

---

[275] ਚੱਲ ਕਾਕਾ ਤੂੰ ਛੋਟਾ ਕੰਮ ਹੀ ਕਰ ਦੇ ਮੇਰਾ. ਆਪਣੇ ਹੀ ਘਰ ਆਣ-ਜਾਣ ਲਈ ਸਾਨੂੰ 10 ਮਿੰਟ ਲੱਗ ਜਾਂਦੇ ਨੇ ਤੇ ਪੁਲਿਸ ਵਾਲੇ ਚਲਾਨ ਨਹੀਂ ਕੱਟਦੇ ਗ਼ਲਤ ਪਾਰਕਿੰਗ ਦਾ ਕਿਸੇ ਨੂੰ ਵੀ. ਸੜਕ ਉੱਤੇ *'double yellow line'* ਲਗਵਾ ਦੇਯੋ ਤੇ ਪੁਲਿਸ ਨੂੰ ਕਹੋ ਗ਼ਲਤ ਖੜ੍ਹੀ ਕਾਰ ਨੂੰ tow ਕਰਵਾ ਦੇਯੋ *(Well, here is a smaller task for you then. It takes us 10 minutes to leave or enter our own house because of wrong parking. Police also does not challan the offenders. Can you ask the police to become more vigilant and also get our roads painted with double yellow lines?)*
[276] ਹੁਣ ਨੀ ਕੋਈ ਤੰਗ ਕਰਦਾ ਆਪਾਂ ਨੂੰ (Now no one dare bother us with a request for votes!)
[277] ਬਾਲਿਗ (Adult or major in age).

having fun at the expense of all the adults as they were hedging bets over various horses.

As a household with nearly half a dozen votes, every candidate was queuing outside to ferry us to the polling booth, after ignoring us for the entire campaigning period. No one's pride in particular, but today we were neighbour's envy indeed. My Bhabi was enjoying this moment of hullaballoo, 'Sarkaar apaan hee te banaani hai'[278] Mother Darling quipped instead, 'Ainwe na apna time kharaab karo. Decision ho gya hai te election Congress ne jitt jaani hai.'[279] Thinking that Mum had come across some election-fixing news in the paper, I asked her to explain. 'Kuch nahin'[280] she pursed her lips and said no more. Unsatisfied, I walked closer to her bed, threatening to caress her cheeks with cold hands. Mum opened a little, 'Main ni keha. Mainu ki pata? Main te house wife haan!'[281] Curiosity had hung the cat by now and as I closed in on Mum, she finally named the person, 'Oh main thorri keha, Ganga Ram ne keha.'[282] With minds running amok about who Ganga Ram was from this sordid world of politics, I lost my wool and as I reached out to the paper Mum was reading, she quickly crumpled the newspaper and held it close to her bosom.

Aggrieved by now, I pulled her soft warm cheek a little with my ice- cold hand and demanded to know, 'Ganga Ram kaun hai?' Stung by the cold treatment, she quickly pulled back and offered a little more information, 'Shimle da hai.'[283] As I stood

---

[278] ਸਰਕਾਰ ਆਪਾਂ ਹੀ ਤੇ ਬਨਾਨੀ ਹੈ (We are the ones who are going to form the government.)

[279] ਐਵੇ ਨਾ ਆਪਣਾ ਟਾਈਮ ਖ਼ਰਾਬ ਕਰੋ. ਫੈਸਲਾ ਹੋ ਗਿਆ ਕੇ ਇਲੈਕਸ਼ਨ ਕਾਂਗਰਸ ਨੇ ਜਿੱਤ ਜਾਣੀ ਹੈ (Don't you waste your time. It has already been decided that Congress is going to win this election.)

[280] ਕੁਝ ਨਹੀਂ (Nothing).

[281] ਮੈਂ ਨਹੀਂ ਕਿਹਾ.. ਮੈਨੂੰ ਕੀ ਪਤਾ ... ਮੈਂ ਤੇ ਇੱਕ housewife ਹਾਂ ... (I didn't say that. Who am I? I am just a housewife?)

[282] ਉਹ ਮੈਂ ਥੋੜੀ ਕਿਹਾ.. ਗੰਗਾ ਰਾਮ ਨੇ ਕਿਹਾ (I told you I am not saying it. Ganga Ram is saying so.)

[283] ਸ਼ਿਮਲੇ ਦਾ ਹੈ (Ganga Ram is from Shimla.)

up with hands curling up in fists to prepare for a mock fight, Mum blew a flying kiss in my direction! Satisfied that she had finally led me to the wall, her own flesh and blood, Mum eventually let me in to her secret with her chin up in the air and a twinkle in her eyes. 'Totaaaah … Shimle da tota Ganga Ram kehnda Congress ne jitt jaana iss vaar te Captain mukhmantri.'[284]

Parties change, leaders change and even seasons change, but one thing that remains constant is my mother's exuberance to celebrate all festivals our vibrant India brings along at regular intervals. I remember one particular morning when our household was coming to life. Dad was almost ready to leave for office, Bhabi[285] was hustling around, Mum was getting the tea in order for everyone. Amidst this organised chaos of the morning, suddenly my phone started chiming in Basant Panchami[286] messages. On this day, the Goddess of knowledge, wisdom and art, Saraswati as well as Lord of Love, Kamadeva are specifically worshipped. The significance of colour yellow in the celebration of Basant Panchami is connected with blossoming flowers of mustard in the fields. People tend to wear yellow clothes and eat yellow-coloured food, even wear yellow hair adornements. Basically, any personification of spring is honoured on this festival.

To brighten up the morning I wished everyone joyous Basant loudly. Mum immediately chimed in, 'Basant hai ajj?

---

[284] ਤੋਤਾ - ਸ਼ਿਮਲੇ ਦਾ ਤੋਤਾ ਗੰਗਾ ਰਾਮ ਕਹਿੰਦਾ ਹੈ ਕਾਂਗਰਸ ਨੇ ਜਿੱਤ ਜਾਣਾ ਇੱਸ ਵਾਰੀ ਤੇ ਕੈਪਟਨ ਮੁੱਖਮੰਤਰੀ (Tarrot parrot from Shimla. The parrot Ganga Ram has confirmed that Congress is going to win and Captain would be the chief minister.)

[285] ਭਾਬੀ (Brother's wife).

[286] ਬਸੰਤ ਪੰਚਮੀ (Festival announcing the advent of spring).

Chal, saareyaan nu sawa mubarak.'[287] Affectionately Mother Darling turned towards Bhabi and said, 'Ajj te pher kuch peele rang da mittha hona chahida hai Bahu Rani.'[288] Calculating which kid to wake up for revision and which one to let sleep longer, Bhabi just fell apart laughing, 'Tuhaanu khaan to ilaava kuchh nahi sujjda savere-savere?!!'[289] Our Mother, the secret of our good health.

Have you ever thought where would we be without our mothers, or even grandmothers? Teenagers hate being dragged to weddings. To complicate matters, most weddings happen over the weekend, when football-fanatic-teens are not just being asked to 'present' a joint family front, but more horrifyingly, sacrifice their weekend matches.

Our neighbour's granddaughter was getting married in the evening and all hell had broken loose. My niece had semester end exams, hence had been respectfully excused. The weight of representing the grandkids now rested on the bony shoulders of my lanky teenaged nephew, who had been counting hours, since days, for the Manchester United v/s Everton match taking place that night. Like a happily neutralised Bua[290], I had been mutely watching him negotiate with every member of the family to be allowed to stay at home to watch the match. Since I too had had the (unwanted) privilege of being the youngest one in my generation, I wanted him to learn bargaining skills and fight for his beliefs from an early age.

---

[287] ਬਸੰਤ ਪੰਚਮੀ ਹੈ ਅੱਜ. ਚੱਲ ਸਾਰਿਆਂ ਨੂੰ ਸਵਾ ਮੁਬਾਰਕ (Today is Basant so my best wishes to everyone on Basant.)

[288] ਅੱਜ ਤੇ ਫੇਰ ਕੁੱਛ ਪੀਲੇ ਰੰਗ ਦਾ ਮਿੱਠਾ ਹੋਣਾ ਚਾਹੀਦਾ ਹੈ ਬਹੁਰਾਣੀ (Daughter-in-law we must have something yellow to eat today then.)

[289] ਤੁਹਾਨੂੰ ਖਾਣ ਤੋਂ ਇਲਾਵਾ ਕੁਝ ਨਹੀਂ ਸੁੱਜਦਾ ਸਵੇਰੇ-ਸਵੇਰੇ (Can you not think of anything beyond food first thing in the morning?)

[290] ਬੂਆ (Father's sister).

My poor nephew lost his case with his father in no time. His mother was telling him just how handsome he would look in his new clothes. His sister could not care less as long as she got to stay at home, grandfather had already gone to sleep and could not be disturbed and his grandmother wanted him next to her at the wedding. The last straw however that won the peace with mutual consent and smiles all around was when my nephew put his arms around my mother and said, 'OK, I will go for the wedding if I am allowed to watch the match on Grandma's phone while all of you socialise there!' Mum tweaked his ear with a grin and signed the deal, 'Eh khachhra kis te chalaa gya?!'[291] Mum agreed and as my nephew ran to his room to get ready, Mum sneaked behind me and whispered with the wickedest of her smiles ever, 'Main apna mobile phone ghar bhull jaawaan?' How could mother even think of it? [292]

Do allow me to share how the same nephew brought an unparalleled joy to this household soon afterwards. In July 2001 just a day after graduating in Economics, I returned home to hold afloat my week old nephew Aman. Much like his father, this little boy is academically brilliant and remained in the top bracket in his class. Then one fine day he grew up to sit his class 10 ICSE Board exams. The results shouted a deliriously high 97.4% marks; 'without attending any tuitions', chimed in his sister. The joy was ours but the hard work was all Aman's. Absolutely PROUD of YOU my boy. Newspapers called to say Aman was third in tri-city but for us, given the amount of sincere effort he had put into his revision in the previous 4 months, our boy was a winner through and through. The drama though continued in the household.

---

[291] ਇਹ ਖਚਰਾ ਕਿਸ ਤੇ ਚਲਾ ਗਿਆ? (From where has this fellow inherited such mischievousness?)
[292] ਮੈਂ ਆਪਣਾ ਮੋਬਾਈਲ ਫੋਨ ਘਰ ਭੁੱਲ ਜਾਵਾਂ? (Should I manage to forget my mobile at home tonight?)

After a joyous trip to the school where Aman was interviewed and the entire family was photographed by over half a dozen national and local newspapers, we really did not know what to do with ourselves. We were basking in the glory of this youngest produce of the house. We had barely gotten used to being blinded by the paparazzi when we were whisked away to meet with the principal of the school. Thanks to the achievement of our little boy, we were treated like royalty in the formidable office of the prim and propa'h principal. For once, we, as parents were leading the conversation and not making small talk.

Finally once we managed to calm ourselves down a little, I overheard a telephone conversation Mum was having with the newspaper boy late at night, 'Tussi na saare paper, har language de kal de jaana!'[293] The following morning Dad could not wait for the newspaper delivery and personally went to buy ALL THE NEWSPAPERS at 5 am itself and then woke up the entire household to read them. Mother Darling who would never miss her morning walk or yoga, quite happily skipped her stretches to pour over the papers. Yes, it was all Aman's hardwork but the kind of joy he had given to everyone in this household, which was bursting at its seams with pride and joy, was incomparable. 'Mool naalo sood pyaara.'[294] Bhabi finally got her bearings and said, 'Mera puttar 9 akhbaaran wich.'[295] Just like Mum, my brother had also not gone to the gym as he had been too busy accepting congratulatory messages.

---

[293] ਤੁਸੀ ਨਾ ਸਾਰੇ ਪੇਪਰ, ਹਰ language ਦੇ ਕੱਲ ਦੇ ਜਾਣਾ! (Please send all the papers, in all languages tomorrow.)

[294] ਮੂਲ ਨਾਲੋਂ ਸੂਦ ਪਿਆਰਾ (An Indian idiom which means that interest is more precious than the principle or the grandkids are more precious than the children.)

[295] ਮੇਰਾ ਪੁੱਤਰ 9 ਅਖਬਾਰਾਂ ਵਿੱਚ (My son is in nine newspapers today.)

Moments like these come around in the life of a select few. I am so glad that our parents have been blessed with two generations of academic achievers. To mark this feat, I gifted Aman a smartphone so that my little one did not have to remain at the mercy of his impish elders. He had earned his digital mobility.

Ours is a family of strange characters. I am often quoted to have started the country's first community-based adventure group called CATS, but I am petrified of anything on four legs. My father loves animals and birds, but is against putting them in cage. My brother can deal with the animals as long as they don't come within 2' of his bodily existence! My mother grew up with animals of all shapes and sizes in her parental home but dislikes them now because she can't deal with their 'mess'. Both the grandchildren in the house would love to have animals, but run away from taking responsibility for their four-legged furry friends. Suffice to say, two generations of this family have grown up without having any animals around. So now imagine the reaction of Mother Superior when she was told by her super-achiever grandson that a black cat had delivered a litter in the backyard of our already overcrowded house.

Grandson: Mubarkaan Grandma. Billi ne bachhe ditte baahar.[296]

Mother Superior: Phitte munh bachhe de ditte billi ne.[297]

Grandson: How can you be so cruel? You ought to be saying congratulations Grandma. They are such cute kittens?

---

[296] ਮੁਬਾਰਕਾਂ Grandma.. ਬਿੱਲੀ ਨੇ ਬੱਚੇ ਦਿੱਤੇ ਬਾਹਰ! (Congratulations Grandma. Cat has delivered babies outside.)

[297] ਫਿੱਟੇ ਮੂੰਹ! ਬਿੱਲੀ ਨੇ ਬੱਚੇ ਦੇ ਦਿੱਤੇ?? *(Good Lord! Cat has delivered kittens?)*

Mother Superior: OK Mubarkaan… bachhe![298]

Grandson: Billi nu mubarkaan deyo.. billi ton laddu manngo![299]

Mother Superior toddled off to fetch milk while the excited grandson looked for an appropriate dish to serve the milk to both the mother cat and the kittens. All is well that ends well.

To live in a house which is planted bang in the middle of shopping streets has its pros and cons. If it means that you don't have to worry too much about feeding the kittens as there is enough fish and Chicken leftovers from the food alley across the road, it also has umpteen cons too. On a Sunday, a day rest as ordained by none else but Lord Himself, the market association across the road put up a 'Chhabeel'[300] to help the commuters beat the heat of the sultry weather. Unfortunately, they also decided to add 'Mata diyaan Bhetaan'[301] on full blast since 9 am.

Initially we had fun trying to guess which filmi song is every 'bhet'[302] based on. However, after 4 hours we were at the end of our tether. Sadly, requests made to the camp organisers fell on deaf ears. Finally, I decided to take matters in my hands and I called the national helpline 100 and asked for Police, to seek help from the uniformed authorities in getting the volume reduced to a more agreeable level. The call got answered within a few seconds and the conversation progressed thus:

---

[298] ਮੁਬਾਰਕਾਂ.. ਬੱਚੇ (OK Congratulations… but kittens??!)

[299] ਬਿੱਲੀ ਨੂੰ ਮੁਬਾਰਕਾਂ ਦੇਯੋ.. ਬਿੱਲੀ ਤੋਂ ਲੱਡੂ ਮੰਗੋ (Congratulate the cat. Ask the cat for the sweets as a celebration of the arrival of her kittens.)

[300] ਛਬੀਲ (Chabeel is a small setup on a thorough way to partake sweetened milk or any other cold sweet non-alcoholic beverage to the passersby.)

[301] ਮਾਤਾ ਦੀਆਂ ਭੇਟਾਂ (Hymns sung in reverence of Mother Goddess).

[302] ਭੇਟ (Hyms).

No. 100: Hello

SD: Sat Sri Akal Ji. Ikk benti karni si jee.[303]

No. 100: Tussi Supreet Dhiman ji bol rahe ho?[304]

SD (smiling inwardly): Haanji[305]

No. 100: Gaddi da number likhwayo jis ne tuhaada baar rokya hoya hai. Main banda bhejda jee!![306]

SD (after recovering from the intial shock): Nahin Veerji aaj te bass 'Mata diyaan Bhetaan' di avaaz halki karwa deyo![307]

No. 100: Hune layo jee.[308]

Mother Superior when heard what had transpired over the phone, was quiet for a bit and then slowly shook her head, 'Rabb ne ik kuri ditti oh vi eho jeyi. Enne te lokaan de munde nahin badnaam hunde thaane wich!!'[309]

All jokes aside, full marks to the cops. Volume was toned down to much more humane levels within minutes. Frustratingly, camp organisers turned up the volume to nuisance levels again half an hour later. We encouraged Dad to pay them a visit this time. The speakers were turned off and the camp packed away. As much as I would like to gloat about

---

[303] ਸਤਿ ਸ੍ਰੀ ਅਕਾਲ.. ਇੱਕ ਬੇਨਤੀ ਕਰਨੀ ਸੀ ਜੀ *(Good day... I have a request to make.)*

[304] ਤੁਸੀ ਸੁਪ੍ਰੀਤ ਧੀਮਾਨ ਬੋਲ ਰਹੇ ਹੋ? *(Are you Supreet Dhiman?)*

[305] ਹਾਂਜੀ *(Yes.)*

[306] ਗੱਡੀ ਦਾ ਨੰਬਰ ਲਿਖਵਾਓ ਜਿਸ ਨੇ ਤੁਹਾਡਾ ਬਾਰ ਰੋਕਿਆ ਹੋਇਆ ਹੈ... ਮੈਂ ਬੰਦਾ ਭੇਜਦਾ ਜੀ!! *(Please share the car registration number which has blocked your driveway.)*

[307] ਨਹੀਂ ਵੀਰਜੀ ਅੱਜ ਤੇ ਬੱਸ ਮਾਤਾ ਦੀਆਂ ਭੇਟਾਂ ਦੀ ਆਵਾਜ਼ ਹੱਲੀ ਕਰਵਾ ਦਿਓ (Thanks brother but it not an illegally parked car today. Instead, can you please get the organisers of Chabeel to tone down the volume of the hymns?)

[308] ਹੁਣੇ ਲਿਧੋ ਜੀ (Sure. Right away.)

[309] ਰੱਬ ਨੇ ਇੱਕ ਕੁੜੀ ਦਿੱਤੀ, ਉਹ ਵੀ ਇਹੋ ਜਿਹੀ ... ਇੰਨੇ ਤੇ ਲੋਕਾਂ ਦੇ ਮੁੰਡੇ ਨਹੀਂ ਬਦਨਾਮ ਹੁੰਦੇ ਥਾਣੇ ਵਿੱਚ! (God blessed me with one daughter, who is more notorious than the boys of other families in the police stations!)

my Dad's clout, our maid told us that the camp organisers had run out of raw materials in reality!

Barely had we survived the religious ceremony when Rakhi[310] arrived. It is a day when the entire household goes through the motions of tying rakhi threads and freshly minted currency notes exchanging hands in return, I am reminded of a rakhi which took place more than two decades ago. I used to be in England those days, along with my only sibling, my dear brother, senior to me by almost half a dozen years. Those were the days of sheer innocence when affection for your kin and kith knew no bounds and the only thing which mattered was who would get to eat the last morsel of home-made full-fat butter dripping allu-parantha shallow fried on cold winter mornings or the last bowl of rajmah refried twice over! I used to be thick as thieves with both my brother and a male cousin. Distance had also failed to dilute our love and concern for each other as our cousin remained in India while we siblings went to England. Since there could not be even a hairwidth difference between my own brother and this cousin, I dutifully posted home one rakhi thread for cousin, as I bought an identical one for my brother in England. Traditions must continue you see.

Upon receiving the envelope, my Mother Darling immediately called my cousin, whom she also loved as her own child, to tell him that he must show up on Rakhi morning for the ritual. Being the considerate and efficient mother that she has always been, Mum rang my cousin on Rakhi morning again to remind him that he must visit home for breakfast and

---

[310] ਰਾਖੀ/ਰੱਖੜੀ (Rakhi is an Indian festival that celebrates the bond between a brother and a sister. All the sisters tie a band around their brothers' wrists, who in return give them gifts and promise to protect them forever.)

Rakhi. Since my cousin also adored Mother Superior, he dutifully showed up, as instructed.

Mum served him his favourite breakfast, topped with a glass of lassi[311]. Then she brought out the Rakhi thali[312] and since there was no girl/sister/woman in sight, it was mutually understood between the chachi-bhateeja[313] duo that Mum would play the role of the missing Chicken and do the Rakhi honours. After the brief duly acted out ceremony, my cousin got up to leave and suddenly Mother Superior found her form, 'Oye! Kithe challeya? Kha leya-pee leya, hunn shagun taan de ke jaa behan da!!!'[314] Traditions must continue you see.

Traditionalist as she might be, Mum ensured that all her children experienced everything in life, right from food, places to sports and clothes. She always stood right behind us, literally having our back. My mother has always rued how none of the females in my Dada-House were allowed to wear sleeveless shirts and blouses. I remember wearing my first elegant sequinned formal spaghetti top, which was actually a birthday present sent by my mother as I was finishing Economics at University of Warwick. I guess it was her way of living her unfulfilled desires through us. Given that she took to mobile technology like a fish at the age of 70, you can just imagine the kind of dreams this woman must have nurtured, which remained unfulfilled due to various reasons. I hope I am able to fulfil some of them at least before it is too late.

---

[311] ਲੱਸੀ (Sweet or salty buttermilk. It is a cooling Indian drink made by churning yogurt and diluting it with water, as per personal preference.)

[312] ਥਾਲੀ (Large/full plate).

[313] ਚਾਚੀ - ਭਤੀਜਾ (Wife of Dad's younger brother and nephew).

[314] ਓਏ! ਕਿੱਥੇ ਚੱਲਿਆ? ਖਾ ਲਿਆ - ਪੀ ਲਿਆ, ਹੁਣ ਸ਼ਗੁਨ ਤਾਂ ਦੇ ਕੇ ਜਾ ਭੈਣ ਦਾ!!! (Hey where do you think you are going? I have fed you well and you are trying to disappear now that the time has come for you to give me a return gift for Rakhi?)

Mum has always taken great pride in the way her kids dress up and carry themselves in public, though what she might say in private spaces is a completely different ball game altogether. I would have to give you a little background before sharing what happens next. I was born and brought up in Chandigarh, a city planned from scratch by the French Architect, Le Corbusier. Approved by none else but the first prime minister of the country, Pt. Jawahar Lal Nehru, the city was to serve as the new independent Indian government's regional capital in Punjab, after the previous capital, Lahore, became part of Pakistan. Chandigarh also has a UNESCO site, The Capitol Complex, which is made up of three concrete buildings: The Palace of Assembly or Legislative Assembly, the Secretariat and the High Court. This is looked upon as the brain, the intellectual base that governs the city.

So when someone gets you a beret from Paris, you have to wear for a heritage walk organised by INTACH (The Indian National Trust for Art and Cultural Heritage). INTACH sensitises the public about the pluralistic cultural legacy of India, while working on the protection of India's living, built and natural heritage. This heritage walk allowed me to flaunt my beret from the highest point of Chandigarh, while hiding my bad haircut. My Mother Darling had one look at me in morning as I was leaving home and she said, 'Tere Nand Lal uncle paunde si eho-jehi topi ... Yaad hai?!!!'[315] I mean, there really is no difference between a chic French beret and a flopping woollen cap aunty would knit for uncle! Bless them all I say.

The beret saga continued as suffering with unabated headache for three days, failing all remedies. I had tried

---

[315] ਤੇਰੇ ਨੰਦ ਲਾਲ Uncle ਪਾਉਂਦੇ ਸੀ ਇਹੋ-ਜਿਹੀ ਟੋਪੀ.. ਯਾਦ ਹੈ?!! (Remember your Nand Lan uncle used to wear a cap like this?)

everything from masala chai[316], coffee, lassi[317], nimbu pani[318], neck exercises, head massage, eye checkup, but to no avail. A muffler around the neck, thick woollen socks and well insulated boots is all I ever need to beat the cold. However, to give Mum a benefit of doubt to her constant nagging about not wearing a cap and also exhausted of this annoying headache, I reached out to my beret in the morning. It was more as a necessity rather than an accessory. I wanted to check if sudden change in weather was causing the headache so I wore it in the house itself today. Mum was of course, completely unaware of my thoughts. When she returned from her morning's mini-shopping trip and saw me wearing my beret, she exclaimed, 'Lae taan, Munni ne pher paa layi apne Nand Lal uncle di topi. Ki gall, uncle enne yaad aaunde ajj-kal tainu?'[319]

God bless my mother who can't spot the difference between a beret and uncle di topi and God bless my uncle's soul who really did love me like a father. It went beyond love, it was absolute and complete trust that uncle put in me for years as far as his medical needs were concerned. I would be the first one who would get a call whenever he would fall ill. I would be the one to get him admitted in hospital each time. Poignantly, I was also the first one to reach the hospital to witness him being resuscitated at 5 am. I saw his heartbeat straightening into one long line, just as his body fell flat on the bed. The tight hugs, indulgence over tea, 21 snacks for Diwali, long goodbyes at the gate and then even after we sat in the car to drive off with the

---

[316] ਮਸਾਲਾ ਚਾਹ (Masala/spiced tea).

[317] ਲੱਸੀ (Buttermilk).

[318] ਨੀੰਬੂ ਪਾਣੀ (Fresh lime water).

[319] ਲੈ ਤਾਂ, ਮੁੰਨੀ ਨੇ ਫੇਰ ਪਾ ਲਈ ਆਪਣੇ Nand Lal uncle ਦੀ ਟੋਪੀ? ਕੀ ਗੱਲ, Uncle ਇੰਨੇ ਯਾਦ ਆਉਂਦੇ ਅੱਜ-ਕਲ ਤੈਨੂ? (Aaah. My kiddo is wearing Nand Lal uncle's cap again? What happened? You missing your uncle again today?)

engine running, I saw them all fall flat on their face that morning. I would never know if it was the beret or the warmth of the relationship with my uncle that took care of my headache. This fleeting thought made me get up and give Mum one tight hug, just like the one which uncle used to give to me.

My mother is a bit hard of hearing in one ear and we took her to an ENT (Eye, Nose and Throat) specialist, who confirmed that she does have a problem, but does not need a hearing aid as yet, but asked us to bring Mum along after a year for a retesting. Mum loved this prognosis because she refuses to even consider hearing aids and somehow managed to dodge a revisit to the ENT for years! Last month I dragged her to an ENT specialist, who confirmed that Mum needs hearing aid to stop the deterioration in her one ear and help the other ear from the extra strain she puts to hear what is being said in the room. Instead of accepting that she needs help, she continued to have an excuse handy to fall back on. Her favourite is that the rest of us don't speak loudly enough! Consequently, the rest of us in the house flit between comical and exasperated situations on a daily, if not hourly, basis.

I thought my mother was a special case as I see all my friend's parents with a hearing aid without much ado. Since Mum has been obstinate about not getting the hearing aid, I thought I would speak with her elder sister or brother so that they may counsel her a little and get her to hear sense. I was over the moon when I saw Massi's[320] number flashing on my phone. Someone in the universe was of course listening to my prayers and had got Mum's elder sister to call. I promptly took the call and started exchanging pleasantries with her. Just before I could raise the issue of hearing aid with her, Massi said to

---

[320] ਮਾਸੀ (Mum's sister).

me, 'Chal hunn phone Mumma nu de per Mumma nu keh de ke ucchii bole. Mera phone nawaan hai!'[321] What do you do eh? They are all as bad as each other! All of them have hearing issues and yet, they always find someone or something to blame!

Life goes on they say, as did my journey to enjoy the presence of my mother in my life. It is not every day that you get to see your septuagenarian Mother turn into a little girl prancing around in pigtails. This is precisely what transpired one fine Sunday, which marked the beginning of weddings of the third generation from my Mum's side. We went expecting to meet the usual set of mamas and maasis,[322] cousins and their kids but nothing had prepared us for what actually unfolded. Over the years we had heard stories about how my Nana-Nani[323] used to run an open loving house, where food was cooked for immediate family of eight, plus at least a dozen staff, plus half a dozen visiting relatives who would remain resident for weeks at end. As nana had seven sisters, four daughters, numerous nieces, it was a strict but equally loving Punjabi household where fun and food never ended!

My brother and I, joined later by Bhabi[324], niece and nephew had often heard Mum and her siblings speak about their 'this Bua[325]' or 'that Massi'. However, for us they might as well be fictional characters since neither had we ever seen or met them, nor was there any photograph, since cameras used to be such a dear commodity in those times. Till this particular Sunday that is!

---

[321] ਚੱਲ ਹੁਣ ਫੋਨ ਮੰਮਾ ਨੂੰ ਦੇ ਪਰ ਮੰਮਾ ਨੂੰ ਦੱਸ ਦੇ ਕੇ ਉੱਚੀ ਬੋਲੇ.. ਮੇਰਾ ਫੋਨ ਨਵਾਂ ਹੈ! (Come on now give the phone to Mum but to tell her to speak loudly, as my phone is new!)

[322] ਮਾਮਾ, ਮਾਸੀ (Mother's brother and sister).

[323] ਨਾਨਾ and ਨਾਨੀ (Mother's father and mother).

[324] ਭਾਬੀ (Brother's wife).

[325] ਬੁਆ (Father's sister).

As perfectly dressed Mother Superior had her appropriately turned out flock sit around a table about to embark on a round of hot coffee on a freezing cold day, a short and sweet elderly lady approached Mum to ask her gently, 'Are you from Chandigarh?' Mum responded equally sweetly, 'Yes'. Pat came the next question, 'Are you so and so, married to so and so?' Mum politely responded, 'Haanji'[326]. Then came the acid test, 'Mainu pehchaaneya?'[327]

All of us got curious by now. Mum's face was a picture of emotions. There was excitement writ large on her face, streaked with a brush of much-deserved embarrassment of course. She was dumb stuck, as she obviously did not have a clue about the identity of this lady who knew too much, to be brushed off lightly and publicly. So my polished Mother softly took the little lady's hand in her own butter soft hands and said, 'Hunn thori jehi help aap nu meri karni payegi. Kuchh apne bare dasso.' [328]

'Main Gurnaam.'[329]

That is all it took for all joy to break loose. Our petite and delicately poised ball of grace, wrapped in fine silks was on her feet in a flash, wow-weeing and giggling loudly as she nearly snowballed this even more petite and delicately framed lady, also wrapped in fine silks, in a big beary hug. Barely had these two gotten over each other when a tall and thinly framed lady nicely wrapped in her finest khadi topped with a 'miss-me-not' charming face and twinkling eyes but not a tooth in her mouth, tapped on Mum's shoulder. Of course Mum did not have a

---

[326] ਹਾਂਜੀ *(Yes).*

[327] ਮੈਨੂੰ ਪਹਿਚਾਣਿਆ? (Do you recognize me?)

[328] ਹੁਣ ਥੋੜੀ ਜਿਹੀ help ਆਪ ਨੂੰ ਮੇਰੀ ਕਰਨੀ ਪਾਏਗੀ. ਕੁੱਛ ਆਪਣੇ ਬਾਰੇ ਦੱਸੋ (You will have to help me out a little here. Please share something about yourself.)

[329] ਮੈਂ ਗੁਰਨਾਮ (Me... Gurnaam.)

clue who she was till she said, 'Nakk te ohi hai'[330] and then it was like watching a duck trying to reach up to an ostrich for a tight hug.

Barely had we gotten over this when a third youngish but formidable looking lady pointed towards my brother and asked, 'Is he your son named so and so?' followed by a random 'Where is your daughter who is named so and so?' Now this nailed us too. We quickly folded our hands and greeted them all, as dutifully as our mother had schooled us. Forget putting a foot wrong, we dared not even bat a wrong eyelid!

Within minutes half a dozen main characters from my mother's childhood revealed themselves amidst warm hugs, kisses, playful pulling of cheeks, gentle tugging of ears and tapping feet. These riot-raising ladies of all hues and colours, of all shapes and sizes were the produce of the same 'khandaan'[331], had all played and grown up in the same courtyard of my nana, eaten from the same plate often, went to same school, lived and laughed while watching each other back till they got married and their lives took amazingly different turns. They had stories to tell and we were all ears. The last they remember meeting 'properly' was about the time when my nana passed away 44 years ago. Yet nothing had changed between them. This one joyous moment confirmed that my nana's open and loving courtyard did indeed exist, nurturing everyone who took shelter under his roof, whether for a few weeks or for a few years. We took a group photograph. For others, it was to save memories. For me, it was a tribute to my mother's father, my nana.

---

[330] ਨੱਕ ਤੇ ਉਹੀ ਹੈ (Nose is the same!)

[331] ਖਾਨਦਾਨ (Family/clan).

Much water has passed under the bridge since this particular aunt and my brother last met more than four decades ago, of which he, a much-loved and charmed nephew, has no recollection and she, a charming and much loving aunt has not forgotten a scene. So the story goes, that Mum and the rest of the feline brigade of the nana's house were not allowed to step out unless absolutely necessary. Think school, school's extra-curricular-related work, gurudwara[332], grocery shopping and occasional clothes/jewellery shopping was never to be done without a chaperone. We are talking about the 50s and 60s mind you, when memories of the partition were still fresh in most minds. Anything remotely related to films amounted to court martial! Nana was too genteel, but it was my towering elder mama with a thundering voice who was considered a terror. Forget home-grown crowd, even visiting female friends were not spared if they were found not following the law and order of the house! However, girls being girls would always find a valid reason to make merry, occasionally of course.

One day the girlie gang of nana's house decided to go watch a film starring a bollywood comedian Mahmood in a theatre, on the pretext of going out to get the bedsheets printed to do embroidery at home during the long summer months. Nani was involved in the plan and she held the fort at home while the rest of the gang skipped out of the house, but the deal was that the girls would take my little brother with them so that even Nani gets some rest at home in their absence. Girls had a great time and best thing was that none knew any better at home.

Fait Accompli. Alas! As was apparently the tradition in nana's house, everyone ate together and would exchange

---

[332] ਗੁਰਦਵਾਰਾ (Sikh temple).

whatever everyone got up to that day. It was a strict household but a very loving one. So my elder mama[333] asked about the girlie-brigade's trip and this cute as hell aunt showed off their newly printed sheets and newly purchased embroidery threads with great flourish. Then mama asked his little nephew about what he saw outside the house. This handsome as hell little one promptly said, 'Mama ji main khel vekheya!'[334]

Obviously alarmed, Mother Darling promptly chimed in to cover up, 'Veerji oh na baandar-baandri da khel si raste wich, oh vekheya si saareyan ne.'[335] This precious brother of a sister yet to be born, having suddenly felt a surge of importance at being asked about the details of his day, felt compelled to immediately correct Mum by adding, 'Nahin nahin Mama ji. Othe baandar nahin, uncle-aunty nachh de paye si.'[336] The rest, as they say, is history!

Umbilically attached to my nana's house, the place where she was born 11 years after the marriage of her parents, the courtyard where she spent a considerable amount of her life, the large double doors through which her 'Doli'[337] left for her new life, this cutest aunt of them all had tonnes of stories to share with all of us. As we were having lunch at that family wedding, she told us how my handsome little brother, the apple of everyone's eyes, used to love COCA-COLA, which would be bought promptly for him. However one day when he was at his crankiest best, the market was shut and COCA-COLA could

---

[333] ਮਾਮਾ (Mother's brother).

[334] ਮਾਮਾ ਜੀ ਮੈਂ ਖੇਲ ਵੇਖਿਆ (Mama ji I saw a play.)

[335] ਵੀਰਜੀ ਉਹ ਨਾ ਬਾਂਦਰ-ਬਾਂਦਰੀ ਦਾ ਖੇਲ ਸੀ ਰਸਤੇ ਵਿਚ, ਉਹ ਵੇਖਿਆ ਸੀ ਸਾਰਿਆਂ ਨੇ. (Brother it was the street play of monkeys. That is what we all had watched.)

[336] ਨਹੀਂ ਨਹੀਂ ਮਾਮਾ ਜੀ. ਉੱਥੇ ਬਾਂਦਰ ਨਹੀਂ, Uncle-Aunty ਨੱਚਦੇ ਪਾਏ ਸੀ (No No Mamaji. They were not monkeys but uncle and aunty who were dancing around the trees.)

[337] ਡੋਲੀ (The car/vehicle in which the bride departs with the groom after marriage).

not be purchased to appease him. Of course, he would have nothing of it and there was a drama in the house. No amount of negotiation or bargaining worked with him.

Quietly, this cute aunt of ours went to the kitchen, boiled tea leaves and sugar in generous amount, sieved it and let it cool. Once this dark-coloured liquid was cold enough, she poured it into my brother's bottle and gave it to him, 'Lae puttar, pee lae[338] COCA-COLA.' He took a sip and observed that COCA-COLA tastes different today to which this resourceful and quick on her feet aunt quickly said, 'Puttar ajj chhutti hai na, isslayi ajj taste farak hai.'[339] Thus, peace was bought in the house for a day. Trick-o-Treat runs in the family I guess!

What none of us realised as we bade goodbyes that Sunday after a sumptuous lunch at the wedding was that this cute bundle of endless stories would collapse the same night, to land in the ICU and be put on the ventilator, and be gone in 5 days. Just when we were warming up to our mother's cousins and had begun to absorb the beautiful lifestyle of our maternal side of the family, the storyteller was snatched away from us. Did you say you would catch up with your aunts and uncles another time eh? Are you sure there would be another time? Do we know who would be next? Get up and say sorry if you messed up, go hug that cousin or nephew who needs his or her soul stitched together. You may be the only hope for that one person. Heart-warming memories are any day much better than heartfelt regrets. Remember, it is not easy to sleep on a soaking wet pillow.

---

338 ਲੈ ਪੁੱਤਰ ਪੀ ਲੈ coca cola (Come my child, here, have your coca cola.)

339 ਪੁੱਤਰ ਅੱਜ ਛੁੱਟੀ ਹੈ ਨਾ, ਇਸਲਈ ਅੱਜ taste ਫਰਕ ਹੈ (Son today is a holiday, that is why it is tasting a little different.)

This one incident took me back to another winter about a decade ago. Most of the elders in our household are fond of Sufi music. Depending on our work schedules and personal engagements, we usually attend concerts; if not collectively, then at least individually. Once Pakistani Qawwal Sher Miandad Khan was due to perform in the royal city of Patiala during the Heritage Festival. He is not a very well known name in Qawalli singing; however, he has the ability to command your hearts once he starts performing. After securing the seats for his concert, all of us piled into the car and reached Patiala to claim our seats in the front row. Sher Miandad Khan's signature pieces at that time used to be Sufi Poet Baba Bulle Shah's 'Raaz diyaan gallan' and a soul-stirring ade to mothers, simply titled 'Maa'. The former connects you with the creator of the universe, while the latter bonds you with your creator on earth.

As 'Maa' was sung on the stage, I noticed that Mum had tears streaming own her plump cheeks. Not wishing to break the spell, I let her be till 'Maa' ended. Just when I was about to put my arm around Mum, I heard my brother ask Mum why was she crying while all her kids and grandkids were around her. Wiping away her tears she said softly, 'Main vi Maa wali haan!'[340] Both of us sitting on each side of our mother were stunned to silence. How easy is it for us to believe that our parents have no other relationships in their lives beyond us and our kids! How selfishly we lay claim to their every emotion! We keep telling everyone around us to 'give us space' but do we give the same space to our parents? We don't own their every living thought just because we were born of them.

---

[340] ਮੈਂ ਵੀ ਮਾਂ ਵਾਲੀ ਹਾਂ (I also have a mother!)

Time kept ticking by and once late at night I noticed that kids had gone to sleep after a day of exams. Brother and Bhabi had hit the sack too after their long evening of socialising. There were only two people awake in the house as the clock ticked closer to midnight. My Mother's daughter who is still playing in her maternal grandfather's home and my Mother's husband, who is known to have dinner by 7 pm and sleep by 8 pm ..., who is watching the cricket match on low volume while sitting only 2' away from the TV! Shall I tell Mother Darling when she wakes up in the morning? I am pretty sure this is something my late aunt would have done with great aplomb.

Days went by and we all went back to our routines, as we all do. My brother was chosen to head the club and that started an endless stream of bouquets for months at end. On the other hand, I would invariably get a mug every time I donated blood. So these two things were in constant supply at home. As flowers would wither and as your maid keeps breaking anything which has a possibility of being broken, including your cherished blood donation mugs, Mother Darling started putting both her kids together. She would plonk the leftover flowers in the chipped mugs and give them a place of pride on the table in the verndah, to welcome everyone from a maid to the master.

During the days running up to Diwali, like the rest of the folks all around, our household also dives into every nook and cranny to autumn clean every speck of dust. Mother Darling also unlocked her pitara[341], commonly referred as 'daaj di peti'[342] to wash, dryclean or simply dry out stuff in the sun. It becomes a trip down the memory lane for Mum also as each

---

[341] ਪਿਟਾਰਾ (Pandora's box).
[342] ਦਾਜ ਦੀ ਪੇਟੀ (Trousseau trunk).

item represents an incident, a moment of pride, someone she has lost over the years, or simply happy times spent before she got married.

Every year Mum manages to pull out something from her pitara which we had not seen previously. This year came the turn of this bright fuschia-coloured bed sheet with matching pillow covers. Mum walked up to me as I was mindlessly tapping away on the laptop, caressing the bedsheet as one would caress a new born, softly and gently. 'Tainu pata eh chaddar main udon kaddhi si, jaddon tera Veer aan wala si. Odhar mainu chaddar kaddhan di chhetti te odhar tere Veer nu aan di chhetti. Ikk maheene de andar tyaar keeta si eh set main. Teri Nani ne kehna kurriye araam ker lae. Meri daadi ne vi kehna tang na ho, hor kurriyaan kaddh den giyaan. Per main aap hathhi kaddi saari.'[343] That gentle face, a little wrinkled, a little crumpled, yet glowing with memories of the era goneby. Before I could get up from my bed to give her one tight hug, she gave a quick whack around my head and said, 'Chal kadde hill ke vi dikha deya ker!'[344]

Taken by absolute surprise at such sudden change in her mood, I just stared at her, open-mouthed. Something nudged inside her. She wrapped my seated self into her standing self, hugging me tight, putting the bedsheet on my shoulders, caressing my hair softly, she said, 'Es Diwali tainu saariyaan khushiyaan milan, sehat channgi rahe, tera har kamm sirae

---

[343] ਤੈਨੂ ਪਤਾ ਇਹ ਚੱਦਰ ਮੈਂ ਉਦੋਂ ਕੱਢੀ ਸੀ, ਜੱਦੋਂ ਤੇਰਾ ਵੀਰ ਆਣ ਵਾਲਾ ਸੀ. ਓਧਰ ਮੈਨੂ ਚੱਦਰ ਕੱਢਣ ਦੀ ਛੇਤੀ ਤੇ ਓਧਰ ਤੇਰੇ ਵੀਰ ਨੂੰ ਆਣ ਦੀ ਛੇਤੀ. ਇੱਕ ਮਹੀਨੇ ਦੇ ਅੰਦਰ ਤਿਆਰ ਕੀਤਾ ਸੀ ਇਹ ਸੈੱਟ ਮੈਂ. ਤੇਰੀ ਨਾਨੀ ਨੇ ਕਹਿਣਾ ਕੁੜੀਏ ਰਾਮ ਕਰ ਲੈ. ਮੇਰੀ ਦਾਦੀ ਨੇ ਵੀ ਕਹਿਣਾ ਤੰਗ ਨਾ ਹੋ, ਹੋਰ ਕੁੜੀਆਂ ਕੱਢ ਦੇਣਗੀਆਂ. ਪਰ ਮੈਂ ਆਪ ਹੱਥੀ ਕੱਢੀ ਸਾਰੀ. *(Do you know that I was carrying your brother when I embroidered this bedsheet set? I was keen to finish the set before your brother arrives and I completed the set within a month. Your grandmother kept asking me to rest and don't stress out. 'Other girls will do it for you', but no, I wanted to complete the set with my own hands.)*

[344] ਚੱਲ ਕਦੇ ਹਿੱਲ ਕੇ ਦਿਖਾ ਦਿਯਾ ਕਰ (Will you move your lazy bones once?)

charrhe, teri har mushkil asaan howe.'[345] Letting her blessings sink in, I hugged her back. Just as I was soaking this moment of tenderness and unadulterated love, Mum said, 'Chal pher uth. Eh teri.'[346] Only a mother knows how to weave and embroider her flock together. She does not needle any vested interests. Go, hug your mothers tight today my friends. If she is not around, go and hug a mother who needs one! Hope you won't wait for a Mother's Day.

---

[345] ਇਸ ਦੀਵਾਲੀ ਤੇਨੂੰ ਸਾਰੀਆਂ ਖੁਸ਼ੀਆਂ ਮਿਲਣ, ਸਿਹਤ ਚੰਗੀ ਰਹੇ, ਤੇਰਾ ਹਰ ਕੰਮ ਸਿਰੇ ਚੜ੍ਹੇ, ਤੇਰੀ ਹਰ ਮੁਸ਼ਕਿਲ ਆਸਾਨ ਹੋਵੇ (May this Diwali you get every happiness, may you be blessed with good health, may you succeed in every endeavor of yours, may every hurdle be removed from your path.)
[346] ਚੱਲ ਫੇਰ ਉੱਠ, ਇਹ ਤੇਰੀ. (Come on, get up. This is yours now.)

'Ek muddat se mirī maañ nahīñ soī 'tābish'

Maiñ ne ik baar kahā thā mujhe Dar lagtā hai.'

- **Abbas Tabish**

Out and About

Parents of one of our eduCATe Scholars, a scholarship programme of Can & Will Foundation, came home to share an update about our eduCATe Scholar Mamta doing medicine at Government Medical College in Patiala. Over a cup of tea they told us about her plans to study towards her MD as she had scored 64/75 in her last set of exams. That's 85% in MBBS. I avoided my mother's glance as I congratulated the proud parents. As soon as they left, I tip-toed out of the house too as I did not want Mum to start enquiring about my own exam result.

As the sun reached high up in the sky, I sat down to have lunch with Mum. Just as I dove into my plate the phone rang and it was our dear eduCATe Scholar Ritika who is doing articleship of Chartered Accountancy profession. Thinking she might be in need of some guidance, I put her call on speakerphone to kill two birds with one stone; I continued to speak with her while polishing off my lunch. Sounding really cheerful about the progress she was making and the fact that her articleship wages would double by next month, she promptly asked me, 'So Ma'am when will you get your exam results?' Mum laughed, I choked.

As I finally got up to leave for work, Mother Darling walked up to me. She assessed me from head to toe as only mothers can do. Finally she opened her mouth, 'Will you take me to tie some loose ends today?' Beginning of the week and I already had a day full. However, since it was the beginning of the week for Mumma also, I was reluctant to hand out a straight no too. To approach the topic cautiously, politely I asked Mum why she wanted to do things immediately? She said with a disarming smile, 'Baad vich pata nahin ki banega iss lai socheya tera result aan to pehlaan thorri shopping ker awaan!'[347] Do I really need enemies to rub salt into my wounds with a mother like this around?

The other day, Mother Superior wanted to run some errands, which she had put off on account of my essays that I had to hand write and submit. So the moment I stepped home this evening, she dragged me back to the car. Since I had no idea where she wanted to go, I was at her mercy for directions, which went something like this:

*On approaching a T-junction – Jiss paason marzi chal, othhe hee pahunchaange! [348]

*Approaching a busy junction with multiple exits, choc-o-bloc in a melee of cars, cows and jaywalkers approaching from all possible directions – Oh jiss passe peeli kameez wala sardar jaa reha hai![349]

*At the roundabout – motorcycle wale pichhe laa lae![350]

---

[347] ਬਾਦ ਵਿਚ ਪਤਾ ਨਹੀਂ ਕੀ ਬਣੇਗਾ ਤੇਰਾ, ਇਸਲਈ ਸੋਚਿਆ ਤੇਰਾ result ਆਣ ਤੋਂ ਤੋਂ ਪਹਿਲਾਂ ਥੋੜੀ shopping ਕਰ ਆਵਾਂ! (God knows what kind of result you would get, so I thought I might as well do some shopping while the mood is still good!)

[348] ਜਿਸ ਪਾਸੋਂ ਮਰਜੀ ਚੱਲ - ਉੱਥੇ ਹੀ ਪਹੁੰਚਾਂਗੇ! (Take any road – We will reach the same place!)

[349] ਉਹ ਜਿਸ ਪਾਸੇ ਪੀਲੀ ਕਮੀਜ਼ ਵਾਲਾ ਸਰਦਾਰ ਜਾ ਰਿਹਾ ਹੈ (See the direction in which that Sikh gentleman in yellow shirt is going?)

[350] ਮੇਟਰਸਾਈਕਲ ਵਾਲੇ ਪਿਛੇ ਲਾ ਲੈ! (Follow the motorcycle rider.)

*Upon finally reaching the destination – Hunn tu car reverse ker ke meri wait ker![351]

Why don't mothers just give us the address? I can travel alone around the world using both public and private transport, but mother won't trust her progeny with a simple local address!

The only time she would let you be is, when you are down and out. For example, the days while tottering between working off my feet or struggling to get off bed due to the long and debilitating spell of chikungunya, I had been noticing how bored stiff Mum had become lately. Almost on a daily basis her plans to go out, or be taken out, scuppered away without much rhyme or reason. Terribly disappointed, Mum bore everything gracefully.

One morning happened to be the day when women celebrate womanhood across the world, but the only woman I wanted to be happy was my Mum. So I asked her to put on her glad rags and get ready for a spin. At first she puckered her nose as she likes to plan her day ahead. She does not take too kindly to the marching orders I tend to deliver to escape her endless interrogation! After a brief reflection which lasted all of 10 seconds, she asked one simple question, 'Kinne waje tyaar howe Maa?'[352] Departure was fixed at 11 am.

Enroute we made a brief pit-stop at a friend's place and together ended up at the North-East India Fair. After browsing through furniture stands, Mum set her eyes on a burgundy scarf, the colour she had been eyeing for 6 years, which 'goes' with her burgundy woollen coat! Trust me when I say my mother is 'The Choosiest Goddess' around. I loved 'Moong Dal' dry pickle but Mum objected to the 'things' moving

---

[351] ਹੁਣ ਤੂੰ ਕਾਰ ਰਿਵਰਸ ਕਰ ਕੇ ਮੇਰੀ ਵੇਟ ਕਰ! *(Now reverse the car and wait for me!)*

[352] ਕਿੰਨੇ ਵਜੇ ਤਿਆਰ ਹੋਵੇ ਮਾਂ? (What time shall I get ready?)

around in the jar. When I pointed it out to the sales girl, at first she could not 'see' anything but then exclaimed, 'Oh! this is normal. You can eat them too.' The vegetarian in me quietly put the jar down and moved to the next stand. We bumped into another set of friends and Mum got busy having a long chat. Mum would have bought a saree or two but since her 7-year-old grandson objected to Grandma's tummy, she let go of her love for sarees. Suits did not match up to her expectation and she did not fancy drinking tea from black stone mugs. Mother Superior is not easy to please you see. Given her standards, at times I wonder how she puts up with me.

As we were about to leave the fair, we bumped into another friend with whom we had had a memorable holiday together. It was turning out to be the kind of day I wanted Mum to have, full of stolen moments of joy away from her mundane life. Mum usually laughs wholeheartedly while reading jokes on WhatsApp; it was even more heart-warming to see her laughing away with her friends at the fair.

Since Mum is always game to try something new, I wanted Mum to try the North-Eastern cuisines. I was taken aback when I was told that their food stalls won't start serving till 2.30 pm! Asking Punjabis to wait for food even a minute after 12 pm is nothing short of a disaster. Instead, I took Mum for her favourite street food, 'Bhalla Paapri' which was followed by yet another favourite, 'Dosa/Uthapam'. As we were about to leave the restaurant, I saw Mum looking longingly at a lady biting into a 'Malaai Kulfi'. Yes! My mother has that incurable sweet tooth. Her favourite confession line being: 'Main nahin khaandi, per mera shareer mithha mangda hai. Mera shareer kehnda hai ke ja, mithha kha!!'[353] Finally, we

---

[353] ਮੈਂ ਨਹੀਂ ਖਾਂਦੀ ਪਰ ਮੇਰਾ ਸ਼ਰੀਰ ਮਿੱਠਾ ਮੰਗਦਾ ਹੈ… ਮੇਰਾ ਸ਼ਰੀਰ ਕਹਿੰਦਾ ਹੈ ਕੇ ਜਾ, ਮਿੱਠਾ ਖਾ *(Personally I don't like sweets at all but what to do when your body demands sugar?)*

reached home where a dear friend had come over with chocolates for Mum. 'Munni, jee khush ho gya aaj te. International Women's Day te saal wich do chaar vaari aa jaana chaahida hai.'[354]

If we look back, it doesn't really take much for our parents to be happy? All they seek is a little bit of our time. Do we ever stop to think that they devoted their young productive years on us while we were busy peeing in our pants or trying to eat our snort? They never calculated how many hours did they spend on bringing us up or taking care of our every need. May be time to reflect a little more on how we prioritise things in life because our parents had no other priority but our well-being and us.

Mother Superior may create all the ruckus to get things done we usually procrastinate, or frog march us to get us to toe the line, or stand in the doorway to get her point across. However, there is something that Mum never does. She rarely asks for anything for herself of much consequence, apart from an odd 'bhalle wali chaat'[355] or a spin around town. So when she does, I usually try to fulfil her politely suggested wish at the earliest possible. This turned out to be one such afternoon.

As I returned home briefly after lunch, Mum gave me a light hug and asked if I had a few minutes to spare. I was about to say that it was a highly inconvenient time since I was scheduled to discuss my 'End Incest' project with a women's platform. However, one look at her disarming smile and that completely undemanding look in her eyes, and I changed my mind.

---

[354] ਮੁੰਨੀ, ਜੀ ਖੁਸ਼ ਹੋ ਗਿਆ ਅੱਜ ਤੇ.. International Women's Day ਤੇ ਸਾਲ ਵਿੱਚ 2–4 ਵਾਰੀ ਆ ਜਾਣਾ ਚਾਹੀਦਾ ਹੈ *(Thank you kid. I am really happy. This day should come two to four times in a year!)*

[355] ਭੱਲੇ ਵਾਲੀ ਚਾਟ (Green bean paste is added with spices, which is then deep fried to make croquets, called bhalla in India. On a bed of bhalla, layers of yogurt, tamarind sauce and spices are added to make this snack.)

Mum wanted to buy a new suit, a nice salwar suit, so shopping time for Mum confirmed. I quickly emailed a note of apology to the team to reschedule the appointment for another day and took Mum to the shops she likes. Now let's not forget that Mum has standards and as by now you all know that she is not easily pleased, so shopping is never a short trip with her. The colours must be different to what she already has in her wardrobe, the embroidery must be finely done, colour combinations must be pleasing and not jarring and the final parameter, 'Mere paaya sohna laggega?'[356] As Mum gets on the nerves of the salesmen, I keep on smiling at them by mouthing little apologies at them. I need them to show the best possible stock to Mum you see, it is not every day that Mum asks for something.

After browsing through stocks in three shops in over an hour, she finally liked one suit that I promptly asked the salesman to pack. As always, Mum tried to hold on to my hand as I took out the card to make the payment by saying, 'Vadda kaun?'[357] As always, I shrugged her off by saying, 'Lambaa Kaun?'[358] This always kind of settles the bill in more than one way.

I thought Mum was done as she had mentioned 'Suit', but when we were walking back to the car, it seems she had 'suits' on her mind as she said, 'Chall dooje paase vi dekh aayiye ki peya hai ohna kol.' [359] Though I was running against a major deadline, still went ahead to the 'other side' of the shopping arcade. We entered one shop and before Mum could dither

---

[356] ਮੇਰੇ ਪਾਇਆ ਸੋਹਣਾ ਲੱਗੇਗਾ? (Would this look nice on me?)

[357] ਵੱਡਾ ਕੌਣ? (Who is the older one?)

[358] ਲੰਬਾ ਕੌਣ? (Who is the tallest of us?)

[359] ਚੱਲ ਦੂਜੇ ਪਾਸੇ ਵੀ ਦੇਖ ਆਈਏ ਕੀ ਪੇਆ ਉਹਨਾ ਕੋਲ (Shall we check out the other side of the market also to check if they have some good stuff?)

about the kind of suit she wanted, I declared loudly that semi-formal winter collection be shown to my Mum. I was trying to cut down the time wastage you see. There was work to catch up for me.

Suit after suit Mum kept on asking to be spread out for her to examine and suit after suit she kept on rejecting. To be honest, I rejected a few as well as embroidery had to be fine on a suit which my Mother Darling wears, patterns must complement her small and round stature, the design must befit her and she must look the best Mum around! As time ticked away, and patience started wearing thin, I stood with the salesman to shortlist the suits to be paraded for Mum. Yes, Mum actually gets the helper staff to hold the suits up and wave around the dupatta to 'get the feel' of the suit! 'Chal beta zaraa suit laa ke dikha hunn!'[360]

Finally, when Mum liked one more suit, we all heaved a sigh of relief and I asked the salesman to pack it before Mum changed her mind. Just as it was to be packed, Mum asked the elderly salesman, 'Length poori hai na?'[361] He assured Mum that it was indeed 'full length' but one look at Mum and we both knew that she was not satisfied. I gave one of those 'apology smiles' to the salesman and asked him to measure it for Mum's satisfaction. Non-verbally he protested, but obliged and asked his man Friday to bring a measuring tape from masterji upstairs.

The salesman held one end of the tape and asked Mum to hold the other end to ensure she stretched the tape as per her liking and decided for herself if it is full length. Now since it is

---

[360] ਚਲ ਬੇਟਾ ਜ਼ਰਾ suit ਲੈ ਕੇ ਦਿਖਾ ਹੁਣ! (Son can you drape the suit on you also so that I can see the fall?)

[361] length ਪੂਰੀ ਹੈ ਨਾ? (I hope you are giving me full length of the suit.)

a pre-printed and pre-cut suit, both sides are obviously of the same length but no, Mum wanted to measure both sides! Then she demanded to measure the length of the fabric for the arms also, precisely at that! Both the salesman and I thought that we were done but Mum had other ideas. She asked the salesman to measure the salwar also. 'Main salwar bhaari paundi haan. Mainu 3 metre di salwar chahidi hai.'[362]

I rolled my eyes enough into my sockets that I am sure I scared the child prancing around us as I heard him yelp. I quickly brought my eyeballs back into place and found the salesman turning a little red in exasperation too. However, I did not want to turn this otherwise-satisfying shopping trip for Mum into a pantomime so I again threw an 'apology smile' at the salesman, with a roll of head this time. He shouted at his man Friday to get the 'steel wala gajj'[363] from the turban counter downstairs to measure the longer fabric length.

Till the man Friday appeared I tried to maintain peace and blood pressures all around by indulging in small talk, which kind of worked. The salesman dramatically took the steel 'gajj' and measured each metre length slowly, so that Mum was able to count each metre length. Both of us heaved a sigh of relief when the salwar fabric turned out to be a couple of inches longer than the 'gajj', which means that Mum has just over 3 metres of salwar length. Fait Accompli. Voila – now Mum can make even a tent out of the salwar fabric! We could buy the suit and finally go home and I could do my work. Alas! That was

---

[362] ਮੈਂ ਸਲਵਾਰ ਭਾਰੀ ਪਾਉਂਦੀ ਹਾਂ. ਮੈਨੂੰ ਤਿੰਨ ਮੀਟਰ ਦੀ ਸਲਵਾਰ ਚਾਹੀਦੀ ਹੈ. *(I wear salwar/bottom, so I need 3 metres length.)*
[363] ਸਟੀਲ ਵਾਲਾ ਗੱਜ *(The steel measuring guage.)*

not to be and Mum had one more question, 'Eh gajj 39" da hai ke 40" da?'[364]

I just could not hold on anymore and blurted out, 'Mumma suit le lo, nahin te main na tuhaanu ethhe hee chhadd jaana hai!'[365] The threat worked! Suit duly paid without any protests, we were back in the car in 5 minutes.

After this episode I refused to even notice Mum's faintest hint of shopping streak. My diligent Mum on the other hand, had started hinting at an outing. Mum had really crossed me big time in her last time, so I was not about to fall in her trap that quickly. So instead of shopping, she started talking about the trailers of the films she had watched recently on YouTube. I did some quick calculations and I thought killing 3 hours in an air-conditioned hall is any day a better deal than being dragged from one shop to the other in search of that perfect suit. When I asked her if she wanted to watch the Punjabi film Qismat starring Sargun and Ammy, the actors she loves, she took all of 10 seconds to agree, complete with a flying kiss. I told Mum to be ready and she dove into her wardrobe, pulled out a suit which, as it happens, I detested. Immediately I blurted, 'Je eh suit paana hai taan aap di film cancel.'[366] Her face dropped. She pursed her lips and dove back into her wardrobe as I tapped away on what she calls my 'dubba'[367], laptop!

After searching high and low she pulled out another suit and coughed to get my attention! One look at the suit and

---

364 ਇਹ ਗੱਜ 39" ਦਾ ਹੈ ਕੇ 40" ਦਾ? *(Is this guage of 39" or 40" length?)*

365 Mumma ਸੂਟ ਲੈ ਲੋ, ਨਹੀਂ ਤੇ ਮੈਂ ਨਾ ਤੁਹਾਨੂੰ ਏਥੇ ਹੀ ਛੱਡ ਜਾਣਾ ਹੈ! (Mumma you better quickly buy the suit, otherwise I am going to just leave you here at the shop itself!)

366 ਜੇ ਇਹ ਸੂਟ ਪਾਣਾ ਹੈ ਤਾਂ ਆਪ ਦੀ ਫਿਲਮ ਕੈਂਸਲ (If you are going to wear this suit to go and watch a film, then your film is cancelled.)

367 ਡੱਬਾ (Box) Mum refers to my laptop as a box.

again I said 'Aap di film cancel.'[368] Mother Superior threw the suit at my face, pulled out a third one and without asking me went ahead to get dressed. As time inched closer to the show and I was still glued to my laptop, dressed to the hilt Mum walked up to me and asked, 'Tu ajje tyaar nahin hona?'[369] Since I wanted to send a couple of emails and I knew I was running against time, I offered a solution, 'Mumma main na ajj injh hee chale jaawangi.'[370]

Mum: Bina nahaate?[371]

Chicken: Haanji.[372]

Mum: Issi terah?[373]

Chicken: Haanji. Nightsuit nahin dress paa ke jawaangi.[374]

Mum: Bina nahaate?[375]

Chicken: Haanji.[376]

Mother Superior: Teri film cancel (Your film cancelled!)[377]

Finally, she got hold of me one Sunday as I was getting ready. Since I was representing CATS at a couple of platforms, I had pulled out my CATS T-shirt to wear. The moment Mother Superior noticed that I had worn THIS T-shirt, and on a Sunday morning, her antennas went into

---

[368] ਆਪ ਦੀ ਫਿਲਮ ਕੈਂਸਲ (Your film stands cancelled.)

[369] ਤੂੰ ਅੱਜੇ ਤਿਆਰ ਨਹੀਂ ਹੋਣਾ? (Are you not going to get ready yet?)

[370] Mumma ਅੱਜ ਨਾ ਮੈਂ ਇੰਝ ਹੀ ਚਲੇ ਜਾਵਾਂਗੀ *(Mum I will go like this.)*

[371] ਬਿਨਾ ਨਹਾਤੇ? (Without a bath?)

[372] ਹਾਂਜੀ *(Yupp.)*

[373] ਇਸੀ ਤ੍ਰਹਾ? (Just like this?)

[374] ਹਾਂਜੀ, Nightsuit ਨਹੀਂ dress ਪਾ ਕੇ ਜਾਵਾਂਗੀ (Yes, but I will change the nightsuit and wear a dress.)

[375] ਬਿਨਾ ਨਹਾਤੇ? *(No bath?)*

[376] ਹਾਂਜੀ *(Yupp.)*

[377] ਤੇਰੀ ਫਿਲਮ ਕੈਂਸਲ! (Your film cancelled.)

overdrive! I usually wear CATS T-shirts only while going out trekking. Mum had missed her outing recently?

Mum: Kithe challi?[378]

CAT: Mumma bas ethhe hee.[379]

Mum: Mainu bina dasse challi billiyaan naal?[380]

CAT: Nahin Mumma, main hee haan, hor koi nahin.[381]

Mum: Chal pher Ma nu naal le ke chal.[382]

CAT: Mumma othe tussi tang ho jayoge. Conference hai.[383]

Mum: Sunday nu kaun conference rakhda hai?[384]

CAT: Mumma sachhi ….[385]

Mum: Eh jhooth bolna kithon sikheya?[386]

CAT (exasperated by now): Mann layo.[387]

Mum: Charhaayi dass kithhe di hai te Maa nu kyun nahi le ke jaana?[388]

CAT: Achha aah vekh layo aap … (I showed her the invite on the laptop).[389]

---

[378] ਕਿੱਥੇ ਚੱਲੀ? (You going somewhere?)

[379] Mumma ਬੱਸ ਇੱਥੇ ਹੀ (Mum just nearby.)

[380] ਮੈਨੂੰ ਬਿਨਾ ਦੱਸੇ ਚੱਲੀ ਬਿੱਲੀਆਂ ਨਾਲ? (You are going with CATS without telling me?)

[381] ਨਹੀਂ Mumma, ਮੈਂ ਹੀ ਹਾਂ, ਹੋਰ ਕੋਈ ਨਹੀਂ (No Mum, I am going alone. There is none going with me.)

[382] ਚਾਲ ਫੇਰ ਮਾਂ ਨੂੰ ਨਾਲ ਲੈ ਕੇ ਚੱਲ (Take Mum along too.)

[383] Mumma ਉੱਥੇ ਤੁਸੀ ਤੰਗ ਹੋ ਜਾਯੋਗੇ, Conference ਹੈ (Mum you will get bored there. It's a conference.)

[384] Sunday ਨੂੰ ਕੌਣ conference ਰੱਖਦਾ ਹੈ? *(Who holds a conference on a Sunday?)*

[385] Mumma ਸੱਚੀ *(Mum honest!)*

[386] ਇਹ ਝੂਠ ਬੋਲਣਾ ਕਿਥੋਂ ਸਿੱਖਿਆ? (Where have you learnt to lie to your Mum?)

[387] ਮੰਨ ਲਯੋ! (Please accept it. I am not lying.)

[388] ਚੜ੍ਹਾਈ ਦੱਸ ਕਿੱਥੇ ਦੀ ਹੈ ਤੇ ਮਾਂ ਨੂੰ ਕਯੂੰ ਨਹੀਂ ਲੈ ਕੇ ਜਾਣਾ? *(Tell where are you headed and not taking Mum along?)*

[389] ਅੱਛਾ ਆਹ ਵੇਖ ਲਯੋ ਆਪ! (Alright.. here.. have a look at this!)

Mum (feeling disappointed a little and then suddenly says with a twinkle in her eyes): eh te do vajje mukk jana … chal uss ton baad kitae challiye … nawaan suit paa ke chlaangi.[390]

The other day I thought of giving Mum an outing of a different kind, especially away from anything which involves measuring fabrics or discussing embroidery or even a film. An engineer by profession, a dear friend Polly Singh has a fascinating hobby, which is taking an interesting art form. He uses scrap from his own factory and from others in the industrial area to make humanoids, which is something that has an appearance resembling a human without actually being one.

Polly's army of humanoids is slowly growing and descended upon the arts exhibition at Punjab Kala Bhawan, a melting pot of art in all its glorious forms. Since Polly is the son of Mother Darling's childhood friend, I thought of taking Mum for the inauguration to kill two birds with one stone. It was a great opportunity to introduce Pollybots to Mum and to get the two old friends together. Mum was the first one to spot Polly's army as we reached the exhibition hall. Seeing his master art pieces for the first time she could not help wondering, 'Munde ne dimaag taan vaddiya laaya hai, per eh phir turran-phirrange vi?!!'[391] Can't take her anywhere!

When taking Mum out for shopping, I usually prefer to do so in the first half of the day as that allows Mum to examine things in daylight, obviating the need to make return trips to exchange stuff, and both of us get to finish the shopping trip

---

[390] ਇਹ ਤੇ 2 ਵੱਜੇ ਮੁੱਕ ਜਾਣਾ.. ਚੱਲ ਉਸ ਤੋਂ ਬਾਅਦ ਕਿਤੇ ਚੱਲੀਏ ... ਨਾਵਟ ਸੂਟ ਪਾ ਕੇ ਚੱਲਾਂਗੀ (This gets over at 2 pm. Come, let's go somewhere after that. I will wear my new suit.)

[391] ਮੁੰਡੇ ਨੇ ਦਿਮਾਗ ਤਾਂ ਵਧੀਆ ਲਾਯਾ ਹੈ ਪਰ ਇਹ ਤੁਰਨ-ਫਿਰੰਗੇ ਵੀ? (The boy has really put his mind to these things, but these bots walk around too?)

with lunch at her favourite restaurant. However, this one time I broke the rule as the footwear Mother Darling had bought during the day in excitement turned out to be wee-bit smaller when she wore it at home in the evening. I agreed to take Mum to the shop as it was only a 2-minute drive away. Trust me, nothing could possibly prepare me for what was in store.

At 8 pm we reached the parking lot and since there was no room to park, I told Mum to call me when she was done so that I would pick her up from the shopfront. Mum pulled a sorry face and said that she left her mobile on charge at home. Seeing that I was turning livid, Mum offered a quick solution. She asked me to wait underneath the largest tree and that is where she will return in 5 minutes after executing the exchange. This sounds simple enough. Right? No!

As soon as Mum left, cops asked me to move the car to avoid a traffic jam in the festive season. I had no choice but to drive around the block to return to the same tree, but there was no sign of Mum. Seeing the cops still stationed there, I drove around the block one more time, but still with no sign of spotting Mum anywhere. Then I decided to park the car and go around each shoe shop to ask about my mother's whereabouts. This exercise took another 15 minutes and finally one shopkeeper said that Mum had exchanged the footwear and left a few minutes ago. Now started the absolutely crazy game of 'Spot the Mother' in the pitch-dark car park as electricity conked off at that precise moment. Taking a deep breath I used my mobile's built-in torch to search the length and width of the car park to find Mum, but to no avail.

I started recalling the number of times my brother was brought back home from the streets as a toddler by neighbours and friends, only because he was exercising his newly developed walking skills. There is no way I was going to abandon my mother at night and go home. Yet there was not much that I could do. Exasperated, I went back to the car and drove it to park right under the tree. I told the cops that they had to cooperate with me as I had lost my mother. They took pity on me and said, 'Go ahead, crowds are thinning too, so no worries.' As I tried to calm myself down by tuning to Adagio with Strings, I got a call on my mobile from an unknown number. Instinctively I knew that it would be Mum. It was Mum! A shopping trip which should have taken 10 minutes ended after more than an hour. Angry, upset, flustered and hungry, neither of us spoke to each other till the following morning.

While we were pouring over the newspapers with our morning tea, Mum nudged me slightly and said, 'Mere naal kal bahut buri hoi.' I reached the tree and could not see the car. I panicked and started checking each car in the parking lot but could not see you anywhere. Then I approached a young man thinking I would borrow his phone to call you. The boy was very kind, but I could not remember your mobile number! The boy offered to look for your car but I could not remember your car's registration number either. All I could tell him was that your car was silver in colour! Then the boy suggested that I call someone else at home to get my number, but I could not recall the mobile numbers of anyone at all. I was scared but I did not want to return home without you. Finally I strung the numbers together and was able to call your Bhabi who confirmed your number. This is how I was able to eventually find you last night in that pitch-dark car park.'

Of course I was upset at Mum for not taking her mobile with her the previous night. However just hearing her out and understanding her concern for her middle-aged daughter who had both the car and a mobile melted my heart. Her only fault was that she has turned forgetful. She forgot her mobile and then in panic she forgot the mobile numbers, and then the car number, and then the make of the car.

Do we ever stop to think that we are all getting there; not the car park, but old age. We are all sliding down the same chute to the good old age where we are all going to loose our marbles, in various compositions and at a different speed perhaps, but it is all 'dust to dust' in the end. Our kids are only going to do to us what we do to our parents. Remember, they are watching, absorbing, even if they are not saying a word. The instinct to protect a toddler son exercising his legs in the middle of the afternoon on the streets or the old mother lost in the car park at night must remain the same.

Not long ago I remember meeting my co-speakers in Indian Institute of Science Education and Research, also called IISER in Bhopal, where I had gone to present my first TEDx talk on incest abuse. One of the speakers Anil Menon shared a little anecdote about his own elderly mother, whose lifelong dream about wearing sleeveless blouse remains unfulfilled. Another co-speaker wove this story beautifully in his talk around 'what would people say'. I was able to link it with my own mother a couple of years later.

Latest summer fashion brought in a lovely replacement for the traditional Punjabi suit women wear called salwar-kameez (bottom and top). Women starting wearing plazzo (of loose cotton pyjama) with kurta (a loose long cotton top). Someone who sweats like a pig, I personally am in favour of anything light and breezy. Somehow, this new trend caught Mum's eye too, but being a traditionalist, she did not have the courage to break the mould. Given that Mum generally sticks to the old rules, I was not interested in buying something she would not wear.

By the by, as with other things in life, Mum started making observations about everyone wearing readymade kurtas with plazzos, wondering out aloud how comfortable they might be in the hot and humid summer. Since she had been doing so for a few weeks, I devised a plan to get her to try this look for herself. However, I knew that if I offered outright to buy plazzo suits then the traditionalist in her would freeze.

So on the pretext of taking her out for a film, I took her to a boutique in the mall and started picking out some loose long tops or kurtas. I nudged her to try some. She blushed but grabbed the kurtas and tried them all. Once she was happy with her kurtas, I suggested that instead of wearing them with the traditional heavy salwar, perhaps she could try a couple of plazzos too. At first she protested, but when even the salesgirl suggested that she try them at least, Mum gave in and went to the try room with a handful of matching plazzos. Trust me if I say she was like a little girl in a candy store. She tried all combinations and permutations of plazzo-kurta sets and finally settled for three sets. They were lovely refreshing summer colours, some with lace and some with embroidery. I was super happy for Mum.

As I paid for them, I asked Mum if she would wear one the very next day. She went quiet. I asked her again and then she mumbled, 'on your birthday'. I knew it was not really going to happen. With money I could buy the plazzo-kurta sets for her, but from where can I buy some courage for her to wear what she wants, without thinking about 'What people might say?'

She was clocking 73 that day, a wife who had laid out her life for her groom, a mother who lived every life for her children, a grandmother who spoilt her grandkids rotten, and yet, where is her share of being a woman? Just a woman! When would she get to live the life she wants, even if it is for a few stolen moments? How many sons and daughters-in-law stand up for their matriarchs and say, 'Go on, we are there for you.' Grandkids complain about their grandparents not being chic, but how often do they spend time making them 'hip and happening'? When would the husbands say to their wives, 'Jaa Simran jaa, jee le apni zindagi'?[392]

Regardless of how unpredictable life can be, it can't be any more unpredictable than our very own Mother Darling. There was this day when I would not have climbed out of bed at all, had it not been for the fact that I was to honour my commitment of presenting a research paper in Ludhiana at Khalsa College for Women, Ludhiana for an international seminar on ethics. Led by a serene and progressive principal, Dr. Mukti Gill and her dedicated faculty, the college is housed in a beautiful 100-year- old building since the days of The Raj. The college is a perfect amalgamation of old and new, both in the building itself and in the character building of its students. And then, of course, my favourite Chaar Yaar was visiting Chandigarh for a concert in the evening. First, I could not miss; second, I did not want to miss; if you know what I mean.

The Faqiri Quartet 'Chaar Yaar', as the name suggests, comprises four musicians – namely, the elderly composer, vocalist and poet Madan Gopal Singh; the ace guitarist, banjo and oud player Deepak Castelino; the young and soulful sarod

---

[392] ਜਾ ਸਿਮਰਨ ਜਾ, ਜੀ ਲੈ ਆਪਣੀ ਜ਼ਿੰਦਗੀ (An extremely popular Hindi film's dialogue, 'Go Simran Go, live your life the way you want to.')

player Pritam Ghosal and a highly regarded multiple percussionist Amjad Khan. Chaar Yaar has traversed the path of Sufi texts dating back to the 12th-13th century, beginning with Baba Farid and Rumi and ending with Khwaja Ghulam Farid of the late 19th century. They have also experimented by incorporating into their music poetry as diverse as that of Brecht, Lorca, Tagore, Puran Singh, Hikmet, Hamzatov, Faiz and Nagarjun, creating musical bridges across cultures. Now imagine an indigenous Baramaah in Punjabi, for example, sung with Simon and Garfunkel's canticle 'Scarborough Fair' or John Lennon's 'Imagine' as 'Socho Zara' or Beatles 'Because' with Iqbal's 'Ye Gumbad-e-Mināi'. You get the picture.

It is not very often that yours truly gets reduced to tears, something Chaar Yaar manages to do each time. In years I have not been able to establish what pulls at my heartstrings when Chaar Yaar perform on the stage; is it their style of music, their choice of pieces, or have they mastered the art of serendipity to connect with the soul of their audience. Guess I would never know. To be honest, I don't even want to find out. I just don't want this magic to end.

Anyway, on my way back from Ludhiana I called up Mother Darling to know if she would like to join me for the Faqiri Quartet in the evening. Mum tossed the idea over a few seconds, hummed and hawwed a little, and then agreed. Traffic enroute delayed me and consequently, we were running late. As soon as I touched the city, I picked up Mum and we dashed towards the concert venue. Given my Mother Darling's tendency to take on any 'roop'[393] at the drop of a hat, I kept mulling over how to encourage Mum to be at her 'best'

---

[393] ਰੂਪ (Avtaar).

behaviour during the evening. Finally, I found a little window while we were waiting for lights to turn green at the Aroma traffic lights. I threw a flying kiss towards Mum and presented my request as gently as I could, 'Mumma, othe na tussi Munni di Ma nahi bann jaana. Othe tussi Supreet di Mumma howoge. Thorra jeha khayaal rakh lena mera.'[394]

I could see her raising her brow in the twinkling traffic lights. That's it. 'You idiot! She is going to walk out of the car right now.' I feared. However, much to my surprise, she plucked my overweight cheek and said, 'Tu chintaa hee nahi ker. Main kuchh nahin kehndi. Main te munh utte ungal rakh ke baithi rehna.'[395]

By the time we reached the auditorium, the concert had already started and soft melody was wafting through the partially open doors. We literally pussyfooted our way to a couple of vacant seats in the aisle to ensure we do not disturb anyone. With every string being pulled on stage, an ounce of stress was finding its way out of the body. Every now and then I would notice Mum tapping her fingers to the beats or lip syncing Bulle Shah. All good things eventually have to come to an end, so did the concert. Everyone rushed to meet the musicians. Mum and I waited for our turn as I wanted to introduce Mum to the Quartet.

Madan ji greeted Mum ever so affectionately, which encouraged Mum to say, 'Parmatma aisa Veer sab nu deve.'[396]

---

[394] Mumma, ਉੱਥੇ ਨਾ ਤੁਸੀ ਮੁੰਨੀ ਦੀ ਮਾਂ ਨਹੀਂ ਬਣ ਜਾਣਾ.. ਉੱਥੇ ਤੁਸੀ Supreet ਦੀ Mumma ਹੋਵੋਗੇ. ਥੋੜਾ ਜੇਹਾ ਖਿਆਲ ਰੱਖ ਲੈਣਾ ਮੇਰਾ (Mum just making a suggestion that you don't turn into your little one's mother there. At the venue you shall be Supreet's Mum. So let's keep the visit a little dignified.)

[395] ਤੂੰ ਚਿੰਤਾ ਹੀ ਨਹੀਂ ਕਰ.. ਮੈਂ ਕੁਛ ਨਹੀਂ ਕਹਿੰਦੀ.. ਮੈਂ ਤੇ ਮੂੰਹ ਉੱਤੇ ਉਂਗਲ ਰੱਖ ਕੇ ਬੈਠੀ ਰਹਿਣਾ! (Don't you worry at all. I promise I won't say anything untoward. In fact, I would sit there with a finger on my lips!)

[396] ਪ੍ਰਮਾਤਮਾ ਐਸਾ ਵੀਰ ਸਭ ਨੂੰ ਦੇਵੇ. (May God bless everyone with a brother like you.)

Mother Darling was really behaving herself and I heaved a sigh of relief. Amjad ji had gone out to catch a breather. While pack-up was in order, Deepak ji also greeted Mum respectfully and declared how he knows Mum from FB. My face dropped as Mum was not aware that I was writing about her antics on FB. Since the cat had been let out of the bag, I just hoped that Mum's questionable hearing would have probably saved the day for me.

Pritam Ji was already in the car when we left the hall. However, he promptly came out to greet Mum and touched her feet. Mum blessed him dutifully and just when I thought I could let my guards down, I overheard Mum ask Pritam ji, 'Aap jitna achha sarod bajaate hain, aap ka kurta uss se bhi achha hai. Kehan se embroidery karwai aap ne?'[397] I just closed my eyes and hoped to disappear in thin air, when I heard Pritam ji respond ever so charmingly, 'Yeh ji meri sasuraal waale mujhe de dete hain. Kehte hain ki stage per ache kapre pehanna karo'[398] With eyes still tightly shut, I broke out in a smile as wide as my mouth could manage, while shaking my head in sheer disbelief, or was it relief or affection for the two people engaged in this conversation?

Allow me to share how Chaar Yaar grew on me and my mother. Years ago Madan ji got to know that I love what is written about brothers in 'Waris Shah di Heer'. Since I missed the concert in Delhi, Madan ji recorded that particular segment and emailed it across to me. Can you imagine how special he

---

[397] ਆਪ ਜਿਤਨਾ ਅੱਛਾ ਸਰੋਦ ਬਜਾਤੇ ਹੈਂ, ਉਸ ਸੇ ਅੱਛਾ ਆਪ ਕਾ ਕੁੜਤਾ ਹੈ. ਕਹਾਂ ਸੇ embroidery ਕਾਰਵਾਈ ਆਪ ਨੇ? (You play sarod beautifully, but your kurta is even better! Where do you get the embroidery done?)

[398] ਯੇਹ ਜੀ ਮੇਰੀ ਸਸੁਰਾਲ ਵਾਲੇ ਮੁਝੇ ਦੇ ਦਿਤੇ ਹੈਂ, ਕਹਿਤੇ ਹੈਂ stage ਪਰ ਅੱਛੇ ਕੱਪੜੇ ਪਹਿਨਾ ਕਰੋ (Aah the kurta? These are actually gifted by my in-laws. They insist that I wear good clothes while performing on stage.)

made me feel with one gesture? He reaffirmed my belief in relationships by making that one thoughtful gesture. The world indeed goes around because of love, care and concern beating inside that human breast.

Months earlier I was part of the post-concert dinner with Chaar Yaar. It was the kind of weather when days are bright and sunny while nights are cold. So you get the picture that I was sitting in the lawns over the dinner table, shivering in my cotton dress without a drape around my shoulders to keep myself from the chill. Pritam ji noticed that and immediately gave me the phulkari that had been gifted to the Faqiri Quartet just minutes ago by the organisers. May Chaar Yaar continue to spread love and warmth through their music for decades to come. May God give me strength to bring more happiness to my mother, one breath at a time.

ਮਾਂ

ਮਾਂ
ਮਾਂ ਬੋਲੀ ਵੀ, ਮਾਂ ਦੇਸ ਵੀ ਹੈ
ਮਾਂ ਆਪਣੇ ਦੇਸ ਦਾ ਵੇਸ ਵੀ ਹੈ

ਮਾਂ ਧਰਮ
ਧਰਮ ਤੋਂ ਪਾਰ ਵੀ ਹੈ
ਇਕਰਾਰ ਲਈ
ਇਨਕਾਰ ਵੀ ਹੈ
ਛਾਂ ਗੁੜ੍ਹੀ ਜਗਾ ਦੀ ਖ਼ੈਰ ਵੀ ਹੈ
ਮਾਂ ਤੱਤੀ ਤਲਖ਼ ਦੁਪਿਹਰ ਵੀ ਹੈ

ਇਸ ਕਰਾਮਾਤ ਨੂੰ ਸਮਝ ਜ਼ਰਾ
ਮਾਂ ਹਾਜ਼ਰ ਨਾਜ਼ਰ ਆਪ ਖੁਦਾ

- ਹਰਿਭਜਨ ਸਿੰਘ

Politically Incorrect Drama Queen

All chuffed from her grandson's academic achievement, I found Mother Darling gloating to her friend, 'Not just my grandson, but my son was also a great achiever in school. Aman has inherited his father's genes of intelligence.' Then pointing towards me Mum fired, 'She used to be like me in maths!' I just stood there in utter amazement at this 'matter of fact' mother of mine.

Later on when we were alone in the car, I quietly said, 'Mother do you remember that I had been awarded state scholarship three times?' Suddenly her face lit up. 'Really? Naaah, I don't. But you never brought anything home! Why did you not claim it?' I explained, 'Mum as per academic record I had been selected for the scholarship, but it was never awarded to me as Dad's income was way higher than their financial criteria cut-off.' I thought this would satisfy her somehow that I was not as academically challenged as she continues to believe. Alas, that was not to be! Mother quipped in chaste Punjabi, 'What a nut-case you are. You should have ticked the SC/ST (scheduled caste/scheduled tribe) column when you filled your forms. You would have been awarded the scholarship in a jiffy!'

Disclaimer: I am not responsible for my mother's politically incorrect, even if factually correct assessment of the academic policies of various Indian governments.

There really is no end to Mum's politically incorrect viewpoints. A few months ago also while going through the morning papers and while sipping her tea, mother quipped, 'Addhi zindagi nikal gayi. Kisae kamm da nahin niklaya. Aur jo iss de haal ne, kissi syaane ne apni kuri vi nahi deni is nu. Dass, Ma di te joon kharaab ker ditti na.'[399] Curiosity killed the CAT so I enquired whom was she referring to in her monologue. Sliding her reading glasses down her nose Mum shot back. 'Ekko te hai ... Rahul Gandhi.'[400]

If this is not enough, as I dutifully picked up my cup of tea one morning, Mum went back to reading the newspapers. Suddenly she let out a chuckle, which did not seem to end. Highly intrigued, I eventually asked what was she reading, even though I was close to asking what had she added to the tea as her new experiment, which had possibly contributed to her bout of happiness first thing in the morning. 'Khabraan sirf tu hee nahi parrdi, main vi Desh di khabar rakhdi haan. Eh sunn. Himachal sarkaar ne Nagaland sarkaar nu arz keeti ke tussi saade baandar apne janglaan wich rakh layo.'[401]

Given that monkeys are a real menace indeed in our beloved Himachal, I wondered what was there to laugh about such a

---

[399] ਅੱਧੀ ਜ਼ਿੰਦਗੀ ਨਿਕਲ ਗਈ. ਕਿਸੇ ਕੰਮ ਦਾ ਨਹੀਂ ਨਿਕਲਿਆ. ਔਰ ਜੋ ਇੱਸ ਦੇ ਹਾਲ ਨੇ ਕਿਸੇ ਸਿਆਾਣੇ ਨੇ ਆਪਣੀ ਧੀ ਨਹੀਂ ਦੇਣੀ ਇੱਸ ਨੂੰ. ਦੱਸ ਮਾਂ ਦੀ ਤੇ ਜੂਨ ਖ਼ਰਾਬ ਕਰ ਦਿੱਤੀ ਨਾ! *(Reached middle age but he has turned out to be good for nothing. And looking at him, no sensible person is going to give his daughter in marriage to him either. In fact, he must have messed up his mother's life.)*
[400] ਇੱਕੋ ਤੇ ਹੈ - ਰਾਹੁਲ ਗਾਂਧੀ (There is only one – Rahul Gandhi.)
[401] ਖ਼ਬਰਾਂ ਸਿਰਫ ਤੂੰ ਹੀ ਨਹੀਂ ਪੜ੍ਹਦੀ, ਮੈਂ ਵੀ ਦੇਸ਼ ਦੀ ਖ਼ਬਰ ਰੱਖਦੀ ਹਾਂ. ਇਹ ਸੁਣ, ਹਿਮਾਚਲ ਸਰਕਾਰ ਨੇ ਨਾਗਾਲੈਂਡ ਸਰਕਾਰ ਨੂੰ ਅਰਜ਼ ਕੀਤੀ ਕੇ ਤੁਸੀ ਸਾਡੇ ਬਾਂਦਰ ਆਪਣੇ ਜੰਗਲਾਂ ਵਿੱਚ ਰੱਖ ਲਿਯੋ *(You are not the only one who reads news. Listen to this, Himachal government sought permission from Nagaland government to send their monkeys to be released in their forests.)*

sensible request as North-East has the lush jungles to let the monkeys monkey around there. As Mum went on, it turned out to be not a sensible exchange between the two states after all. Mum proceeded while almost snorting over her tea, 'Nagaland ne naah ker ditti. Kehnde Himachal ne kehra saade haathi rakhe si jadd assi kuch der pehlaan ohna nu arz keeti si!!'[402] She went on to add, 'Khotte ikathhe hoye saare!'[403]

What Queen's English could not achieve in 300 words, Mother Superior did in one line of good old Punjabi. The other morning bent over the newspapers, Mum is summarising the news that she is reading. 'Dass, agg lagg gayi. Ik banda gaddi charr gaya te teen haspataal di pheri layi pahunch gaye.'[404] I choked on my tea! Punjabi language and mothers are indeed a deadly combination. Mother was reading out the dramatic headlines from the newspapers, which unfortunately believe in grabbing eyeballs by sensationalising news rather than giving factual information.

One winter afternoon, my brother sent a message on our 'family WhatsApp Group', around midday. It was an invite to attend a 'sight and sound show' the same evening, which was dedicated to the life and times of a 'Warrior Saint' from Sikh history. It was an invite-only show and he had the passes for all of us. The only condition my brother laid down was that since the passes asked everyone to be seated by 5.45 pm for 6.15 pm start, he insisted that everyone must be ready to leave home by 5.30 pm. Mum was quick to put her shoes on. Everyone

---

[402] ਨਾਗਾਲੈਂਡ ਨੇ ਨਾਂਹ ਕਰ ਦਿੱਤੀ! ਕਹਿੰਦੇ ਹਿਮਾਚਲ ਨੇ ਕੇਹੜਾ ਸਾਡੇ ਹਾਥੀ ਰਾਖੇ ਸੀ ਜਦੋਂ ਅੱਸੀ ਕੁਝ ਦੇਰ ਪਹਿਲਾਂ ਓਹਨਾ ਨੂੰ ਅਰਜ਼ ਕੀਤੀ ਸੀ? (Nagaland refused saying why should they entertain their request while Himachal had refused Nagaland's request in the past to host their elephants!)
[403] ਖੋਤੇ ਇਕੱਠੇ ਹੋਏ ਸਾਰੇ (Donkeys – the whole lot of them!)
[404] ਦੱਸ, ਅੱਗ ਲੱਗ ਗਈ. ਇੱਕ ਬੰਦਾ ਗੱਡੀ ਚੜ੍ਹ ਗਿਆ ਤੇ ਤਿੰਨ ਹਸਪਤਾਲ ਦੀ ਫੇਰੀ ਲਈ ਪਹੁੰਚ ਗਏ (Aaah – can't believe what is happening all around! One person has taken flight and three have gone on a round of the hospital.)

chimed in unison, sacrificed their evening coffee/snacks and left home in time for a 75-minute show to be held in the open-air makeshift auditorium.

When we reached the venue, we went through the security checks since the chief guest was none else but H.E. Governor of Punjab. Three generations of our family and two of our friends were comfortably seated, eagerly waiting for the show to begin. One does not realise how time flies when one is having fun with friends, provided you are neither hungry, nor cold! On the contrary, the evening was turning out to be chillier than expected and there was neither a morsel to eat, nor a food hawker in sight.

Finally, a gentleman took the mike to introduce the organisation which had organised this 'sight and sound' show, and promptly forgot that introductions are sweet only when in short. Not only did he list all of their projects since inception a couple of decades ago, he repeated them two to three times each to drill home the point. If he was not enough, then there were two other gentlemen who spoke at various lengths about their achievements. Cold had started biting our feet, noses had started running by now amidst the growling bellies. Alas, there was no sign of the show beginning at all. I asked Mum if she was carrying anything to eat and she dug into her handbag and produced a polo tube. We promptly partook it to kill the hunger pangs. We thought they would begin as the clock was hitting 7 pm, but hold on, the team started honouring the sponsors and contributors which again went on for a while. Fortunately for us, a hawker brought a handful of popcorn which Mum immediately purchased for her brood.

We consoled ourselves thinking this might be the end of our misery but then they announced another gentleman to come up on stage to propose a 'Vote of Thanks'. We were laughing silly by now because he was thanking everyone by reading anglicised Punjabi, for a show which had not even begun yet! Surely there could not have been anything more to say after this customary last act, preponed unaccustomisingly. Just as we sunk back into our chairs thinking the show would finally begin, lo and behold, they requested Governor Sa'ab to address the august audience, even though his speech was not in the schedule! Our mother finally lost patience and let out a loud gasp, 'Eh taan nahin hatt.de ajj.'[405]

Work around incest abuse had picked up pace and I must admit that much against my own will, I had started living an erratic life. Once I woke up a little late and though I could have beaten the sunrise to go for my morning walk, I chose to listen to my creaking bones and opted to give it a miss. Instead, to make the most of the time available, I switched on my laptop and started working. Mum pussy footed around me and then gently asked if I wanted the newspapers with my tea. When I responded in the negative, she did not shove them under my nose or walk away with my mobile or slam my laptop shut. She let me be; in fact, she let me get on with my work for the entire day. Mum can be considerate like that actually.

As cows came roaming home with the sun going down, Mum quietly crawled in and spread herself generously on my bed. I did not take my eyes off the screen but I could figure out she was sorting her summer clothes since she was wearing her night shirt with an old salwar! Half reclined, Mum gently

---

[405] ਇਹ ਤਾਂ ਨਹੀਂ ਹੱਟਦੇ ਅੱਜ (Oh these people are incorrigible!)

whispered, 'Munni … O meri Munni'[406]. I looked up slowly and she continued, 'Munni ki kardi payi saver di?'[407] I informed Mum that I was working flat out and not likely to be free for a few hours still.

'Oh meri Munni … Ajj teri Ma bahut thakk gayi.'[408] Mum said and crashed on to the bed. Then with a twinkle in her eyes she raised her head a little and said, 'Chal pher petrol paa uth ke, nahin taan ethhe hee gaddi khari hai teri Mummy dee! Hunn dekh lae ki karna hai tu.'[409] Has she been watching too many TV serials lately? All Mum wanted was a cup of tea!

Mum went on to be a little more specific, 'Munni, chal cha pila vadhiya jee',[410] without specifying what precisely she means by 'vadhiya'[411] at this precise moment of time. I took a risk and presented a nicely laid out tray of tea for Mum. She gulped it down in no time and said, 'Munni, enni ku cha naal te Maa de dand vi gille nahin hoye. Horr banaa ke lya!'[412] How much tea can a person drink? A gallon? May be I should start a 'tea-on-demand' business for all the mothers around – Might as well make some money too.

So you think you can trust your mother? Think again! Mum had been quietly noticing me running around from one end of the house to another as I was finally getting ready to leave home on Saturday afternoon, after a super-hectic week

---

406 ਮੁੰਨੀ ... ਉਹ ਮੇਰੀ ਮੁੰਨੀ (My little one … O my little one!)

407 ਮੁੰਨੀ ਕੀ ਕਰਦੀ ਪਈ ਸਵੇਰ ਦੀ? (What have you been up to since morning?)

408 ਉਹ ਮੇਰੀ ਮੁੰਨੀ ... ਅੱਜ ਤੇਰੀ ਮਾਂ ਬਹੁਤ ਥੱਕ ਗਈ *(Your mother is too tired today.)*

409 ਚਾਲ ਫੇਰ ਪੈਟਰੋਲ ਪਾ ਉੱਠ ਕੇ, ਨਹੀਂ ਤਾਂ ਇਥੇ ਹੀ ਗੱਡੀ ਖਾਰੀ ਹੈ ਤੇਰੀ Mumma ਦੀ! ਹੁਣ ਦੇਖ ਲੈ ਕੀ ਕਰਨਾ ਹੈ ਤੂੰ! (Pep me up with a cuppa or else your Mumma is just going to crash here. Now you decide what do want to do.)

410 ਮੁੰਨੀ ਚੱਲ ਚਾਹ ਪਿਲਾ ਵਧੀਆ ਜੀ (Make a nice cup of tea for me.)

411 ਵਧੀਆ *(Nice).*

412 ਮੁੰਨੀ ਇੰਨੀ ਕੁ ਚਾਹ ਨਾਲ ਤੇ ਮਾਂ ਦੇ ਦੰਦ ਵੀ ਗਿੱਲੇ ਨਹੀਂ ਹੋਏ. ਹੋਰ ਬਣਾ ਕੇ ਲਿਆ *(That was too small a cuppa. Go make another one!)*

purely devoted to assessing applications and holding individual/panel interviews per applicant for our eduCATe Scholar project. Having spent approximately 6 hours to connect the loose ends for every new scholar, making calls to open doors for some, helping others choose the most appropriate career path based on the information they shared during the individual interviews, I thought I had earned my own little break.

Since I was not really done with the eduCATe work as such, I left all the loose paperwork, case scribbles, diaries and registers together with my laptop on charge. Just to make sure no one 'tidies-up' my work, I approached my Mother Darling, who was sitting comfortably, read cross legged, on the comfiest of sofas around. As I slung my handbag across my shoulders, I threw a kiss in Mum's direction and made a polite request, 'Mum please dekh lena ke koi mere kaagaz na cherre. Mera kamm ajje mukkya nahin.'[413] Mum threw a flying kiss back at me with a nod of her well coifed head. Then as if prompted as an afterthought, much against known wisdom, I added, 'Te tussi vi na chherreyo!'[414] Mum gave me a wicked smile and with a toss of her same well coifed head she added, 'Tu chal taan sayi … dekhdi ja ki bann.da!!!'[415] Who could leave the house without bending down to kiss those eyes twinkling with devilish charm?

Yet, the moment you hear your Mother Darling say, 'Tera berra tarr je'[416], trust me, you run, you disappear. Forget any body contact, you avoid all possible eye contact with your Mother Superior and leave home before anyone can say boo to

---

[413] Mumma please ਦੇਖ ਲੈਣਾ ਕੇ ਕੋਈ ਮੇਰੇ ਕਾਗਜ਼ ਨਾ ਛੇੜੇ.. ਮੇਰਾ ਕੰਮ ਅੱਜੇ ਮੁੱਕਿਆ ਨਹੀਂ.. (Mum please make sure that no one moves my stuff. I am not done yet with it yet.)

[414] ਤੇ ਤੁਸੀ ਵੀ ਨਾ ਛੇੜੇਓ (And this applies to you too).

[415] ਤੂ ਚੱਲ ਤਾਂ ਸਹੀ … ਦੇਖਦੀ ਜਾ ਕੀ ਬਣਦਾ!! (Just you wait and watch … see what happens!)

[416] ਤੇਰਾ ਬੇੜਾ ਤਾਰ ਜੇ! *(May God bless you!)*

a goose. Yupp. Such is life dearies. No rest for the old and.. errr … the wicked!

If you think that time or distance helps change things? Think yet again! Fresh from the festive holidays, I took it easy while getting ready for work this morning in a simple pair of black jeans and a crinkly cotton white shirt. As I sat down to have my glass of spiced milk before heading out, Mother Darling sat down to have her own breakfast too. While I was rushing about packing stuff, Mum was eyeing me, without my knowledge or permission.

As I was about to step out, Mum said quietly, 'Ajj na tu oho jehi laggdi hain.'[417] That kind of stopped me in my tracks. Keho jehi? [418] Mother Superior finally unleashed herself with full force, 'Oho.. o jihnaa nu Diwali vandi di hai lifaafeyaan vich pa ke!'[419] Do I still need any more evidence that I was adopted, or perhaps just picked up from the streets to be sheltered?!!

Read on for more evidence. When I returned home after a fortnight down south of India, Mother Darling greeted me at the main gate itself. When I expected her to give me one tight hug and slobber my face with a few kisses, she gave me a clip around the ear instead, 'Paal-Poas ke bheji si … .'[420] I could not believe it! Is this how mothers are supposed to greet their long-lost kids?

Mum took it upon herself to ensure I put back 5 grams I had lost during the trip with a constant supply of Mittha

---

[417] ਅੱਜ ਨਾ ਤੂੰ ਓਹੋ ਜਿਹੀ ਲੱਗਦੀ ਹੈਂ (Today you look like those kind of people.)

[418] ਕਿਹੋ ਜਿਹੀ? *(What kind?)*

[419] ਓਹੋ ..ਓ ਜਿਨ੍ਹਾਂ ਨੂੰ ਦੀਵਾਲੀ ਵੰਡੀ ਜਾਂਦੀ ਹੈ, ਲਿਫਾਫਿਆਂ ਵਿਚ ਪਾ ਕੇ! (Those, the ones who come after Diwali, looking for handouts and leftovers!)

[420] ਪਾਲ-ਪੋਸ ਕੇ ਭੇਜੀ ਸੀ *(I had sent you in good health.)*

Parantha and Halwa[421], Fruit Smoothies. Every couple of days she would come towards me wearing her near-vision glasses, pull the curtains away and conduct a close inspection of my sun burnt, badly freckled face by turning it in all possible directions. Then she would rattle a whole bunch of observations, followed by a set of instructions: 'Aah teriyaan gallhaan te kuch theek ho gayiyaan ne per teri chunjjh da te ajje vi bura haal hai. Aah thoddi vi kharaab hoyi payi hai. Do kaale nishaan eddhar vi ne. Laggi ghumman di hoyi!'[422]

Finally, she would stand up right towering above me, take off her glasses and instruct me with her hands on her hips, 'Main facepack vich ajj aloe vera zyaada pa deaangi. Saver shaam laana hai. Aah naale baahwaan utte vi laa layin. Roz anaar da juice pee ikk maheena je munh theek karna hai. Naale sunscreen do-do ghante baad lagaa. Samajh aayi?'[423] All had been going pretty well. I thought that perhaps my absence had made my Mother Superior less acerbic and more loving for her only daughter. Alas! I made some assumptions too soon.

A couple of Mum's friends came over for high tea and I could overhear bits of their conversation from the adjoining room: 'Haanji Mrs Chopra, Rabb ne taan iss vari tarsaa hee ditta, meenh nahin paa rehaa … O ho, eh te maara hoya … Achha, Mrs Gill da beta aaya hoya hai? … Haanji haanji,

---

[421] ਮਿੱਠਾ ਪਰਾਂਠਾ, ਹਲਵਾ *(Sweet Indian bread and halva; an Indian sweet made with semolina and clarified butter with nuts).*

[422] ਆਹ ਤੇਰੀਆਂ ਗੱਲ੍ਹਾਂ ਤੇ ਕੁਝ ਠੀਕ ਹੋ ਗਈਆਂ ਨੇ ਪਰ ਤੇਰੀ ਚੁੰਜ ਦਾ ਤੇ ਅੱਜੇ ਵੀ ਬੁਰਾ ਹਾਲ ਹੈ. ਆਹ ਠੋਡੀ ਵੀ ਖ਼ਰਾਬ ਹੋਈ ਪਈ ਹੈ. ਦੋ ਕਾਲੇ ਨਿਸ਼ਾਨ ਇੱਧਰ ਵੀ ਨੇ.. ਲੱਗੀ ਘੁੰਮਣ ਦੀ ਹੋਈ! *(Your cheeks look better but your beak still looks questionable. Your chin is also pretty bad. There are two marks over there also.. So much for your passion to travel.)*

[423] ਮੈਂ facepack ਵਿੱਚ ਅੱਜ aloe vera ਜ਼ਿਆਦਾ ਪਾ ਦੇਵਾਂਗੀ. ਸੇਵਰ-ਸ਼ਾਮ ਲੈਣਾ ਹੈ. ਆਹ ਨਾਲੇ ਬਾਹਵਾਂ ਉੱਤੇ ਵੀ ਲਾ ਲਈਂ. ਰੋਜ਼ ਅਨਾਰ ਦਾ juice ਪੀ ਇੱਕ ਮਹੀਨਾ ਜੇ ਮੂੰਹ ਠੀਕ ਕਰਨਾ ਹੈ. ਨਾਲੇ sunscreen 2-2 ਘੰਟੇ ਬਾਅਦ ਲਗਾ. ਸਮਝ ਆਈ? *(I will add more aloe vera to the facepack today. Apply it every morning and evening. Don't forget to apply it on your arms also. Drink pomegranate juice everyday for a month. Also apply sunscreen every 2 hours. Do you understand?)*

meri Madraasan vi aa gayi jee ... Munh kaala karwaa ke murr aayi hai'. [424] Mothers – can't take them anywhere!

Change in weather made me ill despite the extra calories I was eating. I had been under the weather since a couple of days but since 'telling Mum' would get her into a 'super-nuskha'[425] mode, I kept most of the pain away from her. However, since Mum was not aware of the extent of the tummy ache, like a good mother she kept on pestering me to get up and have a bath, which, of course, was out of question given the state I was in. The entire day I kept nodding off in pain and whenever I would have a little control over things, I would check my phone to see if there is any news of a certain Baba being sentenced for sexual offences or listen to some TED Talk using my tiny ear phones. As expected, Mum saw it as an act of sheer defiance, unacceptable at my age!

As the hours ticked away, Mum's patience wore off too. Finally in the evening I felt kind of on top of the pain and thought of checking my phone for the latest news before I headed towards my hamaam. Upon seeing me stir into action from the deep slumber, Mum got up from her seat and immediately came towards me. Expecting some adverse action on account of skipping my shower I prepared myself for an earful, but no, Mum was all concerned about my health. She put her hand gently on my head and asked, 'Saare din di dekhdi payi meri Munni bed ton nahin uthhi. Meri Munni,

---

[424] ਹਾਂਜੀ Mrs Chopra, ਰੱਬ ਨੇ ਤਾਂ ਇੱਸ ਵਰੀ ਤਰਸਾ ਹੀ ਦਿੱਤਾ, ਮੀਂਹ ਨਹੀਂ ਪਾ ਰਿਹਾ ... ਓ ਹੋ, ਇਹ ਤੇ ਮਾੜਾ ਹੋਇਆ ... ਅੱਛਾ Mrs. Gill ਦਾ ਬੇਟਾ ਆਇਆ ਹੋਇਆ ਹੈ? ...ਹਾਂਜੀ ਹਾਂਜੀ, ਮੇਰੀ ਮਦਰਾਸਨ ਵੀ ਆ ਗਈ ਜੀ ... ਮੂੰਹ ਕਾਲਾ ਕਰਵਾ ਕੇ ਮੁੜ ਆਈ ਹੈ! *(Yes Mrs Chopra. God has been very unkind this monsoon. There have hardly been any rains.... That's sad.. Oh really? Mrs Gill's son is over? ...Yes yes, my fairlady has also come from her Madras trip with a blackened face!)*

[425] Super ਨੁਸਖਾ (A concocted solution to deal with any kind of problem, medical or otherwise).

hunn kiddan?'[426] Feeling overwhelmed by her sudden burst of concern, I snuggled up to her and assured her that all was good. With one hand still caressing my hair, Mum said, 'Munni apna phone dikhaayin zara?'[427] Her request made me smile. Unsure of what she was up to, I asked her what she wanted to look at. She replied indulgently, 'Maa teri main, pehlaan phone dikha pher dassdi haan.'[428]

Wondering if she wanted to learn a new feature on the mobile or perhaps she wanted to compare her mobile's model to mine, I asked her lovingly to tell me what she wanted to learn and I would explain. Mother Darling replied with a kiss on my forehead, 'Tu phone de main pher dassdi haan.'[429] Curious to know what Mum wanted to read/see/learn, I handed over my phone to her. I never learn, do I?!!! Next thing I know is that Mother Superior's hand has slipped from my forehead towards my ear in one swift action. Tweaking it a little she thundered as much as her 5' frame would permit, 'Banda bann ke nahaa ke aa pehlaan. Sharam ker kuch, saver di litee jaandi payi hain!'[430]

It is not that Mum does not love me. I think she does but she surely has strange ways of getting the message across. The other day, since I went to sleep early, I woke up early too. With a view of taking advantage of the peace and quiet in the house, I thought I would catch up on some pending work. I had to finalise a proposal and look through the bank stuff for Can & Will also as our eduCATe Scholars would be finishing their

---

[426] ਸਾਰੇ ਦਿਨ ਦੀ ਦੇਖਦੀ ਪਈ, ਮੇਰੀ ਮੁੰਨੀ bed ਤੋਂ ਨਹੀਂ ਉੱਠੀ … ਮੇਰੀ ਮੁੰਨੀ ਹੁਣ ਕਿੱਦਾਂ? (Been watching you since morning and you have not got up from bed… how is my little one feeling now?)

[427] ਮੁੰਨੀ ਆਪਣਾ ਫੋਨ ਦੇਈ ਜ਼ਰਾ (Kid can you give me your phone please?)

[428] ਮਾਂ ਤੇਰੀ ਮੈਂ, ਪਹਿਲਾਂ ਫੋਨ ਦਿਖਾ ਫੇਰ ਦੱਸਦੀ ਹਾਂ (I am your mother! Give me your phone first, then I will tell you.)

[429] ਤੂੰ ਫੋਨ ਦੇ ਮੈਂ ਫੇਰ ਦੱਸਦੀ ਹਾਂ (I told you.. give me your phone first.)

[430] ਬੰਦਾ ਬਣ ਕੇ ਨਹਾ ਕੇ ਆ ਪਹਿਲਾਂ.. ਸ਼ਰਮ ਕਰ ਕੁਝ, ਸਵੇਰ ਦੀ ਲਿਟੀ ਜਾਂਦੀ ਪਈ ਹੈਂ! (Go have a bath first.. you have been lazing around in bed shamelessly since morning!)

semester soon and next semester payments have to be made. Just as I was making these mental calculations, Mother Darling returned from her morning walk. When Mum found me sitting up in bed, she walked up to me and gave me a tight hug. Caressing my head, she gently asked me,

Mum: Ki gall Munni, savere-savere uth gayi.[431]

Chicken: Haanji.[432]

Mum: Tabiyat theek hai? Kuch dukhda te nahin? [433]

Chicken: Nahin Mumma. Raati jaldi so gayi si, isslayi savere jaldi neend khull gayi. [434]

Mum: Good girl. Chal hunn uth gayi hain te baahar ja, walk ker ke aa. [435]

Chicken: Mumma main kamm karan laggi si, walk da time nahin hai. [436]

Her hand slipped from my head towards my neck by now: Bewakoof dekh baahar mausam kinna sohna hai. Chal ja, saer ker ke aa. [437]

Trying to shrug her hand off, I squirmed a little and said: Nahin Mumma, hunn kamm ker lein do, zaroori hai. Raati vi bina khatam keete so gayi si.[438]

---

[431] ਕੀ ਗੱਲ ਮੁੰਨੀ, ਸਵੇਰੇ-ਸਵੇਰੇ ਉੱਠ ਗਈ? (What happened, little one? You got up early today?)

[432] ਹਾਂਜੀ *(Yes.)*

[433] ਤਬੀਅਤ ਠੀਕ ਹੈ? ਕੁੱਛ ਦੁਖਦਾ ਤੇ ਨਹੀਂ? (Is your health okay? Hope no aches and pains?)

[434] ਨਹੀਂ Mumma. ਰਾਤੀ ਜਲਦੀ ਸੋ ਗਈ ਸੀ, ਇਸਲਈ ਸਵੇਰੇ ਜਲਦੀ ਨੀਂਦ ਖੁੱਲ ਗਈ (No Mumma. Slept early last night, so I woke up early this morning.)

[435] ਚੱਲ ਹੁਣ ਉੱਠ ਗਈ ਹੈਂ ਤੇ ਬਾਹਰ ਜਾ, walk ਕਰ ਕੇ ਆ (Aah I see. Since you are up early, you might as well go out for a morning walk.)

[436] Mumma ਮੈਂ ਕੰਮ ਕਰਨ ਲੱਗੀ ਸੀ, walk ਦਾ time ਨਹੀਂ ਹੈ (Mumma I am about to do some work, so don't have the time to go out for a walk.)

[437] ਬੇਵਕੂਫ਼ ਦੇਖ ਬਾਹਰ ਮੌਸਮ ਕਿੰਨਾ ਸੋਹਣਾ ਹੈ. ਚੱਲ ਜਾ, ਸੈਰ ਕਰ ਕੇ ਆ (What a moron you are! See what beautiful weather beckons you outside. Go on, go out for a walk.)

[438] ਨਹੀਂ Mumma, ਹੁਣ ਕੰਮ ਕਰ ਲੈਣ ਦੇ, ਜ਼ਰੂਰੀ ਹੈ, ਰਾਤੀ ਵੀ ਬਿਨਾ ਖਤਮ ਕੀਤੇ ਸੋ ਗਈ ਸੀ (No Mummma, honest. I have some urgent work to hand in, which I did not finish last night.)

Out of the corner of my eye I saw that the hand which I had shrugged off had curled up into a tiny fist: Hae kadar tainu ke rabb ne kinna sohna jahaan banaayea? Bahar Ja, kise chirri nu dekh, jaanwar bhajje phirde, thandi hawa baahar, koi parosi milega, kisse da haal-chaal puchh. Chal nikal baahar!'[439]

When I still dug my heels in that I really wanted to get on with my work and made movements to reach out to my laptop, Mother Superior suddenly emerged from this lovingly cuddly body standing next to my bed and thundered, 'Banda bann ke uth ja, boot pa te baahar nikal, nahin te oh khabar layungi ke tu yaad rakhengi.'[440] Dare I tempt fate! The Chicken just returned after taking pictures of the flowers from the neighbours' gardens, running away from the yapping dogs, crossing the road to avoid the raging bulls, or were they cows?!!

Same evening, as I returned home struggling with my laptop sachel, bag of Can & Will files to work from home, mobile, water bottle and a small box of pinnis made by a friend's mother, I found my own Mother Darling waiting in the verandah. Seeing me spilling over with stuff, she promptly got onto her feet to open the main door and helped me with the stuff I was carrying like a donkey! Once inside the house and having deposited all the stuff in its rightful place, I turned around to head towards the kitchen to get myself some water. However, a cute and cuddly bundle of love was blocking my way.

All of 5', I found my mother tip-toeing on her feet with her arms spread wide. Completely disarmed, I bent down a bit to

---

[439] ਹੈ ਕਦਰ ਤੇਰੂੰ ਕੇ ਰੱਬ ਨੇ ਕਿੰਨਾ ਸੋਹਣਾ ਜਹਾਨ ਬਣਾਇਆ? ਬਾਹਰ ਜਾ, ਕਿਸੇ ਚਿੜੀ ਨੂੰ ਵੇਖ, ਜਾਨਵਰ ਭੱਜੇ ਫਿਰਦੇ, ਠੰਡੀ ਹਵਾ ਬਾਹਰ, ਕੋਈ ਪੜੋਸੀ ਮਿਲੇਗਾ, ਕਿੱਸੇ ਦਾ ਹਾਲ-ਚਾਲ ਪੁੱਛ. ਚੱਲ ਨਿੱਕਲ ਬਾਹਰ! *(Don't you value this beautiful world that God has created? Go outside, spot a bird, the animals are prancing around, there is cool breeze out there, you might meet an odd neighbour. Go outside, meet people and strike some conversations. Go out and enjoy.)*
[440] ਬੰਦਾ ਬਟਨ ਕੇ ਉੱਠ ਜਾ, ਬੂਟ ਪਾ ਤੇ ਬਾਹਰ ਨਿਕਲ, ਨਹੀਂ ਤੇ ਉਹ ਖ਼ਬਰ ਲਯੂਨਗੀ ਕੇ ਤੂੰ ਯਾਦ ਰੱਖੇਂਗੀ! (You better get up, put on your walking shoes and leave the house… or I would sort you out for good!)

fall into her arms and give her one tight hug. Still embracing my frame which is half a foot longer than hers, Mum made a risky jump on her toes but finally conceded, 'Chotti jehi Ma da vi kuchh nahin. Chaallaan maardi reh jaandi hai'[441] How endearing is this now? I wonder when would she actually say to me, 'I love you' though.

There are weeks which just don't seem to end. There are nights which are too long and muggy. There are days which are way too hot and challenging. And when on a day like this you get an invite for a 'Rajmah-Chawal with boondi raita followed by kesar kulfi'[442] lunch, you would even drive out of the way for the comfort food. With tonnes on my mind, I had left home early for a couple of early meetings while Mum must have been tinkering around the house as she rests only when she is ill. After being on the road in the blistering hot sun for 3 hours I reached the home of our ever so loving and caring Chat's home. I was delighted to meet with our dear common friend, a jovial food critic, Babe, who is also part of our Rajmah-Gang.

Just as we sat down around 1 pm, I got a call from Mum and what I hear is a very affectionate tone of voice, 'Munni, tu mainu mill ke nahin gayi?'[443] Sheepishly I mumbled that I had to leave early. 'Tainu pata Mummy tainu miss kardi hai?'[444] Now this is something I was absolutely not prepared for. I expect to be told off about missing lunch, not doing this, blamed for having done that, BUT this was too much to

---

[441] ਛੋਟੀ ਜਿਹੀ ਮਾਂ ਦਾ ਵੀ ਕੁਝ ਨਹੀਂ.. ਛਾਲਾਂ ਮਾਰਦੀ ਰਹਿ ਜਾਂਦੀ ਹੈ (What use is a pint-sized mother. Even if I jump I still can't reach up to you!)

[442] ਰਾਜਮਾਂਹ-ਚਾਵਲ with ਬੂੰਦੀ ਰਾਇਤਾ followed by ਕੇਸਰ ਕੁਲਫੀ (Red kidney beans-rice, spicey yogurt followed by saffron-flavoured ice cream).

[443] ਮੁੰਨੀ ਤੂੰ ਮੈਨੂੰ ਮਿਲ ਕੇ ਨਹੀਂ ਗਈ? (Little one you did not say goodbye to me before leaving home.)

[444] ਤੈਨੂੰ ਪਤਾ Mumma ਤੈਨੂੰ miss ਕਰਦੀ ਹੈ? (Don't you realise that your Mum misses you?)

handle. This is a totally bewildered CAT not knowing which way to turn or what to expect next. As I recovered a bit and actually said, 'Haanji dasso'[445], Mum threw another googly, 'Chal pher Mummy nu ikk selfie bhej!'[446] Flabbergasted I blurted, 'Hain? Kee?'[447] The voice thundered, 'Selfie bhej Mummy nu!'[448] I meekly put the phone down and must have had this incredulous look on my face as both Babe and Chat looked on curiously while Alexa in desi-avataar evesdropped. I told them about the demand for selfie and they merrily posed. I quickly sent the selfie to my Selfie-Queen Mother so that she, who must be obeyed, is satisfied. Mission accomplished, we got down to letting our hair down, at least the ones who could afford to do so.

Babe started narrating the tales of her own mother's telephonic capabilities or the lack of it when Chat's phone rang. Chat got busy over the phone with someone. As Babe and I yapped away, suddenly Chat offered his phone to me. I looked up at him enquiringly and he said one word… just one word … MUM! Yeah, Mum's the word. Till date I am not sure if Mum called Chat to thank him for hosting the lunch or to check if I was indeed having lunch and not sending her an old selfie!

I woke up in the morning at 5, did some work, got overwhelmed by the beautiful weather and got lulled into sleep again by the mild breeze and the vocal orchestra being played by the birds. Such a lovely start to a Sunday! A couple of hours later Mother Darling woke me up with a gentle tap and sat down on my bed. A rush of warmth washed all over me; my

---

[445] ਹਾਂਜੀ ਦੱਸੋ (Yes, please tell me.)

[446] ਚੱਲ ਫੇਰ Mumma ਨੂੰ ਇੱਕ selfie ਭੇਜ! *(Go one then. Send a selfie to Mum.)*

[447] ਹੈਂ? ਕੀ? (What? What did you just say?)

[448] selfie ਭੇਜ Mumma ਨੂੰ! *(Send a selfie to Mum!)*

mommy, my lovely cuddly mommy. No matter how old you become, there really is nothing like being woken up by your mother.

Lovingly stroking my hair Mum said, 'Dekh, tu meri Munni hain. Tera khayaal rakhna mera farz vi hai, te mera haq vi.'[449] Nothing really can beat a mother's gentle touch, and when that touch is coupled with such assuring words, I had died and gone to heaven already.

Almost involuntarily, I curled up a little around my mother's soft body perched comfortably on my bed. This was turning out to be a beautiful 'Maavaan te dhiyaan rall baithiyaan ne maaye'[450] moment. Mum continued, 'Mainu teri bahut chinta ho rahi hai. Saal hee ho gya tu koi saer-exercise nahin kardi. Tu taan meri lambi-lanjhhi dhi hain. Apna haal vekheya hai hun? Fat charrna shuru ho gya!'[451] This kind of woke me up from the slumber! Yet, quietly, smilingly inwardly, I kept listening to her. I wanted to know where she is heading. Mum went on, 'Dekh tu saari umar fit rahi hain, hunn to fat hundi ja rahi hain. Banda bann ja!'[452] There emerged my Chandi-Ma.[453]

'Ajj rakhri hai. Ajj tainu chhutti ditti. Je saver ton tu apni saer ya exercise na shuru keeti, tan pher teriyaan-meriyaan

---

[449] ਦੇਖ, ਤੂੰ ਮੇਰੀ ਮੁੰਨੀ ਹੈਂ, ਤੇਰਾ ਖ਼ਯਾਲ ਰੱਖਣਾ ਮੇਰਾ ਫਰਜ਼ ਵੀ ਹੈ, ਤੇ ਮੇਰਾ ਹੱਕ ਵੀ (See you are my daughter and it is both my right and responsibility to take care of you.)

[450] ਮਾਵਾਂ ਤੇ ਧੀਆਂ ਰੱਲ ਬੈਠੀਆਂ ਨੀ ਮਾਏ (The traditional Punjabi ode celebrating the beautiful bond of mothers and daughters).

[451] ਮੈਨੂੰ ਤੇਰੀ ਬਹੁਤ ਚਿੰਤਾ ਹੋ ਰਹੀ ਹੈ. ਸਾਲ ਹੀ ਹੋ ਗਿਆ ਤੂੰ ਸੈਰ-ਕਸਰਤ ਨਹੀਂ ਕਰਦੀ. ਤੂੰ ਤੇ ਮੇਰੀ ਲੰਬੀ-ਲੰਝੀ ਧੀ ਹੈਂ, ਆਪਣਾ ਹਾਲ ਵੇਖਿਆ ਹੈ ਤੂੰ? Fat ਚੜ੍ਹਨਾ ਸ਼ੁਰੂ ਹੋ ਗਿਆ ਹੈ! *(I am really worried about your health. It has been a year since you have exercised or taken to daily walks regularly. You are my tall and charming daughter but have you looked at yourself lately? You have started accumulating fat lately!)*

[452] ਦੇਖ ਤੂੰ ਸਾਰੀ ਉਮਰ fit ਰਹੀ ਹੈਂ, ਹੁਣ ਤੋਂ fat ਹੁੰਦੀ ਜਾ ਰਹੀ ਹੈਂ. ਬੰਦਾ ਬਣਨ ਜਾ! (See all your life you have remained fit. Now you have started becoming fat. You better sort yourself out soon!)

[453] ਚੰਡੀ-ਮਾਂ (My devilish mother).

gallan!'[454] I wonder if I can get my Mother Superior booked for body shaming or mental cruelty on a child. I am told the children can dial 1098 to register their complaints against abuse with CHILDLINE!

Can we possibly be politically incorrect and not talk about what transpired during the politically motivated days of demonetisation? The torturous times when people had to queue for hours in the sun to get their hands on only Rs. 2000/- and then you could not spend those notes as no one had appropriate or enough legal currency notes to give back to you! Worst was the deadline within which you had to hand in all the banned currency notes, after which it would become a criminal offence to be in possession of old notes. The whole country was relying on barter system. Mind you, I am talking from the perspective of housewives who had to go out and buy regular groceries and run their households, not the entities who had stashed away millions and zillions of black money.

Housewives were also badly affected on another front due to the banning of old currency overnight, as their rainy day stash had to be suddenly declared and their financial credibility got questioned by their own family members. Sons and daughters-in-law took the cash from them and never returned on the pretext of sending grandkids abroad or to buy a new car or to construct another room on the terrace. Regardless, since husbands and sons were mainly at work, it was these very housewives who were asked to queue up at the bank to get the currency exchanged, 4000 at a time!

---

[454] ਅੱਜ ਰੱਖੜੀ ਹੈ. ਅੱਜ ਤੈਨੂੰ ਛੁੱਟੀ ਦਿੱਤੀ. ਜੇ ਸੇਵਰ ਤੋਂ ਤੂੰ ਆਪਣੀ ਸੈਰ ਯਾ ਕਸਰਤ ਨਾ ਸ਼ੁਰੂ ਕੀਤੀ, ਤਾਂ ਫੇਰ ਤੇਰੀਆਂ-ਮੇਰੀਆਂ ਗੱਲਾਂ! (On account of Rakhi today I will let you off but from tomorrow onwards you must follow a daily regime of fitness … or else!)

Without getting involved in a deeper politically incorrect monologue, let's get back to how demotisation affected our Mother Darling. I heard a commotion arising out of Mum's room as Bhabi[455] had gone to give Mum her bowl of cereals. A bewildered voice mixed with an exasperated voice raised my curiosity. Suddenly both of them emerged out of the room and walked towards me. Mum muttering away, 'Berra tarr je iss Modi da. Garmiyaan de kappreyaan utte gaaj sutti te sardi de kappreyaan nu ki pata?'[456] As I raised my eyebrow with wonderment, Bhabi burst open, 'Aah Mummy nu saambh lo. 15 din pehlaan viaah jaan lagge golden purse wichhon 4000/- nikalya si. Oh mushkil naal adjust keeta te ajj hunn juraab wichon 500 de note kaddhi baithe ne. Meri bass hai!'[457]

Har Har Modi … Har Ghar Modi![458] Then Mum stands there wringing her hands like a 2-year-old child, beseeching eyes full of disbelief, almost claiming visually, 'don't know how it happened!'

A couple of weeks later, spring cleaning my handbags was like diving into a Pandora's box full of surprise Christmas joy. I opened my cherished orange summer bag and it jingled with some copper. The cerise pink bag had some old paying-in stubs dating back to 2004, to remind me wistfully that I used to be rich once upon a time. The old white one had more charming

---

[455] ਭਾਬੀ (Brother's wife).

[456] ਬੇੜਾ ਤਰ ਜੇ ਇੱਸ ਮੋਦੀ ਦਾ ... ਸਰਦੀਆਂ ਦੇ ਕੱਪੜਿਆਂ ਉੱਤੇ ਗਾਜ ਸੁੱਟੀ ਤੇ ਸਰਦੀਆਂ ਦੇ ਕੱਪੜਿਆਂ ਨੂੰ ਕੀ ਪਤਾ? (God bless Mr. Modi! He declared demonetisation in November when winter wardrobe was out. How were we to know about odd cash lying in summer clothes?)

[457] ਆਹ ਮੰਮੀ ਨੂੰ ਸਾਂਭ ਲਓ. 15 ਦਿਨ ਪਹਿਲਾਂ ਵਿਆਹ ਜਾਣ ਲੱਗੇ ਗੋਲਡਨ ਪਰਸ ਵਿੱਚੋ 4000/- ਨਿਕਲਿਆ ਸੀ. ਉਹ ਮੁਸ਼ਕਿਲ ਨਾਲ ਅਡਜਸਟ ਕੀਤਾ ਤੇ ਅੱਜ ਹੁਣ ਜੁਰਾਬ ਵਿੱਚੋ 500/- ਦੇ ਨੋਟ ਕੱਢੀ ਬੈਠੇ ਨੇ! ਮੇਰੀ ਬੱਸ ਹੈ! *(Look at your mother! Fifteen days ago she found Rs. 4000/- from her golden purse while getting ready for a wedding. I had such trouble in adjusting that money and today she has found another bunch of Rs. 500/- notes from her socks! I have had enough.)*

[458] ਹਰ ਹਰ ਮੋਦੀ - ਹਰ ਘਰ ਮੋਦੀ! (Hail Modi – Hail Modi; An election slogan of Modi government).

stuff. I took out an old newspaper cutting narrating the story of Fauja Singh from 2011. The brown waist bag had painkillers, Volini gel and best of all, my old pedometer. I felt chuffed when I flipped it open and it still worked. The battery had not leaked or burnt out. I had run 11.2 kilometres in 1 hour 27 minutes the last time I used it, which was 7 April 2013 at 5.47 am. I rightfully patted myself on the back, completely ignoring the 3 kg extra weight my feet are carrying now, making all the difference between a fit and a fat CAT!

The mellow yellow bag's slip pocket had the much defunct Spice Privilege Card of all things. I came across my first ever blood donor card in India from Rotary Blood Bank. I also found silver coins still in gift pouches, which I always used to carry with me in the past. These were to save me from embarrassing myself as I used to forget almost all birthdays and wedding anniversaries. Most 'old' CATS would vouch for this habit of mine.

I also felt blessed at not having lost the Krishna card given to me by a dear centurion blood donor in 2010. Then there was the birthday wishes card Mum had written to accompany the bouquet long ago. Found a few girlie things also such as my long forgotten jelly gloss, nail file, nail paint remover wipes, hairpins, soap paper and tampons representing their design evolution over the years.

Then my fingers found some more papers in the red bag. It was a deep pocket and it took a little while for me to extract the papers due to my painful and swollen fingers. I assumed they would be some old envelopes from CATS treks or more bank stubs. As I finally managed to pull them out, they turned out to be notes. Horrifyingly, all 500s. Uncomfortably more than the

Rs. 5000/- deposit allowed. Bhabi simply shook her head while Mother Superior had a hearty laugh.

'Chal hunn apniyaan juraabaan vi check ker lai', she insisted.[459]

____

[459] ਚੱਲ ਹੁਣ ਆਪਣੀਆਂ ਜੁਰਾਬਾਂ ਵੀ ਚੈੱਕ ਕਰ ਲਈ! *(Come let's check your socks also!)*

मां

बेसन की सोंधी रोटी पर खट्टी चटनी जैसी माँ ,
याद आता है चौका-बासन, चिमटा फुँकनी जैसी माँ ।

बाँस की खुर्री खाट के ऊपर हर आहट पर कान धरे ,
आधी सोई आधी जागी थकी दुपहरी जैसी माँ ।

चिड़ियों के चहकार में गूँजे राधा-मोहन अली-अली ,
मुर्गे की आवाज़ से खुलती, घर की कुंड़ी जैसी माँ ।

बीवी, बेटी, बहन, पड़ोसन थोड़ी-थोड़ी सी सब में ,
दिन भर इक रस्सी के ऊपर चलती नटनी जैसी मां ।

बाँट के अपना चेहरा, माथा, आँखें जाने कहाँ गईं ,
फटे पुराने इक अलबम में चंचल लड़की जैसी माँ ।

- निदा फ़ाज़ली

The Other Mothers

As time has gone by, experiencing the highs and lows of my mother's life from very close quarters, I guess at some level my mother has made me less selfish. She has helped me become a more generous person: giving towards others, gentle towards my own being, kind in my soul. And then a mother is a mother no matter which way you look. Observing my mother made me so much alive to the other mothers around me too. Allow me to share my Biji with you as I woke up in Biji's bed one winter morning. Snuggled in her blanket, I was overwhelmed by the memories of my ever so hip, chic and loving Biji. We had no blood ties and I was not born off her, but she loved me like her own. She just walked into our lives one winter evening and became an inseparable part of our family.

Born around 1927 in Lahore to a doctor father and a home minister mother, she had graduated in maths and English in 1947 from Lahore, the original Punjab University. She married into a very spiritual family, worked all her life to shoulder the responsibilities of her small family of three excellent kids. Biji was a widow for the last three decades of her life. Confident, independent and using her own words, 'obstinate', she stayed by herself in her own house till the last 5 years of her life.

All of 5' in height, Biji was equally round, much like my own mother to be honest. Biji was a great story teller and we would often sit around her to ask her endless questions about her life gone by, right from her childhood, to her getting married, though she put her foot down when my brother asked her where she had gone to spend her honeymoon! Full of wisdom and yet untouched by malice, Biji took pride in all of us. Since her own loving kids were in different cities and countries, we became her family in lieu. She also played the Dowager-matriarch for us. She would always have a chocolate for our kids, token and significant gifts for the ones in the middle and love for everyone. She never missed a single Rakhi[460] as she tied the sacred thread on my father's wrist.

Biji liked the fact that I could carry almost anything I wore, with grace. Since I would drop by her home as I headed off to office in the mornings, she could figure out my day's schedule from the clothes I had selected to wear that day. 'Site work hai ajj?'[461] Biji would ask if she saw me wearing flats on my feet (2"-4" heel was 'normal office day' you see.) If she saw me with a long skirt but with a scarf in the summer, 'Ajj kisi de bhog layi jaana hai?'[462]

One day I got dressed to dust and clear off paperwork in office and hence was wearing my 'lazy old clothes'. Biji did not like what she saw but did not want to burst my bubble either.

---

[460] ਰੱਖੜੀ (Rakhi is an Indian festival that celebrates the bond between a brother and a sister. All the sisters tie a band around their brothers' wrists, who in return give them gifts and promise to protect them forever.)

[461] site work ਹੈ ਅੱਜ? (You have site work today?)

[462] ਅੱਜ ਕਿਸੀ ਦੇ ਭੋਗ ਲਈ ਜਾਣਾ ਹੈ? (Do you have to attend someone's last prayers today in the temple?)

So she just said, 'Supreet, go get my purse.' Sensing it odd for Biji to say so since she knew I was in a hurry and won't be able to go out to run her errands, I asked Biji what did she want to do with the purse? 'Let's go and buy some clothes for you!'

Mothers will always be mothers I guess who always want to see their daughters well dressed and well behaved. Mothers can be quite unforgiving towards themselves too I noticed. Biji was also very fond of going for long drives during the heavy summer monsoons, which would bring the much-needed relief from the scorching sun in North India. I would invariably pick up Mother Darling from home and then get Biji into the car to drive away for an hour or so. This used to be enough excitement for Biji as then exhaustion laced with hunger pangs would take over both the mothers in the car. Fond of Sagar Ratna's Dosa and Sindhi's Chana-Bhatura, the graceful ladies would make the decision about the meal of the day.

I remember driving towards Biji's home on one such evening after yet another ladies' day out in the rains. Just as Biji stepped out of the car, her foot lost grip on the slippery, muddy, grassy footpath and she landed on her rear end with one loud thud. Both Mumma and I panicked and dashed out of the car to check if Biji was OK and help her get back to feet. Biji sprang back to her feet like one of those life-size bouncy toys which keep bouncing back despite being punched on the nose by hundreds of visitors at the local fairs. Even before we could ask about her well-being, Biji asked us instead, 'Mainu kisi ne girdi nu dekhya taan nahin?'[463] Not a care in the world about any injuries she might have sustained during the fall, but she cared enough in case the world laughed at her fall.

---

[463] ਮੈਨੂੰ ਕਿਸੀ ਨੇ ਗਿਰਦੀ ਨੂੰ ਦੇਖਿਆ ਤੇ ਨਹੀਂ? *(I hope no one saw me tumbling down.)*

Yet another series of incidents led me to another mother, Polly's Mum. Some summers ago Polly got in touch with me as he needed blood donors for his beloved father. Since this comes naturally to CATS, we did the needful. A few days later I noticed Polly had posted his father's picture on FB, sharing his loss. The very next morning as Mum was reading the newspaper, she expressed her shock at the demise of her childhood friend's husband, and of course it was the same picture. This is when the penny dropped that Polly and I are connected in ways more than one. So Polly and I conspired to get these old neighbours and schoolmates from 1950s to 1960s to meet one lazy Sunday.

In a flash they both settled down to talk about old and new times alike. Childhood ties are special, especially when you are friends and not tied down by blood relationships. While chatting away their lives, Auntie suddenly turned to me and asked, 'Desi cheezaan kha leindi hain?'[464] With a smile I responded, 'Only if you have made something!' Smilingly she pulled out a tiffin full of 'gulgule.'[465] Punjabi mothers can't really think beyond food when they want to express love. And we love this friend of our Mother Darling and the best part is, I have her mobile number – Direct connection with another mother when my own holds me to ransom!

Mothers come in all shapes and forms and here is another one whom I stumbled upon, quite by accident to be honest. I had a thumping headache one evening and I needed masala chai made in a particular manner, something you don't get in the cafes. Since my dear friend Madhvi's house was the closest as I finished the last

---

[464] ਦੇਸੀ ਚੀਜ਼ਾਂ ਖਾ ਲੈਂਦੀ ਹੈਂ? (Are you fond of old traditional Punjabi food?)

[465] ਗੁਲਗੁਲੇ (Gulgule is a Punjabi sweet made by deep frying sweet wheat flour batter.)

meeting of the day, I literally walked into her home to grab a large mug of tea, and found Madhvi grossly occupied with some exquisitely embroidered squares. It turned out that these embroidered squares came stitched with a very beautiful story. Madhvi's mother was much like my own, an epitome of patience and resilience, an elegant lady who took great pride in her person as well as appearance. She was an aesthete and patronised craft and promoted crafts persons. It has been years since her mother passed away but Madhvi has held on to quite a few of her mother's belongings, which in her own words are enough to last her for two to three lifetimes more!

I often see Madhvi wearing her Mum's shawls, scarves etc. What you see here is something her Mum had worn decades ago. Upon inheriting Mum's wardrobe, Madhvi got them redesigned into a fresh suit. Eventually that suit got wornout but Madhvi was taking off the embroidered squares so that Mum's elegant love could be carried forward to another suit or a dupatta[466]. A mother's love never ends. Her daughter carries a mother's love deep in her heart, wears it on her sleeve, or covers her head with it. Of a mother long gone and and a daughter not just keeping her alive in her heart, but keeping her along in every possible way. I guess this relationship of our lives is the beautiful patchwork of love and care, laced with concern needled into every living breath of our lives, and beyond.

I managed to make home in many a mother's heart to satiate my lust for that 'special mug of tea'. Vipin was a dear heart, someone you could trust your life with, but could not trust the cup of tea he would make! In fact, it was always his wife Smriti or his beloved mother, a frail yet graceful octogenarian lady who

---

[466] ਦੁਪੱਟਾ (Long scarf worn with a Punjabi suit).

would make the tea, which would lift your soul and sorrows with each sip.

Vipin's mother was only 3 years old when she had lost her entire immediate family in the Quetta earthquake. Brought up by her uncle and his loving family, partition in 1947 brought in another upheaval in her life. She got married into a family and supported her husband's wish to continue his studies, who eventually become an academician. She graced every challenge with her resilience. She brought up her only child with the values which made him a much-loved teacher and sought-after friend. This is one mother who despite her tiny frame holds the wisdom and warmth of the whole universe in her lap. Whenever I get tired of fighting the battles with the wicked world, I go home to aunty and let her wash away my soul with her gentle touch, and that magical mug of tea of course.

The lure of the same mug of tea often takes me to another friend of mine, a fine gentleman in his 70s, the kinds God does not make anymore. He fawns over you lovingly, and yet minces no words when he finds you are losing the plot. Fondly called Chat by friends, he is the one who takes absolute pride in your work and indulges you with your favourite kidney beans (rajmah) and rice lunch. However, when facing a deadline, he would even withhold that much-needed cup of tea till you have completed the task at hand. If he finds you have been behaving appropriately lately, then he would reward you by serving you tea in his mother's favourite bone china cup.

I remember once over tea Chat shared an incident with me, which I have long forgotten. However, what I do recall is that I summed the incidence with an old Urdu couplet,

Na jaane kya kaha jaati huyi maujon ne saahil se,
Ke maujein ab tak saahil se apna sar patakti hain.[467]

Suddenly this son of a titled 'Sardar Saheb', an officer of the Provincial Civil Service from independence times, Chat looked up at me with misty eyes and said, 'My mother used to recite this couplet often.' We both fell silent for a while. He went on to share his remembrances of his beloved mother with me, whom he addressed as Biji. She was the gentlest of souls one could imagine – quite befitting her name Shanti – meaning peace and calmness. Forget twisting any child's ear, she never even raised her voice to scold any of them. She would laugh off Chat's demand when he would ask his mother to make 'half-a-roti'[468]!

He demanded that it not be torn off in half from a whole roti, but made exactly half in size, life a half-moon! Only mothers can indulge us so I guess and when they leave, they leave behind this huge hole of heartache which can never be filled, not even with tears. Had you ever imagined that a cuppa-cha might evoke such a train of thought? Life is nothing but a collection of small incidents, which we tend to file away in the race of the big promotion, the big car or a big house. Now imagine this big house, where you have parked your big car, which you bought with your big promotion, but without a mother to bless you!

The cup of tea turned into a round of drinks at the terrace of Anant Mann and Siddharth Wig not long ago. As a bunch of close friends were discussing everything under the huge

---

[467] ਨਾ ਜਾਣੇ ਕਿਆ ਕਹਾ ਜਾਤੀ ਹੁਈ ਮੌਜੋ ਨੇ ਸਾਹਿਲ ਸੇ (Who knows what the shore said to the receding waves).
ਕੇ ਮੌਜੇ ਅਬ ਤਕ ਸਾਹਿਲ ਸੇ ਅਪਨਾ ਸਰ ਪਤਕਤੀ ਹੈਂ (That till this day the waves are crashing their heads on the shore).

[468] ਰੋਟੀ (Indian bread made from wheat in a round shape, like a full moon).

mango tree hanging towards the terrace, Siddharth's thoughts wandered off towards his own beloved mother whom we lost a couple of years ago. 'Mum would always be the first one to hear the koel sing and she used to be filled with so much joy as koel singing is the sure sign of advent of spring with expectation of a bumper crop of mangoes.' Taking a sip from his single malt he quietly added, 'Koel sang this morning and I was the first one to notice her sing.' The rest, he left unsaid.

With much left unsaid, my mind wandered off to Anant's mother who is lovingly called 'Ammi Ji' by everyone in the family. This deceptively frail but formidable in character Ammi Ji has this most amusing habit of saying, 'Achhh'. It is neither a fully formed Punjabi affirmation 'Achhaa' meaning yes, nor a half hearted British acknowledgement 'Aah'. It usually leaves her kids and grandkids wondering for days whether Ammi Ji was happy with what you had shared with her, was she internalising the situation and hence left her thoughts mid-air, or was she simply expressing clear dispproval at the prat you had made of yourself yet again!

In Anant's own words, 'Diminutive but hard-as-nails lady is my mother. Nobody messes with her. She must have been the first person I laid my eyes on, and ever since then I have seen her preside over everything and everyone around her with aplomb. She never read any books on feminism but she threw the rules and rule books of patriarchy out of the window when she got married at the age of 20 and made her own rules to mark her space. I did not fully understand it then, but the partnership of my parents was something astonishing.

As a child I wanted to fit in with my friends and their homes, yet our home was nothing like theirs. My school teacher parents ran our house as a great team. When she was washing clothes, he would be hanging them out to dry. When she was making rotis, he was washing the utensils and cleaning the kitchen. When she was sitting at the sewing machine sewing clothes for the entire house, including the covers for the radio, fans, even the sewing machine itself, he would be watering the plants and readying the soil for the next batch of vegetables. Later they would both sit with the radio on making monthly budget. So there, all the lessons in feminism for my brother and I; we both resisted then, mind you! We thought we were born in a weird house, but we both absorbed it all like little sponges. She ages with the country, midnight's child that she is. She is milder now, mellower, but nobody still messes with her. She is still making her own rules, still hard to please. Every year I think I have grown up enough and done well enough to earn her approval but it is a very hard commodity, her approval. I love her to bits though. Everything is right with the world when she is around.'

Trust me, I can vouch for what Anant says about her mother! I had barely met her mother at the Valedictory Lecture held at PGIMER (Chandigarh) in honour of Dr. N.N. Wig when somehow, the conversation veered towards the days when Anant walked into Dr Wig's household as a daughter-in-law. Ammi Ji shared that all she saw at their beautiful home was the huge library full of books; books of all shapes, colours and sizes, books on all possible topics one could imagine, but all the books were in English. Being a teacher and a voracious reader herself in multiple languages, a habit she had inculcated in Anant too, her immediate thoughts were, 'Acchhhh! At least my daughter knows more languages than they do!'

Then there is a very young quadragenarian mother who sort of confirms that mothers remain the same, regardless of which decade they embraced motherhood. My dear friend Ashish Arora is not just an adventure enthusiast with CATS, he is also a regular blood donor who has never missed a blood donation camp. However, like all mothers, his mother would always be anxious each time he donated blood. To begin with she tried to dissuade Ashish gently by saying that there are others who donate too, so why does he need to give his pint of red every three months? When that did not work, she started suggesting that perhaps he should donate at alternate camps. When that failed too, she gave up on suggestions but not on her motherly instincts.

When Ashish would reach home after every blood donation camp, she would notice the band-aid on his arm, quietly go to the kitchen and feed him all the nutritious food and fruit juices to make up for the donated fluid. This went on for years. When Ashish donated blood for the 25th time, CATS honoured him with a glad trophy. He went home and handed the trophy to his mother. She gently took the trophy in her hands, kissed his forehead and instead of going to the kitchen to make up for the fluid loss, she went to their little temple at home and placed the trophy along with the prayer books. With this one action, the creator, the caregiver and the creation became one.

Mothers are special and they have the most distinct ways to remain calm amidst the chaos. I love stopping by the ever-welcoming Bhatia household for a cup of tea or to literally put my feet up for a short while. However, one particular evening when I walked into the house, everything was in sixes and sevens as the house was under renovation. Our most beautiful Dr. Nirmal Bhatia was trying to make some space liveable for the night with the army of cleaners under her command. Noticing the clutter, I immediately offered to leave so that she could get on with her work in peace. However, the moment she heard I wanted to make myself scarce, without batting an eyelid she waved me in, 'Come on straight in. You are part of the process!'

Mind you there is another mother whom I have never had the honour of meeting, but whom I respect tremendously for the daughter she has raised. Rita Kaul's Mum was only 14 years old when she got married. She had studied till class 8 but she was fiercely passionate about the education of her children. During the uncertain and anxiety-filled Naxalite days in 1970s, the situation was quite volatile in their hometown Calcutta. Academic schedules had taken a backseat in educational institutions due to violence on campuses. Such was the courage in the heart of this middle school pass mother that to ensure uninterrupted quality education, she decided to send her daughter away to the another part of the country.

Rita came to Chandigarh to persue psychology, a city where she knew not a single soul. Mind you, those were the days when Kalka Mail train would take 3 days to reach Chandigarh and even a trunk call took 3-4 days to materialise. What a wonderful foresight of a mother who bore all the anxieties to give wings to her daughter. Perhaps because she had faith in her upbringing. She taught Rita to always speak her mind, but gently. To dream the impossible, but work hard to achieve it. To ensure she remains financially independent. To share the joys with others but reflect on sorrows alone to strengthen her future decision making. Finally, to love everyone who touches her life. May us daughters have half the wisdom to follow our heroines' principles.

Just like Rita, another dear friend Savita Bhatti calls her mother a mighty braveheart, who in return calls Savita her 'Laadli', a beloved daughter. Walking down the memory lane, Savita remininced, 'Every birthday my mother would stitch frocks for my sister and me, wearing which I would wait at the gate of our house for friends to arrive. To be honest, I used to be more eager to see what gifts they would be bringing for me. As a child, you have the luxury of expressing displeasure, without being politically correct. It did not help that I could never hide my disappointment even if I tried with the skin of my teeth! So I would rudely tell my friends, "Why have you brought this Enid Blyton book for me? I have already read it." Heaven save the friends who brought toffee boxes!'

With a sense of pride in her soul, Savita continued, 'I firmly believe that mothers are the gentlest and most effective police officers God ever made. Mum told me politely, yet in no uncertain terms, that this shouldn't happen again. She taught me the importance of valuing people in my life, beyond the price tags. She trained me to rise above disappointments as every fresh morning brings in hope for a better future. Luckily, since then I have been receiving perfect gifts.' Savita laughed and added with glistening eyes, 'I am often left wondering if Mum and God had some secret pact going whereby God told Mum that if you take care of your precocious kid, I will look after the gifts.'

Savita smiled and added that seeing her mother now confined to bed, she finally understands what unconditional love is. 'Mum speaks little now, but her eyes light up when she sees my sister Naina and me. That joy is more than a thousand words of eloquence.' Someone who has loved and lost so much, Savita scribbled a heartfelt note in honour of her mother, 'My

Mom, I owe everything to you: my existence, my growth, my thoughts and my smile. Balbir, I truly am blessed to be your "laadli".'

Let these thoughts sink in as I share another mother with you, a mother I had not expected to meet at all. I attended an interesting session which was called 'Circle of Gratitude' by Grey Shades as a special invitee. The rising number of senior citizens and the changing trend of families moving from a joint to a nuclear family are causing a huge gap in the lives of the elderly. The demanding lifestyles of today's work culture for the children, lack of meaningful activities or even the space for engagement coupled with the digital revolution has resulted in decreased social participation and interaction, making the elderly more prone to psychological, emotional and social insecurities. The young team of Grey Shades led by Inderpreet and Wyonna has kickstarted a happiness project involving the senior citizens in fun-filled activities.

So during this session, after the fluffy, touchy, feely bits, we were all handed colour papers and crayons and asked to use these to express gratitude to who so ever we wanted to thank. Thinking of my maker, I quickly drew some scrolls over the paper to write Mother Darling and a little heart.

I had planned to bring it home and give it to Mum. However the facilitator asked us to share a story of gratitude before she would let us have tea. An elderly lady, a rolly-polly mother who spoke before me, shared her pain of losing two kids. If we are nothing without our mothers, do we realise the pain we leave behind when we walk out of the lives of our mothers, knowingly or unintentionally? I presented this poster to that mother instead. Theek keeta na?[469]

If you happen to think that you have time, you will make that phone call tomorrow, or buy that gift during the sales, or take Mum out on a vacation once the exams of your kids would get over, do think again. An extremely dear friend of my mother suddenly passed away about a decade ago due to medical negligence. Aunty was such a hospitable lady that her front door was barely ever locked. Many a relative stayed in their house to study and build their careers, but she looked upon herself as only a provider and not a claimant to their success. Their refrigerator, television set and telephone was used by the entire neighbourhood, yet she never creased her brow. There was always a smile on her gentle face, a sane piece of advice and a warm hug to put your pieces together. All of us were left aghast at the unexpected demise of aunty; however, the rituals had to be performed.

Given the generosity of her character, there was not a soul which did not turn up for her last prayers. The temple's hall was full with mourners. The priest paid beautiful tributes to aunty. An odd relative read out an obituary too. Deep inside, we were all grieving at a personal level, yet were keeping a brave face to help keep the immediate family together. It was a collective and almost unexpected loss. I recall Mum putting her arm around the shoulders of aunty's elder son to comfort him, and then she said softly, 'Vekh tere Mumma da kinna pyaar si saryaan naal, ajj saare pahunche ne.'[470] With tears in his eyes

---

[469] ਠੀਕ ਕੀਤਾ ਨਾ? (I made the right decision. Right?)

[470] ਵੇਖ ਤੇਰੇ Mumma ਦਾ ਕਿੰਨਾ ਪਿਆਰ ਸੀ ਸਾਰਿਆਂ ਨਾਲ, ਅੱਜ ਸਾਰੇ ਪਹੁੰਚੇ ਨੇ. (See how much your mother loved everyone? Today everyone has reached to pay their respects to her.)

he turned around to fall into Mum's arms and said, 'Saare
aaye, bas ik Mummy nahin aayi.'[471]

---

471 ਸਾਰੇ ਆਏ, ਬੱਸ ਇੱਕ Mummy ਨਹੀਂ ਆਈ *(Everyone came, but for Mummy.)*

An Ode to Women

ਭੰਡਿ ਜੰਮੀਐ ਭੰਡਿ ਨਿੰਮੀਐ ਭੰਡਿ ਮੰਗਣੁ ਵੀਆਹੁ ॥

Bhand jammīai bhand nimmīai bhand mangaṇ vīāhu.
Of woman are we born, of woman conceived.
To woman engaged and married.

ਭੰਡਹੁ ਹੋਵੈ ਦੋਸਤੀ ਭੰਡਹੁ ਚਲੈ ਰਾਹੁ ॥

Bhandahu hovai dostī bhandahu chalai rāhu.
Woman are befriended.
By woman is the civilisation continued.

ਭੰਡੁ ਮੁਆ ਭੰਡੁ ਭਾਲੀਐ ਭੰਡਿ ਹੋਵੈ ਬੰਧਾਨੁ ॥

Bhand muā bhand bhālīai bhand hovai bandhān.
When woman dies, woman is sought for.
It is by woman that the entire social order is maintained.

ਸੋ ਕਿਉ ਮੰਦਾ ਆਖੀਐ ਜਿਤੁ ਜੰਮਹਿ ਰਾਜਾਨ ॥

So kio mandā ākhīai jit jameh rājān.
So why speak ill of her?
From her, kings are born.

– Shri Guru Granth Saheb (page 473)

Author's Bio

An entrepreneur, an adventure enthusiast, a philanthrope and a researcher, Supreet Dhiman dons several hats with aplomb. A trained management professional, she creates be-spoke and exquisite landscaping products out of natural stone with StoneArt.

Following her undying enthusiasm to help make this world a better place to live for everyone, she is raising environmental concerns through Chandigarh Adventures Treks and Sports (CATS), the first community-based adventure sports group in the country. A regular blood donor herself, she heads a blood donation drive that sends blood donors 24/7 to 10 regional hospitals to meet medical emergencies. Passionate about transforming lives of the underprivileged through education, she is currently expanding 'eduCATe Scholars', a sustainable livelihood creation programme of Can & Will Foundation. Deeply entrenched in humanitarian causes, coupled with her willingness to ask difficult questions while chartering unknown territories, led her to research a social taboo that has helped raise voice to acknowledge and 'End Incest'.

A voracious reader, a compassionate human being and an incorrigible daughter, she is a Paul Harris Fellow from Rotary International and Board Member of Association of British Scholars. If there is one thing that Supreet has learnt and imbibes in life, it is the value of relationships both at work and in personal life, which is reflected in this book documenting her relationship with her mother.

A TEDx and Josh Talks speaker, Supreet is in demand to convey innovative ideas and key messages through storytelling, which she delivers in multiple languages.

Links to TEDx Talks:

India's Dirty Little Secret: http://bit.ly/TEDxIIM-Indore-Incest

The Question of Education: http://bit.ly/TEDxUBSpu-Education

Links to Projects:

If you wish to support education, click www.canandwillfoundation.org
If you wish to join the fight against incest abuse, click endincest.org

To join the blood donation drive, send a message to 98144-14440

To join adventure sports activities, email: cats.chd@gmail.com
To get in touch with the author, email: contact@supreetdhiman.com

Project Brief: Can & Will Foundation mentors, supports, guides and grooms intelligent students who wish to achieve more than their current resources permit, till they become financially independent.

Our Achievement: A registered charity since 2010, Can & Will Foundation has had the privilege of serving 170 such students under the project 'eduCATe Scholars'. Thirty-five eduCATe Scholars are currently enrolled in prestigious colleges, and their annual fee budget is Rs. 15.82 lakhs.

Scholars are studying BTech, MBBS, BEd, BCom, BCA, Pharmacy, Nursing, Law etc. Of the 25 who have graduated, 17 are working and rest are preparing for competitive or higher studies. We feel privileged that our eduCATe Scholars are working in institutions such as Medanta Hospital (Gurgaon), Tata Memorial Hospital (Mumbai), British School (Gurgaon) and Max Super Speciality Hospital (Mohali). Internships are held at Bharat Electronics Ltd. (Panchkula), Maxxon Constructions (Punjab) etc.

Our Strengths: Can & Will Foundation goes beyond providing merely a cheque to our eduCATe Scholars. We invest time, resources and efforts in every eduCATe Scholar to provide learning opportunities for career optimisation and professional goals fulfilment, which produces role models in their respective local communities.

Some Links for More Information:

Website: www.canandwillfoundation.org
FB: https://www.facebook.com/canandwillfoundation
A short 2-minute video sharing a case study and project details:
http://bit.ly /Funds4educatescholars-2019
TEDx The Question of Education:
http://bit.ly/TEDxUBSpu-Education

Help us create more Role Models through funds.

Project brief: Research-driven, action-based registered charity End Incest Trust has created a dual model of awareness and advocacy related to sexual abuse within families, while offering support to the participants since 2017. The aim is to use judiciously designed programmes for a forearmed childhood and a forewarned society.

Our research findings include, but are not limited to, the following:

- Most vulnerable age for victims is 7-18 years
- Most perpetrators fall in the age bracket of 12-30 years
- All victims are NOT females
- 40% of the respondents have been a WITNESS to incest
- 1 in 5 have been a VICTIM of incest
- 92% of the victims never share/disclose their trauma to anyone

Most vulnerable groups are in schools, colleges and universities:

- Children (7-12 years)
- Teenagers and young adults
- Financially, physically and emotionally vulnerable individuals

Achievements in last 1 year without any funding:

- 923 sensitised through research participation
- 5680 lives touched through direct awareness initiatives

- 257 witnesses positively assisted

- 117 victims counselled

- 13 victims remain in touch

- 52 direct awareness camps in 11 Indian states and union territories

- 2 fully functional chapters in Chandigarh (tier II) & Ludhiana (tier IV)

Some Links for More Information and to Request Awareness Workshops:

Website: www.endincest.org

FB Page: https://www.facebook.com/endincest/

Research Link: http://bit.ly/END-incest-research

The Multicity Approach: http://bit.ly/endincest-multicity

A 9-minute documentary: http://bit.ly/Challenging-Incest-Abuse

TEDx India's Dirty Little Secret: http://bit.ly/TEDxIIM-Indore-Incest

Help us save and protect lives through funds.